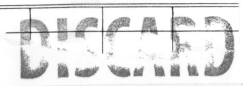

*Religious Controversies
of the Nineteenth Century:
Selected Documents*

Religious Controversies
of the Nineteenth Century:
SELECTED DOCUMENTS

EDITED BY

A. O. J. Cockshut

University of Nebraska Press

LINCOLN

Publishers on the Plains

UNP

Editorial matter © A. O. J. Cockshut 1966

All rights reserved

Library of Congress Catalog card number 66–18225

Parts of this book in excess of 500 words may not be reproduced in any form without permission in writing from the publisher

Contents

General Introduction

SEEN in retrospect, the religious situation of England in 1815, the year of Waterloo, seems distinctly odd. This makes it all the more important to remember that to most people living then it did not seem odd at all. The Church of England possessed almost a monopoly of power and influence; and the vital point here was not the pre-eminence ensured to it then, as now, by the constitution, but its monopoly of higher education. Irish Catholics and English dissenters very seldom had the intellectual training to argue on equal terms with the Anglicans. But the traditions of both had an inner strength, as yet inarticulate. The Anglicans made the mistake, excusable enough on the information they had, of underrating it.

It is a commonplace to say that the Church of England is full of anomalies. The odd thing about the years just before and after 1815 was that scarcely anybody noticed them. The first odd thing was that the most powerful religious movement of the time, the Evangelical movement, cut right across the barrier between Anglicanism and dissent. The immense gulf in social tone and public privilege reflected no difference at all in theology, in religious sensibility or in moral principles. In the year 1815, Charles Simeon was fifty-six, and had already been the incumbent of Holy Trinity, Cambridge for thirty-two years. Educated at Eton, he had been vice-provost of King's in 1790. He shared in fact, all the privileges of the Anglican monopoly except the stipend of his office which he renounced. He laboured with enormous zeal for a religious system, which most of his fellow-Anglicans distrusted, and which many dissenters actively supported. Yet these last were excluded from universities altogether.

The Church of England was emphatically a Protestant church. A deep horror of Popery was the common pride of devout Evangelicals and of three-bottle squires, whose chief interest in religion derived from the money they could make by selling church patronage. Everyone wanted the Church to be Protestant, and everyone was certain that it was Protestant. There was, indeed, a High Church school, represented, for instance, by Henry Phillpotts, aged thirty-seven in 1815, and destined as bishop of Exeter, some thirty-five years later, to be the

I

protagonist of the Gorham case. But, though Phillpotts and others were High Church in the sense that they believed in the Apostolic Succession, episcopal authority, and the importance of the sacramental tradition, they were just as anti-Catholic as the Evangelicals. Perhaps even more so, for they were even more patriotic and xenophobic; and Phillpotts himself would soon be writing bitter pamphlets attacking Catholic Emancipation.

When it is to everyone's interest to ignore an obvious fact, it can remain in obscurity for a long time. And it was eighteen years from 1815 before anyone pointed out that the formularies of the Church of England are not Protestant at all; that its creeds are identical with those of the Roman Church; that bishops were supposed to have a religious function, and not just to sit in the House of Lords and bow down to the Royal Family; and that practices, which Protestants held in horror, such as auricular confession, are advised by the Prayer Book. When the Tractarians drew attention to these and other facts, which were quite undeniable, a large part of the public was outraged. And this is what we should expect; for people do not mind being told what they do not know. They mind being told what they know and will not admit. They minded, for instance, being told by Ibsen, in *Ghosts*, that venereal disease may be hereditary.

In some ways, then, the key figure in the history of the church in the first half of the century is not Wilberforce or Simeon or Keble, but the anonymous bishop who, on reading Newman's tract on the Apostolic Succession, could not tell whether he held the doctrine or not. Nothing could illustrate more clearly the extent to which the Church had lost sight of its intellectual foundations. It was not that the bishops were stupid or uneducated men. It was rather that, taking the everlasting Protestantism of England for granted, and not guessing how soon indifference and worldliness might be replaced by active unbelief, they applied their minds to other questions, and forgot to ask themselves what they were supposed to be.

This deep theological confusion was matched by an equal administrative confusion. The inequality of clerical incomes was startling even in an age when great inequalities were part of the accepted order. In one case Peel, the chief architect of Reform on these matters, found that Trinity College, Cambridge were paying 1·2 per cent, £24 out of £2,000, of the income of one living to the man who did the work. The story of the marked improvement that occurred in this respect between 1828 and 1860 can be studied in Olive Brose's excellent *Church and Parliament* (1959) to which I am indebted for the last example. But the purely administrative history lies outside the scope of this book.

The Evangelical remedy for this unsatisfactory state of affairs was clear and simple. Dismissing both theological and administrative difficulties as irrelevant to the main issue, they put their trust in the growth of 'vital religion'. This meant a lively conviction of being a sinner, followed by conversion, that is, a belief that Christ had died to save the sinner personally. Without this experience intellectual acceptance of Christian doctrine, church-going and good works were vain. In the first third of the nineteenth century, they had immense success and influence. The abolition of slavery, the decline of duelling and many other improvements can be attributed in large measure to their work. But they were in a vulnerable position. For they laid all the stress on feeling, not thought. Their children, unable or unwilling to maintain the emotional temperature at which their parents had lived, did not, as a rule, maintain the tradition. Thus Leslie Stephen, who was born into the Evangelical élite, became an agnostic; while of Wilberforce's children, one, Samuel, became a High Church bishop, and several others became Roman Catholics. All these were men of considerable gifts; and it may be said that the early nineteenth-century Evangelicals were robbed of their natural successors, and that their actual successors, in the mid-Victorian period, were not worthy of them. Their Sabbatarianism, which had been experienced as a glorious gift to the Creator of part of the time which he had given them, and as a real aid to holiness, became in many mid-Victorian households no more than a boring, negative habit. Then again, just because their feelings were so strong, and their ideals so lofty, they paved the way for a set of hypocritical canters, who were embalmed for ever by Dickens and Trollope in characters like Stiggins and Slope. For all these sad developments the early Evangelicals should not be blamed.

A second school of thought is associated especially with the names of Thomas Arnold and A. P. Stanley, Dean of Westminster. Like the Evangelicals they attached little value to theology. But they were more concerned with the moral and educational influence of Christianity on the nation as a whole than with the drama of salvation in the individual soul. Distressed by the endless proliferation of sects in Protestantism, but basically Protestant in their rejection of ecclesiastical authority, they found their principle of unity in the State. They saw the Church of England as the State in its religious aspect; they wished the formulas of the Church to be interpreted with complete liberality, so that they would exclude nobody who did not exclude himself. They rejoiced in the Royal Supremacy, because, they thought, it meant that the Church could be truly national and comprehensive. Stanley, in particular, realized better than the Evangelicals the strength of the influence of public worship. Here again, they considered that the Church of England had an immense advantage in the venerable dignity of its liturgy, over the impromptu prayers of the dissenters. This school came to be known as the Broad Church.

A third reaction to the dangerous situation of the early nineteenth century is represented by the Oxford Movement or Tractarians. Though they held many of the same doctrines as the old High Church school represented by Phillpotts, they differed profoundly from them in spirit. They accepted the connection between Church and State, not out of conservatism, or subservience to the throne, but because they believed that the Catholic Church was a divinely founded institution, that the Church of England was the true heir in these realms of the undivided Church, and that it was the duty of the State to conform itself to this state of affairs. It is a nice irony that the movement which was soon to be accused of Romanizing, began with Keble's Assize sermon; this proclaimed that the suppression of bishoprics in the Church of Ireland, a body of unimpeachable Protestantism, amounted to national apostasy. The Tractarians, and especially Newman, were aware of the intellectual character of the struggle. They knew that the Church could not support itself for long on its temporal privileges. To resist unbelief, it needed a clear theoretical basis and courageous leaders. To a generation that was accustomed to regard appointments to bishoprics as part of the system of aristocratic patronage, it must have been startling to find that the bishops were being told by a devout member of the Church that he could wish them nothing better than the spoiling of their goods and martyrdom. This was meant in all sincerity, but no doubt Newman was well aware that it would sound to many a strange or even a malicious remark.

In their earnestness, their devotion to the Church, and in their awareness that it had reached a moment of great danger, the Oxford leaders of 1833 were at one. This concealed for a considerable time the great differences between Hurrell Froude, Keble, Newman and Pusey, differences not only of temperament but of theology and spiritual outlook. Hurrell Froude, brother of the now more famous J. A. Froude, died in 1836, only three years after the movement began.

4

But the influence of his arresting personality was always present. A lover of paradox, who delighted to shock, impulsive, cruel at times both to others and to himself, he detested what he considered the cant and hypocrisy of popular Protestantism and the worldliness of the old High Church party in equal measure. Having no talent for compromise he would surely have landed the other Oxford leaders in trouble years before they reached it of their own accord, had not persistent ill-health and then an early death prevented him.

John Keble was venerated by those who knew him as a saint; his gentle and profoundly spiritual temper formed a hidden reserve of strength for the others. But, though a fine scholar of the old-fashioned kind, he was not a profound thinker, and had little sense of the spirit of the age. He saw the movement not as a revolution or even a revival, but as a simple act of continuity with the High Church practices he had known in his boyhood. Like some of the Evangelical leaders of the previous generation, he was immensely influential, but left no lasting intellectual monument.

Newman was an immensely complex personality about whom much has been and will continue to be written. More than any other man mentioned in this book, except Coleridge, his thought, subtle, humane, and profoundly original, is alive today. His allegiance to the Church of England was, like Keble's, devoted and selfless; but unlike Keble's, it was essentially conditional. He was devoted to it as a branch of the Catholic Church. When he came to doubt its claim to this status, he ceased to write and work for it. When he came to disbelieve its claim, he left it; and in all this he was perfectly consistent in his principles. It was his judgment of facts that had changed. Unlike Keble's, or indeed Pusey's, his thought was dynamic, and he believed that growth was the only evidence of life. He was intolerant of what he called 'paper systems'; and from the first he had misgivings as to whether his version of Anglicanism might prove to be no more than another of these. It seems likely that, though they always revered him, the other Oxford leaders never altogether understood him.

Pusey, immensely learned in theological history, put his trust in antiquity; he advised his followers to look always to the first six centuries. This meant, in effect, that disputed points must be settled by an appeal to scholars; there was a great gulf between this and Newman's view of a living, contemporary authority, and of growth as the sign of life in doctrine as in other things. It was inevitable that in the end they would diverge. A touching monument to their mutual

5

affectionate incomprehension came many years later, in 1865, when Newman had been a Roman Catholic for twenty years. Pusey's *Eirenicon*, or letter of peace to Roman Catholics, was devoted mainly to a highly coloured account of excesses, both learned and popular, in Roman devotions to the Blessed Virgin. It was a mass of detailed accusations rather than a calm statement of differing principles. Newman, in his reply was moved to say 'You discharge your olive branch as if from a catapult.'

With Newman lost to the Church of England, Froude dead, and Keble too modest and retiring to be a leader, Pusey became in time the acknowledged leader of the Tractarians, who came to be known by their opponents as Puseyites. This term of abuse generally included an accusation of ritualism; a subject which roused the later Victorians to heights of passionate denunciation. As the English, in their public life, their treatment of royalty, and even in their way of drinking port, are traditionally the most ritualistic people in Europe, the antipathy to ritual in religion faithfully reflects the abiding horror of Rome; it is difficult, but it is essential for an understanding of the period, to realize just how strong this was. In the circumstances, Newman's unquestioned victory in his other great public controversy is all the more remarkable.

Charles Kingsley was a clergyman, of the school popularly known as 'muscular Christians'. The popular title was justified to this extent at least in Kingsley's novels; strikingly unlike life in this as in other respects, the man who is in the right always has the better straight left. In his novel *Westward Ho*, he had worked himself into a state of great indignation against the Roman Church, and had represented the cold-blooded murder of a Catholic bishop in America by Elizabethan sea-dogs as in some obscure way justified. In reviewing J. A. Froude's *History of England* he remarked casually, and probably with no very strong intention to annoy: 'Truth for its own sake has never been a virtue of the Roman clergy. Father Newman informs us that it need not and on the whole ought not to be.' As Newman had never informed them of any such thing, the only thing for Kingsley to do, when a protest was made, was to apologize. This he refused to do, and he contented himself with accepting Newman's assurance that his words had not had the meaning he had ascribed to them. Not only was this admission made in a grudging and sneering tone, but it was manifestly inadequate. For as Newman had never made the statement complained of at all, there could be no question of misinterpretation. It has often been said that Kingsley did not understand what it was all about; it is true that his

6

intellectual powers were limited, but it is not credible that any man of education can fail to distinguish between misinterpreting a man's words, and ascribing to him words he never used. Newman was sufficiently disturbed to re-examine old documents and letters, and then to write with extraordinary speed his most famous book, the *Apologia*, a spiritual autobiography. The annihilating dialectical defeat which this book administered to Kingsley was well deserved, but comparatively unimportant. The contemporary importance of the book lay in giving Protestants a clearer view than many of them had ever had before of Roman Catholics as men with a sense of truth and honour not necessarily inferior to their own. Kingsley's reaction was another statement containing more false accusations, and containing the sentence, memorable in view of Newman's immense superiority to himself both in intellect and good temper, 'If I am to bandy words it must be with sane persons.'

But the affair contained a deeper irony than this. Kingsley was a canon of the Church of England, yet he tended to reject or deprecate all specifically Christian moral principles, and place all his trust in the rough-hewn truth and honour of the healthy, sporting Englishman. Yet he alone of all the leading figures in Victorian religious history publicly committed a dishonourable act, and refused to admit it when it had become obvious to all that he had done so.

We have been anticipating, and must now return to the early years of the Oxford Movement. The Oxford leaders, and Newman in particular, were fond of grouping the forces opposed to them under the general heading of 'liberalism'; and this word of many meanings is more likely than any other theological term of the nineteenth century to lead to misunderstanding today. It had nothing to do with politics; it meant rather the idea that a man's religious convictions were simply a matter of his personal taste, that he had no duty to believe anything in particular, and that in moral questions he had no duty to conform himself either to revelation or to reason. Liberals, in Newman's sense, denied any unchanging truth in religion, maintained that everything was relative, and that a doctrine that was useful at one time might be harmful at another. To show the degree of change the world has undergone, it will be enough to give a single example. The South African doctrine of apartheid would be a perfect example of liberalism in Newman's sense. The Church and Scripture maintain that all men are 'of one blood'; scientific investigation discerns no fundamental differences of race. Belief in apartheid is therfore 'liberal' in the sense that

7

it is just a convenient self-interested opinion of a dominant group. But, of course, it is also true that the Tractarians were opposed to a number of ideas, such as the idea of the lay state, which would be described as liberal today.

Before long the authorities of the Church, and of the exclusively Anglican University of Oxford, were driven to stern measures against the Tractarians. W. G. Ward, one of Newman's most impetuous followers, who was to become many years later one of his strongest opponents inside the Roman Church, was declared unfit to teach. Tract XC (1841) in which Newman attempted to reconcile the Thirty-nine Articles with Roman doctrines, was the subject of an adverse resolution by the Oxford Hebdomadal Board, and so forth. Now, on the whole, these authorities have had a very bad press. It is always more natural to sympathize with the hunted than the hunters; and Newman was so much more brilliant than all his persecutors and opponents, and so much more selfless and single-minded than most of them, that this natural tendency is intensified. There can be no doubt at all that the enemies of the Tractarians made errors of tact and judgment, and that, in some cases their theological learning was extremely sketchy. All the same (and this is the point so many commentators have chosen to ignore) they were proved right by time in their main contention. They maintained that Tractarian principles were or might be subversive of Anglican loyalty; and they were proved right when so many Tractarians, including the greatest, left the Church of England. What they failed to discern, and this was surely excusable at the time, was that there was more than one set of Tractarian principles, as I have tried to outline above. Keble was in the main stream of the Anglican tradition, and Newman was not. But those who condemned the whole movement as incompatible with Anglican principles were no further from the truth than those who make out that if only Newman had had an understanding bishop, he and all the other converts might have died as Anglicans. Newman's decision was inevitable, unless he had lacked the courage to take it, for it was the conclusion of years of careful thought.

The twenty years that followed Newman's reception into the Roman Church in 1845 were years of conflict, doubt and agony. Everyone who cared deeply for religion found himself fighting on several fronts at once. In 1847, the Hampden case showed the curious double edge of so many Victorian religious problems. From one point of view, the clerical and lay petitions against Hampden's appointment as bishop of Hereford might be seen as the work of a narrow and irresponsible pressure group. The actual complaint made against him was that he had been considered by the University of Oxford unfit to teach theology. The controversy was exclusively doctrinal; no imputation was made on Hampden's character or learning. Hampden was the kind of Latitudinarian Protestant who has generally found a place in the Church of England; and many people felt that the easy-going rule of bored Prime Ministers was preferable to the rule of dons and theologians.

But Hampden's opponents maintained that the Church was entitled to be consulted before it had bishops imposed on it by the Crown, that a man in whom so many of the clergy had no confidence could not possibly carry out his episcopal duties effectively. Behind all these rather obvious arguments lay a much more vital question. Was the Church of England a part of Christ's Church or was it a department of State?

This question appeared in a much more acute form about three years later with the Gorham case. For the Hampden case only concerned the choice of a man for a position, and there are many ways of choosing men for high office. None of them is perfect, and the relative value of different methods will remain a matter of controversy. But the Gorham case roused the slumbering question of the control of the State over doctrine. It was also a reminder of the complete theological incompatibility of two of the traditional schools of Anglican thought. Gorham was a clergyman of Calvinist views. Calvinists, believing that God has decreed from all eternity which souls do and which souls do not belong to the Elect, cannot accept the doctrine of Baptismal Regeneration. Gorham could accept infant baptism, the traditional Anglican practice, but only as a solemn sign of the future conversion and grace which it was hoped the child might one day be granted. Phillpotts, bishop of Exeter, and, as we have seen, a High Churchman of the old eighteenth-century school, held that no one who did not accept that baptism was an effective sign, washing away the guilt of Original Sin, was qualified for the Anglican ministry. He would have refused to ordain Gorham, had he not been already ordained. As it was, he refused to present him to a living in his diocese.

Lengthy letters and interviews followed; both men were learned and argumentative. Phillpotts maintained that the Prayer Book was, in his sense, Catholic. Gorham took his stand on the Articles, as warranting Calvinist doctrines. That was a familiar dispute, though it had seldom

9

if ever in the past been conducted by bishop and clergyman face to face for many hours on end. But the point that so deeply disturbed High Churchmen, particularly those of the new Oxford school, was this. The matter went for final adjudication to a court set up by the State, and this court did not merely decide on the justice and wisdom of the bishop's action. That would have been a blow to the Church's dignity, but might have been accepted with some resignation. But it was much worse than that. A civil court decided whether Baptismal Regeneration was part of the doctrine of the Church of England, and found that it was not an indispensable requirement of the faith. To men like Gladstone and Manning, archdeacon of Chichester, this seem to undercut the whole basis of their faith, if the Church accepted it. For it would mean that the faith of the Church of England was not the universal faith of a world-wide Church, but whatever the State liked to say it was. The Church officially made no move to resist, though Phillpotts wrote a spirited letter to the Archibshop of Canterbury, in effect excommunicating him for acquiescing in the judgment. So Manning and some others decided that the Church had shown that it was not what they had maintained it was, a portion of the Catholic Church, and so left it and became Roman Catholics. Gladstone remained, though, rather oddly for such an intellectual man, he never explained how he reconciled the judgment and its acceptance with his view of the Church.

In the same year, 1850, the Pope set up a new hierarchy of bishops in England, and appointed Cardinal Wiseman the first Archbishop of Westminster. Wiseman had been educated abroad, and so had escaped the blighting effect of educational handicaps on most English and Irish Catholics. The change was in reality only administrative, as there had been Vicars Apostolic in England, appointed by Rome, since time immemorial. But a large section of public opinion was alarmed; and the alarm was turned to political account by the Premier, Lord John Russell, who skilfully interwove the alarm over 'Papal Aggression' with the disquiet already existing among Protestants about the behaviour of the Tractarians. The point on which indignation was particularly strong was that the new bishops were to take their titles from English cities, while the Vicars Apostolic had been titular dignitaries of places far distant. This was treated as a kind of claim to govern English territories, though the Anglican bishops could have testified how little secular power was conferred by the freedom to use the name of a city in one's signature. The Ecclesiastical Titles Bill was one of those forcible-feeble

English measures which provided penalties which no one really intended should be carried out. Gladstone saved the credit of the House of Commons by a logically unanswerable speech against the Bill, which was, however, passed by a large majority. It was never enforced, and soon forgotten. But Russell's transient success here showed how touchy opinion had become on religious questions.

Another, and a much more impressive testimony to this fact, came in the same year with the publication of Tennyson's *In Memoriam*. Perhaps it is this, rather than the more celebrated *Origin of Species* nine years later, which should be regarded as the *locus classicus* of the impact of scientific speculation on religious life. For Tennyson, as well as being the finest craftsman in verse of his time, was a man of religious temperament, of no very fixed and certain beliefs, who had an extraordinary sensitiveness to current scientific ideas.

Tennyson had been convinced by his reading of the geologists that the earth was immensely old, and he had absorbed the salient points of the idea of evolution.

For the first time in literature there appears a time-scale of aeons instead of centuries; the hills, formerly considered as unchangeable, dissolve like mists; not just individual animals but whole species disappear in the struggle for existence. The idea of a loving God is seen as infinitely precious, but also as threatened.

The purpose of this volume is to present texts which are comparatively inaccessible, and therefore *In Memoriam* does not appear. But for every student of the religious history of the period it should be one of the key texts.

Essays and Reviews (1860) introduced an entirely new note into religious controversy, because it caused many people to wonder whether infidelity, instead of being only an external threat, was not gaining ground within the Church itself. The seven contributors were men of respectability, weight and scholarly distinction, and six of them were clergyman. Frederick Temple was headmaster of Rugby and was to become, more than thirty years later, Archbishop of Canterbury. Jowett, professor of Greek at Oxford, and later Master of Balliol, was on the way to becoming the most celebrated Oxford figure of his time. Mark Pattison (supposed by some to have inspired George Eliot in her portrayal of Casaubon in *Middlemarch*) and Professor Baden Powell were also notable figures at Oxford. Rowland Williams, H. B. Wilson and C. W. Goodwin were scholars of somewhat less fame until *Essays and Reviews* brought them into the limelight. The

Essayists were soon given the popular nickname 'Septem contra Christum'. This was, of course, quite unfair, but shows the bitterness of the controversy raised.

The general tendency of the volume was to deprecate dogma and to lay the greatest possible stress on the moral content of Christianity. It became less a revelation than an endorsement of the highest aspirations of an English scholar and gentleman. For the first time, German Biblical Criticism, which a select few had been studying for many years, came right into public notice.

Both the High Church and Low Church parties, in different ways, were perplexed and angry. The same touchiness of public opinion which we have seen in the Papal Aggression scare manifested itself in a different direction here. When Williams and Wilson were chosen to be prosecuted for heresy, it was rather as representatives of the others than because their essays were particularly obnoxious. But the essayists were in a stronger position than appeared at first sight. What might really be thought subversive was their tone, their hidden suggestion that the childish doctrines of Christianity were dissolving like a mist before the sun of Victorian scholarship and enlightenment. But it must never be forgotten that all doctrinal questions in the Victorian Church were decided by lay courts, with or without ecclesiastical assessors, who judged by the standards of evidence prevailing in the civil courts. They were precluded from assessing the general tendency of a theological work; what they judged was its compatibility with the Thirty-nine Articles. Now as Newman had demonstrated in Tract XC some twenty years before that the Articles might mean many things which they had not in the past been supposed to mean, the Thirty-nine Articles obviously composed a document of extraordinary difficulty for lawyers. Accustomed to documents that try to close every loophole that subtlety and malice might discover, they were now faced with a document that read at least as if it had been meant to leave as many loopholes as possible. In these circumstances, any prosecution for heresy was likely to fail, and this one duly failed. It was particularly exasperating for the orthodox because Wilson, one of the accused, had maintained in his essay on the national church that the only moral obligation incurred by the assent to the Articles, which was and still is required of every clergyman, was the strictly legal obligation. Now the courts, in judging Wilson, found that the legal obligation was so vague as almost to lack substance.

So it was that the courts in effect decided that the Church of England was what Stanley and others always wanted it to be, a national association of men who called themselves Christians, and who accepted the ultimate authority of the Crown in religious matters. Amid all the vagaries of doctrine this last was, for the courts, the crucial point. This was the idea which neither Free Churchmen nor Roman Catholics would accept. But, of course, no decision of the courts could convince those, whether Puseyite or Evangelical, who remained in the Church of England and who had entirely different ideas of its true nature.

The relation of the Church to the State was a difficult question enough when the scene was restricted to England. But in the Colenso case, which dragged on through the 1860's, a yet more intractable problem arose. What was the relation of Church and State overseas? Colenso, when he published his book on the Pentateuch, was bishop of Natal; both he and his metropolitan Robert Gray, bishop of Capetown, had been appointed under Letters Patent from the Crown, and one provision of these was that the metropolitan had the right to inquire into and adjudicate upon complaints against the bishop of Natal. Gray tried Colenso for heresy, found him guilty and deposed him from his bishopric. An appeal to the Privy Council led to a decision which was equally startling for both parties. The Privy Council found that, as South Africa had a government of its own, the powers conferred by the Letters Patent were illegal and void. Therefore Gray's verdict had no legal validity, but, on the other hand, the Church in South Africa had become an autonomous body independent of the State, and therefore Colenso could not look to the State to defend his claim. The English bishops saw their opportunity to escape from State control abroad if not at home, and so they consecrated a new bishop of Natal, Macrorie. A judgment of the English courts, known as the Romilly judgment, confirmed Colenso in the temporal rights and emoluments of his see, and so for some fourteen years until Colenso's death in 1883, there were two rival bishops of Natal.

The theoretical importance of all this was that the decision of the Privy Council split the Anglican Church into two bodies, which though maintaining unity and communion with each other, were, in legal terms, entirely distinct. All parts of the Anglican Communion abroad became independent bodies, and in these a power vacuum was left by the withdrawal of the Crown from its traditional authority. The new governments of the self-governing dominions had no intention of taking over the former royal powers in this matter; so power passed by default to the bishops, who professed a general loyalty and obedience to the Archbishop of Canterbury. But in England the Crown had not abdicated at all; the Archbishop of Canterbury was still appointed by the Crown, that is, by the man who happened at the time to command a majority of votes in the House of Commons. Many years later, the rejection of the Prayer Book of 1928 by the House of Commons was to show that this secular control of the Church in England was certainly not a dead letter. The Colenso case, then, clearly indicated confusions in the theoretical basis and juridical status of the Church of England which remain unresolved.

This was the last of the full-dress Victorian controversies, and the remaining years of the century were calmer. The excitement, in the Lincoln case, of having an English bishop on trial for ritualistic practices was mitigated by the cool and balanced judgment delivered in the case by Archbishop Benson. The various parties in the Church of England realized that they could not finally oust each other, and began to live together in greater tolerance.

There is one respect in which both this introduction, and the documents which follow, are unavoidably unbalanced. The Free Churches, which were immensely important and influential, hardly make an appearance. For the great strength of non-conformity was of the kind that does not leave documents and literary monuments behind. The two pillars of its strength were the corporate life of the chapel and the eloquence of the outstanding preacher like Spurgeon. Much of the nation's solidity, moral idealism and material success had its source and inspiration here. There are a few books which give a vivid picture of the life of the chapels, which was certainly much more intense and exciting than is generally realized today. The novels of W. Hale White (sometimes known by the name of one of his characters, Mark Rutherford) give a unique impression of the small chapels in the country; and C. M. Davies's *Unorthodox London* gives some fascinating glimpses of the style of the great popular preachers in the capital.

Perhaps this caveat should be extended, in a rather different sense, to the Church of England also. There were plenty of bitter disputes as the following pages will show; and we are right in a way to concentrate on these for their great historical and intellectual interest. But there must have been many devout people who were little touched by them, and whose religious experience was just as it would have been in another age.

I

WILLIAM WILBERFORCE: *Practical View of the Prevailing Religious Conceptions of Professed Christians in the Higher and Middle Classes in this Country Contrasted with Real Christianity*

Chapter 3, section 4; Chapter 7, section 1

Born to independent wealth and position in 1759, Wilberforce was M.P. at twenty-one. This eloquent appeal for Evangelical religion was published in 1797, about halfway through his long and arduous campaign against the slave trade which began about 1787. Those whose idea of Evangelical Protestantism is derived from Victorian novels, or from autobiographical accounts of childhood miseries (like Augustus Hare's), may be surprised by the balance, the intellectual force, and the sincere benevolence of Wilberforce's statement of faith. There is nothing pedantic about his reverence for Scripture; he sees it as a whole system of salvation, not as an arbitrary collection of texts. Though intentionally urging the strict and solemn duty of believing and acting as a Christian he has sympathy for those he feels to be misguided. 'Let us also hope that he who searches the heart, sees the right dispositions in many who use the mistaken and dangerous language to which we have objected.' He firmly rejects the over-convenient view to which his theological school has sometimes tended, that belief alone without the fruits of belief in conduct is amply sufficient for salvation. When he says that the tree is known by its fruits, he was referring to a Biblical text which he never forgot, though some Victorian Evangelicals did.

The section on gloom and pleasure shows that the Victorian Sunday was a perversion of the ideas of the earlier generations of Evangelicals. In general, one can say, few schools of religious thoughts have had a worse press; and Wilberforce, perhaps the greatest of the school, should be read carefully to redress the balance.

IF it be true then, that, in contradiction to the plainest dictates of Scripture, and to the ritual of our established Church, the sanctifying operations of the Holy Spirit (the first fruits of our reconciliation to God, the purchase of our Redeemer's death, and his best gift to his true disciples), are too generally undervalued and slighted; if it be also true, that our thoughts of the blessed Saviour are confused and faint, our affections towards him languid and lukewarm; little proportioned to what they, who at such a price have been rescued from ruin, and endowed with a title to eternal glory, might be justly expected to feel towards the author of that deliverance; little proportioned to what has been felt by others, ransomed from the same ruin, and partakers of the same inheritance: if this, let it be repeated, be indeed so, let us not shut our eyes against the perception of our real state; but rather endeavour to trace the evil to its source. We are loudly called on to *examine well our foundations*. If any thing be *there* unsound and hollow, the super-structure could not be safe, though its exterior were less suspicious. Let the question then be asked, and let the answer be returned with all the consideration and solemnity which a question so important may justly demand, whether, in the grand concern of all, *the means of a sinner's acceptance with God*, there be not reason to apprehend, that the nominal Christians whom we have been addressing, too generally en-tertain very superficial and confused, if not highly dangerous notions? Is there not cause to fear, that with little more than an indistinct and nominal reference to Him who 'bore our sins in his own body on the tree,' they really rest their eternal hopes on a vague, general persuasion of the unqualified mercy of the Supreme Being; or that, still more erroneously, they rely in the main, on their own negative or positive merits? 'They can look upon their lives with an impartial eye, and congratulate themselves on their inoffensiveness in society; on their having been exempt, at least, from any gross vice, or if sometimes accidentally betrayed into it, on its never having been indulged habitually; or, if not even so,' (for there are but few who can say this, if the term vice be explained according to the strict requisitions of the Scriptures) 'yet on the balance being in their favour, or on the whole not much against them, when their good and bad actions are fairly weighed, and due allowance is made for human frailty.' These con-

siderations are sufficient for the most part to compose their apprehensions; these are the cordials which they find most at hand in the
moments of serious thought, or of occasional dejection; and sometimes perhaps in seasons of less than ordinary self-complacency, they
call in also to their aid the general persuasion of the unbounded mercy
and pity of God. Yet persons of this description by no means disclaim
a Saviour, or avowedly relinquish their title to a share in the benefits
of his death. They close their petitions with the name of Christ; but
if not chiefly from the effect of habit, or out of decent conformity
to the established faith, yet surely with something of the same ambiguity of principle, which influenced the expiring philosopher, when
he ordered the customary mark of homage to be paid to the god of
medicine.

Others go farther than this; for there are many shades of difference
between those who flatly renounce, and those who cordially embrace
the doctrine of Redemption by Christ. This class has a sort of general,
indeterminate, and ill understood dependence on our blessed Saviour.
But their hopes, so far as they can be distinctly made out, appear
ultimately to rest on the persuasion that they are now, through Christ,
become members of a new dispensation, wherein they will be tried by
a more lenient rule than that to which they must have been otherwise
subject. 'God will not now be extreme to mark what is done amiss;
but will dispense with the rigorous exactions of his law, too strict indeed for such frail creatures as we are, to hope that we can fulfil it.
Christianity has moderated the requisitions of Divine Justice; and all
that is now required of us, is thankfully to trust to the merits of Christ
for the pardon of our sins, and the acceptance of our sincere though
imperfect obedience. The frailties and infirmities to which our nature
is liable, or to which our situation in life exposes us, will not be severely
judged; and as it is practice that really determines the character, we
may rest satisfied, that if, on the whole, our lives be tolerably good,
we shall escape with little or no punishment, and through Jesus Christ
our Lord, shall be finally partakers of heavenly felicity.'

We cannot dive into the human heart, and therefore shall always
speak with caution and diffidence, when, from external appearances or
declarations we are affirming the existence of any internal principles
and feelings; especially as we are liable to be misled by the ambiguities
of language, or by the inaccuracy with which others may express
themselves. But it is sometimes not difficult to any one who is accustomed, if the phrase may be allowed, to the anatomy of the human

mind, to discern, that generally speaking, the persons who use the above language, rely not so much on the merits of Christ, and on the agency of Divine Grace, as on their own power of fulfilling the moderated requisitions of Divine Justice. He will hence therefore discover in them a disposition, rather to extenuate the malignity of their disease, than to magnify the excellence of the proffered remedy. He will find them apt to palliate in themselves what they cannot fully justify, to enhance the merit of what they believe to be their good qualities and commendable actions, to set, as it were in an account, the good against the bad; and if the result be not very unfavourable, they conceive that they shall be entitled to claim the benefits of our Saviour's sufferings as a thing of course. They have little idea, so little, that it might almost be affirmed that they have no idea at all, of the importance or difficulty of the duty of what the Scripture calls 'submitting ourselves to the righteousness of God;' or of our proneness rather to justify ourselves in his sight, than, in the language of imploring penitents, to acknowledge ourselves guilty and helpless sinners. They have never summoned themselves to this entire and unqualified renunciation of their own merits, and their own strength; and therefore they remain strangers to the natural loftiness of the human heart, which such a call would have awakened into action, and roused to resistance. ALL THESE THEIR SEVERAL ERRORS NATURALLY RESULT FROM THE MISTAKEN CONCEPTION ENTERTAINED OF THE FUNDAMENTAL PRINCIPLES OF CHRISTIANITY. They consider not that Christianity is a scheme for 'justifying *the ungodly*,'[1] by Christ's dying for them, *'when yet sinners:'*[2,3] a scheme for reconciling

[1] Rom. iv. 5.
[2] Ibid. v. 6–8.
[3] The Writer trusts he cannot be misunderstood to mean that any, continuing sinners and ungodly, can, by believing, be accepted, or finally saved. The following chapter, particularly the latter part of it, (Sect. 6) would abundantly vindicate him from any such misconstruction. Meanwhile he will only remark, that true faith (in which repentance is considered as involved) is in Scripture regarded as *the radical principle of holiness*. If the root exists, the proper fruits will be brought forth. An attention to this consideration would have easily explained and reconciled those passages of St Paul's and St James's Epistles, which have furnished so much matter of argument and criticism. St James, it may be observed, all along speaks not of a man, who *has* faith, but who *says* that he hath faith. He contrasts pretended, imperfect, dead faith, with real, complete, living faith. This surely must appear decisively clear to those who observe that the conclusion which he deduces from his whole reasoning in verses 23 & 26, respects *faith* – Abraham *believed* God, &c. *Faith without works*, &c. It is his great object to assert and establish the right kind of faith, and only to deny the utility or value of that which falsely usurps the name. – Vide James ii. 14, &c. &c.

us to God – '*when enemies;*' and for making the fruits of holiness *the effects, not the cause,* of our being justified and reconciled: that in short, it opens freely the door of mercy, to the greatest and worst of penitent sinners; who obeying the blessed impulse of the grace of God, whereby they had been awakened from the sleep of death, and moved to seek for pardon, may enter in, and, through the regenerating influence of the Holy Spirit, be enabled to bring forth the fruits of Righteousness. But they rather conceive of Christianity as opening the door of mercy, that those, who on the ground of their own merits could not have hoped to justify themselves before God, may yet be admitted for Christ's sake, on condition of their having previously satisfied the moderated requisitions of Divine Justice. In speaking to others also of the Gospel scheme, they are apt to talk too much of terms and performances on our part, on which we become entitled to an interest in the sufferings of Christ; instead of stating the benefits of Christ's satisfaction as extended to us freely, 'without money and without price.'

The *practical* consequences of these errors are such as might be expected. They tend to prevent that sense which we ought to entertain of our own natural misery and helplessness; and that deep feeling of gratitude for the merits and intercession of Christ, to which we are wholly indebted for our reconciliation to God, and for the will and the power, from first to last, to work out our own salvation. They consider it too much in the light of a contract between two parties, wherein each, independently of the other, has his own distinct condition to perform; man – to do his duty; God – to justify and accept for Christ's sake: If they fail not in the discharge of their condition, assuredly the condition in God's part will be faithfully fulfilled. Accordingly, we find in fact, that they who represent the Gospel scheme in the manner above described, give evidence of the subject with which their hearts are most filled, by their proneness to run into merely moral disquisitions, either not mentioning at all, or at least but cursorily touching on, the sufferings and love of their Redeemer; and are little apt to kindle at their Saviour's name, or, like the apostles, to be betrayed by their fervor into what may be almost an untimely descant on the riches of his unutterable mercy. In addressing others also whom they conceive to be living in habits of sin, and under the wrath of God, they rather advise them to amend their ways as a preparation for their coming to Christ, than exhort them to throw themselves with deep prostration of soul at the foot of the cross, there to obtain pardon, and find grace to help in time of need.

The great importance of the subject in question will justify the writer in having been thus particular. It has arisen from a wish that on a matter of such magnitude, it should be impossible to mistake his meaning. But after all that has been said, let it also be remembered, that, except so far as the instruction of others is concerned, the point of importance is the internal disposition of the mind; and it is to be hoped, that a dependence for pardon and holiness may be placed where it ought to be, notwithstanding the vague manner in which men express themselves. Let us also hope, that he who searches the heart, sees the right dispositions in many who use the mistaken and dangerous language to which we have objected.

If the preceding statement of the error so generally prevalent concerning the nature of the Gospel offer be in any considerable degree just, it will then explain that langour in the affections towards our blessed Saviour, together with that inadequate impression of the necessity and value of the assistance of the Divine Spirit, which so generally prevail. According to the soundest principles of reasoning, it may be also adduced as an additional proof of the correctness of our present statement, that it so exactly falls in with those phenomena, and so naturally accounts for them. For even admitting that the persons above mentioned, particularly the last class, do at the bottom rely on the atonement of Christ; yet, on their scheme, it must necessarily happen, that the object to which they are most accustomed to look, with which their thoughts are chiefly conversant, and from which they most habitually derive complacency, is rather their own qualified merit and services, though confessed to be inadequate, than the sufferings and atoning death of a crucified Saviour. The affections towards our blessed Lord therefore (according to the theory of the passions formerly laid down) cannot be expected to flourish, because they receive not that which was shewn to be necessary to their nutriment and growth. If we would love him as affectionately, and rejoice in him as triumphantly, as the first Christians did; we must learn like them to repose our entire trust in him, and to adopt the language of the apostle, 'God forbid that I should glory, save in the cross of our Lord Jesus Christ'[1] – 'Who of God is made unto us wisdom and righteousness, and sanctification, and redemption.'[2]

Doubtless there have been too many, who, to their eternal ruin,

[1] Gal. vi. 14.   [2] 1 Cor. i. 30.

have abused the doctrine of Salvation by Grace; and have vainly trusted in Christ for pardon and acceptance, when by their vicious lives they have plainly proved the groundlessness of their pretensions. The tree is to be known by its fruits: and there is too much reason to fear that there is no principle of faith when it does not decidedly evince itself by the fruits of holiness. Dreadful indeed will be the doom, above that of all others, of those loose professors of Christianity, to whom at the last day our blessed Saviour will address those words, 'I never knew you; depart from me, all ye that work iniquity.' But the danger of error on this side ought not to render us insensible to the opposite error: an error against which in these days it seems particularly necessary to guard. It is far from the intention of the writer of this work to enter into the niceties of controversy. But surely without danger of being thought to violate this design, he may be permitted to contend, that they who in the main believe the doctrines of the Church of England, are bound to allow, that our dependence on our blessed Saviour, as alone the meritorious cause of our acceptance with God, and as the means of all its blessed fruits and glorious consequences, must be not merely formal and nominal, but real and substantial; not vague, qualified, and partial, but direct, cordial, and entire. 'Repentance towards God, and faith towards our Lord Jesus Christ,' was the sum of the apostolical instructions. It is not an occasional invocation of the name of Christ, or a transient recognition of his authority, that fills up the measure of the terms, *believing in Jesus*. This we shall find no such easy task: and, if we trust that we do believe, we should all perhaps do well to cry out in the words of an imploring suppliant, (he supplicated not in vain) 'Lord, help thou our unbelief.' We must be deeply conscious of our guilt and misery, heartily repenting of our sins, and firmly resolving to foresake them: and thus penitently 'fleeing for refuge to the hope set before us,' we must found altogether on the merit of the crucified Redeemer our hopes of escape from their deserved punishment, and of deliverance from their enslaving power. This must be our first, our last, our only plea. We are to surrender ourselves up to him to 'be washed in his blood,'[1] to be sanctified by his Spirit, resolving to receive him for our Lord and Master, to learn in his School, to obey all his commandments.

It may perhaps be not unnecessary, after having treated so largely on this important topic, to add a few words in order to obviate a

[1] Rev. i. 5.

charge which may be urged against us, that we are insisting on nice and abstruse distinctions in what is a matter of general concern: and this too in a system which on its original promulgation was declared to be peculiarly intended for the simple and poor. It will be abundantly evident, however, on a little reflection, and experience fully proves the position, that what has been required is not the perception of a subtile distinction, but a state and condition of heart. To the former, the poor and the ignorant must be indeed confessed unequal; but they are far less indisposed than the great and the learned, to bow down to that 'preaching of the cross, which is to them that perish foolishness, but unto them that are saved the power of God, and the wisdom of God.' The poor are not liable to be puffed up by the intoxicating fumes of ambition and wordly grandeur. They are less likely to be kept from entering into the straight and narrow way, and, when they have entered, to be drawn back again, or to be retarded in their progress, by the cares or pleasures of life. They may express themselves ill: but their views may be simple, and their hearts humble, penitent, and sincere. It is, as in other cases; the vulgar are the subjects of phæno-mena, the learned explain them: the former know nothing of the theory of vision or of sentiment; but this ignorance hinders them not from seeing and thinking; and though unable to discourse elaborately on the passions, they can feel warmly for their children, their friends, their country.

After this digression, if that be indeed a digression which, by remov-ing a formidable objection, renders the truth of the positions we wish to establish more clear and less questionable, we may now resume the thread of our argument. Still intreating therefore the attention of those, who have not been used to think much of the necessity of this undivided, and, if it may be so termed, unadulterated reliance, for which we have been contending: we would still more particularly address ourselves to others who are disposed to believe that though, in some obscure and vague sense, the death of Christ as the satisfaction for our sins, and for the purchase of our future happiness, and the sanctifying influence of the Holy Spirit, as to be admitted as fundamental articles of our creed, yet that these are doctrines so much above us, that they are not objects suited to our capacities; and that turning our eyes therefore from these difficult speculations, we should fix them on the practical and moral precepts of the Gospel. 'These it most concerns us to know; these therefore let us study. Such is the frailty of our nature, such the strength and number of our temptations to evil, that, in reducing the Gospel morality to practice, we shall find full employment: and by attending to these moral precepts, rather than to those high mysterious doctrines which you are pressing on us, we shall best prepare to appear before God on that tremendous day, when "He shall judge every man according to his WORKS.".'

'Vain wisdom all, and false philosophy!'

It will at once destroy this flimsy web, to reply in the words of our blessed Saviour, and of his beloved Disciple – 'This is the work of God, that ye *believe* in him whom he hath sent.'[1] 'This is his *commandment*, that we should *believe* on the name of his Son Jesus Christ.'[2] In truth, if we consider but for a moment the opinions of men who argue thus, we must be conscious of their absurdity. Let the modern Unitarians reduce the Gospel to a mere system of ethics, but surely it is the highest degree unreasonable to admit into our scheme all the grand peculiarities of Christianity, and having admitted, to neglect and think no more of them! 'Wherefore' (might the Socinian say) 'Wherefore all this costly and complicated machinery? It is like the Tychonic astronomy, encumbered and self-convicted by its own complicated relations and useless perplexities. It is so little like the simplicity of nature, it is so unworthy of the divine hand, that it even offends against those rules of propriety which we require to be observed in the imperfect compositions of the human intellect.'[3]

Well may the Socinian assume this lofty tone, with those whom we are now addressing. If these be indeed the doctrines of Revelation, common sense suggests to us that from their nature and their magnitude, they deserve our most serious regard. It is the very theology of Epicurus to allow the existence of these 'heavenly things,' but to deny their connection with human concerns, and their influence on human actions. Besides the unreasonableness of this conduct, we might strongly urge also in this connection the profaneness of thus treating as matters of subordinate consideration those parts of the system of Christianity, which are so strongly impressed on our reverence by the dignity of the person to whom they relate. This very argument is indeed repeatedly and pointedly pressed by the sacred writers.[4]

Nor is the profane irreverence of this conduct more striking than its ingratitude. When from reading that our Saviour was 'the brightness of his Father's glory, and the express image of his person, upholding

1 John, vi. 29.   2 1 John, iii. 23.
3 Nec Deus intersit, &c.   4 Vide Heb. ii. 1. &c.

23

all things by the word of his power,' we go on to consider the purpose for which he came on earth, and all that he did and suffered for us; surely, if we have a spark of ingenuousness left within us, we shall condemn ourselves as guilty of the blackest ingratitude, in rarely noticing, or coldly turning away, on whatever shallow pretences, from the contemplation of these miracles of mercy. For those baser minds, however, on which fear alone can operate, that motive is super-added; and we are plainly forewarned, both directly and indirectly, by the example of the Jewish nation, that God will not hold them guilt-less who are thus unmindful of his most signal acts of condescension and kindness. But as this is a question of pure Revelation, reasonings from probability may not be deemed decisive. To Revelation there-fore we must appeal; and without entering into a laboured discussion of the subject, which might be to trespass on the reader's patience, I would refer him to the sacred Writings themselves for complete satisfaction. We would earnestly recommend it to him to weigh with the utmost seriousness those passages of Scripture wherein the peculiar doctrines of Christianity are expressly mentioned; and farther, to attend, with due regard, to the illustration and confirmation, which the conclusions resulting from those passages incidentally receive from other parts of the word of God. They who maintain the opinion which we are combating, will thereby become convinced that their's is indeed an *unscriptural* Religion; and will learn, instead of turning off their eyes from the grand peculiarities of Christianity, to keep these ever in view, as the pregnant principles whence all the rest must derive their origin, and receive their best support.[1]

Let us then each for himself solemnly ask ourselves, whether *we* have fled for refuge to the appointed hope? And whether we are habitually looking to it, as to the only source of consolation?

[1] Any one who wishes to investigate this subject, will do well to study atten-tively M'LAURIN's Essay on Prejudices against the Gospel. – It may not be amiss here to direct the reader's attention to a few leading arguments, many of them those of the work just recommended. Let him maturely estimate the force of those terms, whereby the Apostle in the following passages designates and characterizes the whole of the Christian system. 'We preach Christ crucified.' – 'We determined to know nothing among you, save Jesus Christ, and him crucified.' The value of this argument will be acknowledged by all who consider, that a system is never designated by an immaterial or an inferior part of it, but by that which constitutes its prime consideration and essential distinction. The conclusion suggested by this remark is confirmed by the Lord's Supper being the rite by which our Saviour himself commanded his Disciples to keep him in

'Other foundation can no man lay:' there is no other ground for dependence, no other plea for pardon; but *here* there *is* hope, even to the uttermost. Let us labour then to affect our hearts with a deep conviction of our need of a Redeemer, and of the value of his offered mediation. Let us fall down humbly before the throne of God, imploring pity and pardon in the name of the Son of his love. Let us beseech him to give us a true spirit of repentance, and of hearty undivided faith in the Lord Jesus. Let us not be satisfied till the cordiality of our belief be confirmed to us by that character with which we are furnished by an inspired writer, 'that to as many as believe, Christ is

---

remembrance; and indeed a similar lesson is taught by the Sacrament of Baptism, which shadows out our souls being washed and purified by the blood of Christ. Observe next the frequency with which our Saviour's death and sufferings are introduced, and how often they are urged as practical motives.

'The minds of the Apostles seem full of this subject. Every thing puts them in mind of it, they did not allow themselves to have it long out of their view, nor did any other branch of spiritual instruction make them lose sight of it.' Consider next that part of the Epistle to the Romans, wherein St Paul speaks of some who went about to establish their own righteousness, and had not submitted themselves to the righteousness of God. May not this charge be in some degree urged, and even more strongly than in the case of the Jews, against those who satisfy themselves with vague, general, occasional thoughts of our Saviour's mediation; and the source of whose habitual complacency, as we explained above, is rather their being tolerably well satisfied with their own characters and conduct? Yet St Paul declares concerning those of whom he speaks, as concerning persons whose sad situation could not be too much lamented, that he had great heaviness and continual sorrow in his heart, adding still more emphatical expressions of deep and bitter regret.

Let the Epistle to the Galatians be also carefully examined and considered; and let it be fairly asked, what was the particular in which the Judaizing Christians were defective, and the want of which is spoken of in such strong terms as these; that it frustrates the grace of God, and must debar from all the benefits of the death of Jesus? The Judaizing converts were not immoral. They seem to have admitted the chief tenets concerning our Saviour. But they appear to have been disposed to trust *not wholly, be it observed also, but only in part*, for their acceptance with God, to the Mosaic institutions, instead of reposing entirely on the merits of Christ. Here let it be remembered, that when a compliance with these institutions was not regarded as conveying this inference, the Apostle shewed by his own conduct, that he did not deem it criminal; whence, no less than from the words of the Epistle, it is clear that the offence of the Judaizing Christians whom he condemned, was what we have stated; that their crime did not consist in their obstinately continuing to adhere to a dispensation the ceremonial of which Christianity had abrogated, nor yet that it arose out of the sacrifices of the Levitical law, being from their very nature without efficacy for the blotting out of sin. – Vide Hebrews, x. 4, &c. – It was not that the foundation on which they built was of a sandy nature, but that they built on *any other* foundation than that which God had laid in the Gospel; it was not that they fixed their confidence on a false or a defective object, but that they did not direct it exclusively to the only true object of Hope held forth to us by the Gospel.

precious;' and let us strive to increase daily in love towards our blessed Saviour; and pray earnestly, that 'we may be filled with *Joy* and *Peace* in believing, that we may abound in *Hope* through the power of the Holy Ghost.' Let us diligently put in practice the directions already given for cherishing and cultivating the principle of the Love of Christ. With this view let us labour assiduously to increase in knowledge, that our affection to the Lord who bought us, may be deeply rooted and rational. By frequent meditation on the incidents of our Saviour's life, and still more on the astonishing circumstances of his death; by often calling to mind the state from which he proposes to rescue us, and the glories of his heavenly kingdom; by continual intercourse with him of prayer and praise, of dependence and confidence in dangers, of hope and joy in our brighter hours, let us endeavour to keep him constantly present to our minds, and to render all our conceptions of him more distinct, lively, and intelligent. The title of Christian is a reproach to us, if we estrange ourselves from him after whom we are denominated. The name of Jesus is not to be to us like the Allah of the Mahometans, a talisman or an amulet, to be worn on the arm, merely as an external badge and symbol of our profession, and to preserve us from evil by some mysterious and unintelligible potency; but it is to be engraven deeply on the heart, there written by the finger of God himself in everlasting characters. It is our sure and undoubted title to present peace and future glory. The assurance which this title conveys of a bright reversion, will lighten the burdens, and alleviate the sorrows of life; and in some happier moments, it will impart to us somewhat of that fulness of joy which is at God's right hand, enabling us to join even here in the heavenly Hosannah. 'Worthy is the Lamb that was slain, to receive power and riches, and wisdom, and strength, and honour, and glory, and blessing.'[1] – 'Blessing, and honour, and glory, and power, be unto him that sitteth upon the throne, and unto the the Lamb for ever and ever.'[2]

CHAPTER IV

WHAT has been now remarked, concerning the habitual feelings of the real believer, may suggest a reply to an objection common in the mouths of nominal Christians, that we would deny men the innocent amusements and gratifications of life; thus causing our Reli-

[1] Rev. v. 12.   [2] Ib. 13.

gion to wear a gloomy forbidding aspect, instead of her true and natural face of cheerfulness and joy. This is a charge of so serious a nature, that although it lead into a digression, it may not be improper to take some notice of it.

In the first place, Religion prohibits no amusement or gratification which is *really* innocent. The question, however, of its innocence, must not be tried by the loose maxims of wordly morality, but by the spirit of the injunctions of the word of God; and by the indulgence being conformable or not conformable to the genius of Christianity, and to the tempers and dispositions of mind enjoined on its professors. There can be no dispute concerning the true end of recreations. They are intended to refresh our exhausted bodily or mental powers and to restore us, with renewed vigour, to the more serious occupations of life. Whatever therefore fatigues either body or mind, instead of refreshing them, is not fitted to answer the designed purpose. Whatever consumes more time, or money, or thought, than it is expedient (I might say *necessary*) to allot to mere amusement, can hardly be approved by any one, who considers these talents as precious deposits, for the expenditure of which he will have to give account. Whatever directly or indirectly must be likely to injure the welfare of a fellow-creature, can scarcely be a suitable *recreation* for a Christian, who is 'to love his neighbour as himself;' or a very consistent *diversion* for any one, the business of whose life is to diffuse happiness.

But does a Christian never relax? Let us not so wrong and vilify the bounty of Providence, as to allow for a moment that the sources of innocent amusement are so rare, that men must be driven, almost by constraint, to such as are of a doubtful quality. On the contrary, such has been the Creator's goodness, that almost every one of our physical and intellectual, and moral faculties (and the same may be said of the whole creation which we see around us) is not only calculated to answer the proper end of its being, by its subserviency to some purpose of solid usefulness, but to be the instrument of administering pleasure.

> Not content
> With every food of life to nourish man,
> Thou mak'st all nature beauty to his eye
> And music to his ear.

Our Maker also, in his kindness, has so constructed us, that even mere vicissitude is grateful and refreshing – a consideration which should prompt us often to seek, from a prudent *variation of useful pursuits,* that recreation, for which we are apt to resort to what is altogether *unproductive* and *unfruitful*.

Yet rich and multiplied are the springs of innocent relaxation. The Christian relaxes in the temperate use of all the gifts of Providence. Imagination, and taste, and genius, and the beauties of creation, and the works of art, lie open to him. He relaxes in the feast of reason, in the intercourses of society, in the sweets of friendship, in the endearments of love, in the exercise of hope, of confidence, of joy, of gratitude, of universal good-will, of all the benevolent and generous affections; which, by the gracious appointment of our Creator, while they disinterestedly intend only happiness to others, are most surely productive of peace and joy to ourselves. O! little do they know of the true measure of man's enjoyment, who can compare these delightful complacencies with the frivolous pleasures of dissipation, or the coarse gratifications of sensuality. It is no wonder, however, that the nominal Christian should reluctantly give up, one by one, the pleasures of the world; and look back upon them, when relinquished, with eyes of wistfulness and regret: because he knows not the sweetness of the delights with which true Christianity repays those trifling sacrifices; and is wholly unacquainted with the *nature* of that pleasantness which is to be found in the ways of Religion.

It is indeed true, that when any one, who has long been going on in the gross and unrestrained practice of vice, is checked in his career, and enters at first on a religious course, he has much to undergo. Fear, guilt, remorse, shame, and various other passions, struggle and conflict within him. His appetites are clamorous for their accustomed gratification; and inveterate habits are scarcely to be denied. He is weighed down by a load of guilt, and almost overwhelmed by the sense of his unworthiness. But all this ought in fairness to be charged to the account of his past sins, and not to that of his present repentance. It rarely happens, however, that this state of suffering continues very long. When the mental gloom is the blackest, a ray of heavenly light occasionally breaks in, and suggests the hope of better days. Even in this life it is found an universal truth, that 'They that sow in tears,' provided they be really tears of penitence and contrition, 'shall reap in joy.' 'The broken and contrite heart God never did, nor ever will, despise.'

Neither, when we maintain, that the ways of Religion are ways of pleasantness, do we mean to deny that the Christian's internal state is, through the whole of his life, a state of discipline and warfare. Several of the causes which contribute to render it such, have been already pointed out, together with the workings of his mind in relation to them: but if he has solicitudes and griefs peculiar to himself, he has 'joys also with which a stranger intermeddles not.'

'Drink deep,' however, 'or taste not,' is a direction full as applicable to Religion, if we would find it a source of pleasure, as it is to knowledge. A little Religion is, it must be confessed, apt to make men gloomy, as a little knowledge is to render them vain: hence the unjust imputation often brought upon Religion by those, whose degree of Religion is just sufficient, by condemning their course of conduct, to render them uneasy; enough merely to impair the sweetness of the pleasures of sin, and not enough to compensate for the relinquishment of them by its own peculiar comforts. Thus these men bring up, as it were, an ill report of that land of promise, which in truth abounds with whatever in our journey through life, can best refresh and strengthen us.

We have enumerated some sources of pleasure which men of the world may understand, and must acknowledge to belong to the true Christian; but there are others, and those of a still higher class, to which they must confess themselves strangers. To say nothing of a qualified, I dare not say an entire exemption from those distracting passions and corroding cares, by which they must naturally be harassed, whose treasure is within the reach of mortal accidents; the Christian has a humble quiet-giving hope of being reconciled to God, and of enjoying his favour; he has a solid peace of mind, (which the world can neither give nor take away,) resulting from a firm confidence in the infinite wisdom and goodness of God, and in the unceasing care and kindness of a gracious Saviour, and he has persuasion of the truth of the divine assurance, that all things shall work together for his good.

When the pulse indeed beats high, and we are flushed with youth, and health, and vigour; when all goes on prosperously, and success seems almost to anticipate our wishes; then we feel not the want of the consolations of Religion: but when fortune frowns, or friends forsake us; when sorrow, or sickness, or old age, comes upon us, then it is, that the superiority of the pleasures of Religion is established over those of dissipation and vanity, which are ever apt to fly from us when we are most in want of their aid. There is scarcely a more melancholy sight to a considerate mind, than that of an old man, who is a stranger to those only true sources of satisfaction. How affecting, and at the same time how disgusting, is it, to see such an one awkwardly catching at the pleasures of his younger years, which are now beyond his reach; or feebly attempting to retain them, while they mock his endeavours and elude his grasp! To such an one, *gloomily* indeed does the evening of life set in! All is sour and cheerless. He can neither look backward with complacency, nor forward with hope; while the aged Christian relying on the assured mercy of his Redeemer, can calmly reflect, that his dismission is at hand, and that his redemption draweth nigh: while his strength declines, and his faculties decay, he can quietly repose himself in the fidelity of God: and at the very entrance of the valley of the shadow of death, he can lift up an eye, dim perhaps, and feeble, yet occasionally sparkling with hope, and confidently looking forward to the near possession of his heavenly inheritance, even 'to those joys which eye hath not seen, nor ear heard, neither hath it entered into the heart of man to conceive.'

Never were there times which inculcated more forcibly, than those in which we live, the wisdom of seeking a happiness beyond the reach of human vicissitudes. What striking lessons have *we* had of the precarious tenure of all sublunary possessions! Wealth, and power, and prosperity, how peculiarly transitory and uncertain! But Religion dispenses her choicest cordials in the seasons of exigence, in poverty, in exile, in sickness, and in death. The essential superiority of that support which is derived from Religion is less felt, at least it is less apparent, when the Christian is in full possession of riches, and splendour, and rank, and all the gifts of nature and fortune. But when all these are swept away by the rude hand of time, or the rough blast of adversity, the true Christian stands, like the glory of the forest, erect and vigorous; stripped indeed of his summer foliage, but more than ever discovering to the observing eye the solid strength of his substantial texture;

> Pondere fixa suo est, nudosque per aëra ramos
> Attollens, trunco non frondibus efficit umbram.

2

S. T. COLERIDGE: *'Lay Sermons'* and *'Church and State'*

Part of *Lay Sermons*; chapters V and VI of *Church and State*

It is very difficult to select from Coleridge in such way as to give any idea of the power and influence of his thought. His endless digressions and his occasional obscurity tend to mask the importance of what he is saying. But Newman recognized him as a great precursor of the Oxford Movement, and Mill saw in him one of the two most influential thinkers of the whole century. Coleridge's thought cannot be summarized, but we can note one or two points. He sees everything as organic, as against the fashionable mechanistic philosophy. Thus in religious terms he prepares the way for the recovery of the forgotten doctrine of the Church as the Body of Christ. He feels always that we are members one of another. Then he defends the Church Establishment as so many others had done; but in a new way. He distinguishes between the Church as a Divine Society, of which the English Church can only be a part, and the secular functions of an establishment actually existing, which include teaching and civilizing the people. He also attempts to give a more spiritual meaning to the idea of Royal Supremacy, and his attitude to Henry VIII and the Reformation is markedly ambivalent.

His attack on Unitarians and Quakers should not be regarded primarily as an episode in past sectarian quarrels. The essential point that Coleridge was trying to establish was that Christianity was strange, mysterious and capable of making unlimited demands on the intellectual and the moral faculties; in fact, that it was a *revealed* religion, not a higher form of common sense. In maintaining this he had more than Unitarians against him. He was opposing the whole tradition of *Paley's Evidences*, which remained for more than a hundred years the standard theological textbook at the exclusively Anglican University of Oxford.

The sharp distinction Coleridge makes between Christianity and worldly prudence was much more startling to his first readers than it is to us; for both the tepid conformism of the thoughtless majority in a 'Christian country' and the prevailing theological tone of more devout circles tended to identify the two.

THERE is a third influence, alternately our spur and our curb, without which all the pursuits and desires of man must either exceed or fall short of their just measure. Need I add, that I mean the influence of religion? I speak of that sincere, that entire interest, in the undivided faith of Christ which demands the first-fruits of the whole man, his affections no less than his outward acts, his understanding equally with his feelings. For be assured, never yet did there exist a full faith in the divine Word, (by whom not immortality alone, but light and immortality were brought into the world) which did not expand the intellect while it purified the heart; which did not multiply the aims and objects of the mind, while it fixed and simplified those of the desires and passions. If acquiescence without insight; if warmth without light; if an immunity from doubt given and guaranteed by a resolute ignorance; if the habit of taking for granted the words of a catechism, remembered or forgotten; if a sensation of positiveness substituted – I will not say, for certainty, but – for that calm assurance, the very means and conditions of which it supersedes; if a belief that seeks the darkness, and yet strikes no root, immovable as the limpet from its rock, and like the limpet fixed there by mere force of adhesion; – if these suffice to make us Christians, in what intelligible sense could our Lord have announced it as the height and consummation of the signs and miracles which attested his Divinity, that *the Gospel was preached to the poor?* In what sense could the Apostle affirm that believers have received, not indeed the wisdom of this world that comes to nought, but the wisdom of God, that we might know and comprehend the things that are freely given to us of God? or that every Christian, in proportion as he is indeed a Christian, has received the Spirit that searcheth all things, yea, *the deep things of God himself?* – On what grounds could the Apostle denounce even the sincerest fervour of spirit as defective, where it does not bring forth fruits in the understanding?[1] Or again: if to believe were enough, why are we com-

[1] Brethren! be not children in understanding: howbeit, in malice be ye children but in understanding be men.

manded by another Apostle that, *besides this, giving all diligence we should add to our faith manly energy and to manly energy knowledge?* (2 Pet. i. 5.) Is it not especially significant, that in the divine economy, as revealed to us in the New Testament, the peculiar office of Redemption is attributed to the Word, that is, to the intelligential wisdom which from all eternity is with God, and is God; that in Him is life, and the life is the light of men?

In the present day we hear much, and from men of various creeds, of the plainness and simplicity of the Christian religion: and a strange abuse has been made of these words, often indeed with no ill intention, but still oftener by men who would fain transform the necessity of believing in Christ into a recommendation to believe him. The advocates of the latter scheme grew out of a sect that were called Socinians, but having succeeded in disbelieving far beyond the last foot-marks of the Socini, have chosen to designate themselves by the name of Unitarians. But this is a name, which in its proper sense, can belong only to their antagonists: for unity or unition, and indistinguishable unicity or sameness, are incompatible terms: while in the exclusive sense in which they mean the name to be understood, it is a presumptuous boast, and an uncharitable calumny. Their true designation, which simply expresses a fact admitted on all sides, would be that of Psilanthrophists,[1] or assertors of the mere humanity of Christ. It is the interest of these to speak of the Christian religion as comprised in a few plain doctrines, and containing nothing not intelligible, at the 'first hearing', to men of the narrowest capacities. Well then, (it might be replied) we are disposed to place a full reliance on the veracity of the great Founder of the Christian religion, and likewise – which is more than you yourselves are on all occasions willing to admit – on the accuracy and competence of the writers, who first recorded his acts and sayings. We have learned from you, whom, – and we now wish to hear from you – what we are to believe. In answer to this request we are referred to a particular fact or incident, recorded of Jesus, by his biographers, the object and purpose of which was, we are

---

[1] New things justify new terms. *Novis in rebus licet nova nobis verba confingere.* –, We never speak of the unity of attraction, or of the unity of repulsion; but of the unity of attraction and repulsion in each one corpuscle. The essential diversity of the ideas, unity and sameness, was among the elementary principles of the old logicians; and the sophisms grounded on the confusion of these terms have been ably exposed by Leibnitz, in his critique on Wissowatius, the acutest, perhaps, of all the learned Socinian divines, when Socinian divines were undeniably men of learning.

told, to produce belief of certain doctrines. And what are these? Those without the previous belief of which, no man would, or rather, according to St Paul's declaration, could become a convert to Christianity; doctrines, which it is certain that Christ's immediate disciples believed, not less confidently, before they had acknowledged his mission, than they did afterwards. Religion and politics, they tell us, require but the application of a common sense, which every man possesses, to a subject in which every man is concerned. To be a musician, an orator, a painter, or even a good mechanician, presupposes genius; to be an excellent artisan or mechanic requires more than an average degree of talent; but to be a legislator or a theologian, or both at once, demands nothing but common sense! Now, I willingly admit that nothing can be necessary to the salvation of a Christian which is not in his power. For such, therefore, as have neither the opportunity nor the capacity of learning more, sufficient, doubtless, will be the belief of those plain truths, and the fulfilment of those commands, which to be incapable of understanding, is to be a man in appearance only. But even to this scanty creed the disposition of faith must be added: and let it not be forgotten that though nothing can be easier than to understand a code of belief, four-fifths of which consist in avowals of disbelief, and the remainder in truths, concerning which (in this country at least) a man must have taken pains to learn to have any doubt; yet it is by no means easy to reconcile this code of negatives with the declarations of the Christian Scriptures. On the contrary, it requires all the resources of verbal criticism, and all the perverse subtlety of special pleading, to work out a plausible semblance of correspondency between them. It must, however, be conceded that a man may consistently spare himself the trouble of the attempt, and leave the New Testament unread, after he has once thoroughly persuaded himself that it can teach him nothing of any real importance that he does not already know. St Paul indeed thought otherwise. For though he too teaches us, that in the religion of Christ there is *milk for babes*: yet he informs us at the same time, that there is *meat for strong men*: and to the like purpose one of the Fathers has observed that in the New Testament there are shallows where the lamb may ford, and depths where the elephant must swim. The Apostle exhorts the followers of Christ to the continual study of the new religion, on the ground that in the mystery of Christ, which in other ages was not made known to the sons of men, and in the riches of Christ which no research could exhaust, there were contained all the treasures of knowledge and wisdom. Accordingly in that earnestness of spirit, which his own personal experience of the truth inspired, he prays with a solemn and a ceremonious fervour, that being *strengthened with might in the inner man, they may be able to comprehend with all saints what is the breadth and length and depth and height*, of that living principle at once the giver and the gift of that anointing faith, which in endless evolution *teaches us of all things, and is truth.* For all things are but parts and forms of its progressive manifestation, and every new knowledge but a new organ of sense and insight into this one all-inclusive verity, which, still filling the vessel of the understanding, still dilates it to a capacity of yet other and yet greater truths, and thus makes the soul feel its poverty by the very amplitude of its present, and the immensity of its reversionary, wealth. All truth indeed is simple, and needs no extrinsic ornament. And the more profound the truth is, the more simple: for the whole labour and building-up of knowledge is but one continued process of simplification. But I cannot comprehend, in what ordinary sense of the words the properties of plainness and simplicity can be applied to the Prophets, or to the writings of St John, or to the Epistles of St Paul; or what can have so marvellously improved the capacity of our laity beyond the same class of persons among the primitive Christians; who, as we are told by a fellow Apostle, found in the writings last-mentioned many passages hard to be understood, which the *unlearned* as well as the unstable, were in danger of wresting and misinterpreting. I can well understand, however, what is and has been the practical consequence of this notion. It is this very consequence, indeed, that occasioned the preceding remarks, makes them pertinent to my present subject, and gives them a place in the train of argument requisite for its illustration. For what need of any after-recurrence to the sources of information concerning a religion, the whole contents of which can be thoughly acquired at once, and in a few hours? An occasional remembrancing may, perhaps, be expedient; but what object of study can a man propose to himself in a matter of which he knows all that can be known, all at least, that it is of use to know? Like the first rules of arithmetic, its few plain and obvious truths may hourly serve the man's purposes, yet never once occupy his thoughts. But it is impossible that the affections should be kept constant to an object which gives no employment to the understanding. The energies of the intellect, increase of insight, and enlarging views, are necessary to keep alive the substantial faith in the heart. They are the appointed fuel to the sacred fire. In the state of perfection all other faculties may, perhaps, be swallowed up in love; but it is on the wings of the Cherubim, which the ancient Hebrew doctors interpreted as meaning the powers and efforts of the intellect, that we must first be borne up to the pure empyrean: and it must be Seraphs and not the hearts of poor mortals, that can burn unfuelled and self-fed. *Give me understanding (exclaimed the royal Psalmist) and I shall observe thy law with my whole heart. Teach me knowledge and good judgment. Thy commandment is exceeding broad: O how I love thy law! it is my meditation all the day. The entrance of thy words giveth light, it giveth understanding to the simple. I prevented the dawning of the morning: mine eyes prevent the night-watches, that I might meditate upon thy word.* Now where the very contrary of this is the opinion of many, and the practice of most, what results can be expected but those which are actually presented to us in our daily experience?

Thus, then, there is one class of men[1] who read the Scriptures, when

[1] Whether it be on the increase, as a sect, is doubtful. But it is admitted by all – nay, strange as it may seem, made a matter of boast, – that the number of its secret adherents, outwardly of other denominations, is tenfold greater than that of its avowed and incorporated followers. And truly in our cities and great manufacturing and commercial towns, among lawyers and such of the tradesfolk as are the ruling members in book-clubs, I am inclined to fear that this has not been asserted without good ground. For, Socinianism in its present form, consisting almost wholly in attack and imagined detection, has a particular charm for what are called shrewd knowing men. Besides, the vain and half-educated, whose Christian and surnames in the title pages of our magazines, lady's diaries, and the like, are the successors of the shame-faced Critos, Phileleutheroses, and Philaletheses in the time of our grandfathers, will be something: and now that Deism has gone out of fashion, Socinianism has swept up its refuse. As the main success of this sect is owing to the small proportion which the affirmative articles of their faith (*rari nantes in gurgite vasto*) bear to the negative, (that is their belief to their disbelief) it will be an act of kindness to the unwary to bring together the former under one point of view. This is done in the following catalogue, the greater part if not the whole of which may be authenticated from the writings of Mr Belsham.

1. They believe in one God, professing to differ from other Christians only in holding the Deity to be unipersonal, the Father alone being God, the Son a mere, though an inspired and highly gifted, man, and the Holy Spirit either a synonyme of God, or of the divine agency, or of its effects.

2. They believe men's actions necessitated, and consistently with this affirm that the Christian religion (that is, their view of it) precludes all remorse for our sins, they being a present calamity, but not guilt.

3. They believe the Gospels though not written by inspiration, to be authentic histories on the whole: though with some additions and interpolations. And on the authority of these writings confirmed by other evidence, they believe in the resurrection of the man Jesus Christ, from the dead.

4. On the historic credibility of this event they believe in the resurrection of the body, which in their opinion is the whole man, at the last day: and differ from other Churches in this only, that while other Christians believe, that all

they do read them, in order to pick and choose their faith: or (to speak more accurately) for the purpose of plucking away live-asunder, as it were from the divine organism of the Bible, textuary morsels and fragments for the support of doctrines which they had learned beforehand from the higher oracle of their own natural common-sense.

---

men will arise in the body, they hold that all the bodies that had been men will arise.

5. A certain indefinite number of mankind thus renewed to life and consciousness, it is the common belief of them all, will be placed in a state of happiness and immortality. But with respect to those who have died in the calamitous condition of unreformed sinfulness, (to what extent it is for the supreme Judge to decide) they are divided among themselves. The one party teach, that such unhappy persons will be raised only to be re-annihilated: the other party contend, that there will be a final restoration of all men, with a purgatory or state of remedial discipline, the severity and duration of which will be proportioned to the kind, degree, and obstinacy of the disease, and of which therefore every man is left to his own conjectural hopes and fears: with this comfort however to the very worst, (that is, most unfortunate and erroneous of mankind) that it will be all well with them at last. In this article they differ from the Papists in having no hell, and in placing their purgatory after, instead of before, the day of judgment.

6. Lastly, as they hold only an intellectual and physical and not a moral, difference in the actions and characters of men, they not being free agents, and therefore not more responsible beings than the true beasts, although their greater powers of memory and comparison render them more susceptible of being acted on by prospective motives – (and in this sense they retain the term, responsibility, after having purified it by the ex-inanition of its old, and the transfusion of a new, meaning) – and as they with strict consequence, merge all the attributes of Deity in power, intelligence, and benevolence, (mercy and justice being modes, or rather perspective views, of the two latter; the holiness of God meaning the same or nothing at all; and his anger, offence, and hatred of moral evil, being mere metaphors and figures of speech addressed to a rude and barbarous people) they profess to hold a Redemption – not however by the Cross of Christ, except as his death was an evidence of his sincerity, and the necessary preliminary to his Resurrection; but – by the effects which this fact of his Resurrection, together with his example, and his re-publication of the moral precepts (taught indeed long before, but as they think, not so clearly, by Moses and the Prophets) were calculated to produce on the human mind. So that if it had so happened, that a man had been influenced to an innocent and useful life by the example, precepts, and martyrdom of Socrates, Socrates, and not Christ, would have been his Redeemer.

These are all the positives of the modern Socinian Creed, and even these it was not possible to extricate wholly from the points of disbelief. But if it should be asked, why this resurrection, or re-creation is confined to the human animal, the answer must be, – that more than this has not been revealed. And so far all Christians will join assent. But some have added, and in my opinion much to their credit, that they hope it may be the case with the brutes likewise, as they see no sufficient reason to the contrary. And truly, upon their scheme, I agree with them. For if man be no other or nobler creature essentially, than he is represented in their system, the meanest reptile, that maps out its path on the earth by lines of slime, must be of equal worth and respectability, not only in the sight of the Holy

Sanctas Scripturas frustant ut frustrent. Through the gracious dispensations of Providence a complexity of circumstances may co-operate as anti-dotes to a noxious principle, and realise the paradox of a very good man under a very evil faith. It is not denied that a Socinian may be as honest, useful and benevolent a character as any of his neighbours; and if he thinks more and derives a larger portion of his pleasures from intellectual sources, he is likely to be more so. But in such instances (and that they are not infrequent, I am, from my own experience, most willing to bear witness), the fruit is from the grafts, not from the tree. The native produce is, or would be, an intriguing, overbearing, scorn-ful and wordly disposition; and in point of fact, it is the only scheme of religion that inspires in its adherents a contempt for the understandings of all who differ from them.[1] But be this as it may, and whatever be its effects, it is not probable that Christianity will have any direct influence on men who pay it no other compliment than that of calling by its name the previous dictates and decisions of their own mother-wit.

One, but by a strange contradiction even before man's own reason. For remove all the sources of esteem and the love founded on esteem, and whatever else pre-supposes a will and therein a possible transcendence to the material world; mankind, as far as my experience has extended, (and I am less than the least of many whom I could cite as having formed the very same judgment) are on the whole distinguished from the other beasts incomparably more to their dis-advantage, by lying, treachery, ingratitude, massacre, thirst of blood, and by sensualities which both in sort and degree it would be libelling their brother-beasts to call bestial, than to their advantage by a greater extent of intellect. And what indeed, abstracted from the free-will, could this intellect be but a more showy instinct of more various application indeed, but far less secure, useful, or adapted to its purposes, than the instinct of birds, insects, and the like. In short, as I have elsewhere observed, compared with the wiles and factories of the spider, or with the cunning of the fox, it would be but a more efflorescent, and for that very cause a less efficient, salt to prevent the hog from putrifying before its destined hour.

Well may the words of Isaiah be applied and addressed to the teachers and followers of this sect, or rather, I would say, to their tenets as personified – *The word of the Lord was unto them, precept upon precept, line upon line, here a little and there a little, that they might go and fall backward, and be broken and snared. Wherefore, hear the word of the Lord, ye scornful men that rule this people! Because ye have said, We have made a covenant with death, and with hell are we at agreement! Your covenant with death shall be annulled, and your agreement with hell shall not stand. For your bed is shorter than that a man can stretch himself upon it, and the covering narrower than that he can wrap himself in it.* – xxviii.

[1] A Calvinist, or Moravian, for instance, would lament over a disbeliever in their peculiar tenets, as over one from whom the gift of faith had been hitherto withholden; but would readily join in attestation of his talents, learning, good morals, and all natural gifts. – 1827.

Still, however, the more numerous class is of those who do not trouble themselves at all with religious matters, which they resign to the clergyman of the parish. But whilst not a few among these men consent to pray and hear by proxy; whilst others, more attentive to the prudential advantages of a decorous character, yield the customary evidence of their Church-membership; but, this performed, are at peace with themselves, and

> think their Sunday's task
> As much as God or man can fairly ask; –

there exists amongst the most respectable laity of our cities and great towns, an active, powerful, and enlarging minority, whose industry, while it enriches their families, is at the same time a support to the revenue, and not seldom enlivens their whole neighbourhood: men whose lives are free from all disreputable infirmities, and of whose activity in the origination, patronage, and management both of charitable and of religious associations, who must not have read or heard? and which who that has will dare deny to be most exemplary? After the custom of our forefathers, and their pure household religion, these, in so many respects estimable persons, are for the greater part in the habit of having family-prayer, and a portion of Scripture read every morning and evening. In this class, with such changes or sub-stitutions as the peculiar tenets of the sect require, we must include the sensible, orderly and beneficent Society of the Friends. Here then, if any where, (that is, in any class of men; for the present argument is not concerned with individuals,) we may expect to find Christianity tempering commercial avidity and sprinkling its holy damps on the passion of accumulation. This, I say, we might expect to find, if an undoubting belief in the threats and promises of Revelation, and a consequent regularity of personal, domestic, and social demeanour, sufficed to constitute that Christianity, the power and privilege of which is so to renew and irradiate the whole intelligential and moral life of man, as to overcome the *spirit of the world*. If this, the appointed test, were found wanting, should we not be forced to apprehend, nay, are we not compelled to infer, that the spirit of prudential motive, however ennobled by the magnitude and awfulness of its objects,[1]

---

[1] And in this alone, Paley, by a use of terms altogether arbitrary, places the distinction between prudence and virtue, the former being self-love in its appli-cation to the sum of pain and pleasure that is likely to result to us, as the conse-quence of our actions, in the present life only; while the latter is the same self-love, that together with the present consequences of our actions, takes in likewise the

and though as the termination of a lower, – it may be the commencement (and not seldom the occasion) of a higher state, – is not, even in respect of morality itself, that abiding and continuous principle of action, which is either one with the faith spoken of by St Paul, or its immediate offspring. It cannot be that spirit of obedience to the commands of Christ, by which the soul dwelleth in him, and he in it; and which our Saviour himself announces as a *being born again*. And this indispensable act, or influence, or impregnation, of which, as of a divine tradition, the eldest philosophy is not silent; which flashed through the darkness of the pagan mysteries; and which it was therefore a reproach to a master in Israel, that he had not already known; this is elsewhere explained, as a seed which, though of gradual development, did yet potentially contain the essential form not merely of a better, but of another life; – amidst all the frailties and transient eclipses of mortality making, I repeat, the subjects of this regeneration not so

---

more important enjoyments or sufferings which, accordingly as we obey or disobey His known commands, God has promised to bestow, or threatened to inflict, on us in the life to come.[a] According to this writer, it becomes the duty of a rational free agent (it would be more pertinent to say, of a sentient animal capable of forecast) to reduce his will to an habitual coincidence with his reason, on no other ground, but because he believes that God is able and determined either to gratify or to torment him. Thus, the great principle of the Gospel, that we are bound to love our neighbours as ourselves and God above all, must, if translated into a consistency with this theory of enlightened self-love, run thus: On the ground of our fear of torment and our expectation of pleasure from an infinitely powerful Being, we are under a prudential obligation of acting towards our neighbours as if we loved them equally with ourselves; but ultimately and in very truth to love ourselves only. And this is the work, this the system of moral and political philosophy cited as highest authority in our Senate and Courts of Judicature? And (still worse!) this is the text-book for the moral lectures at one of our Universities, justly the most celebrated for scientific ardour and manly thinking. It is not without a pang of filial sorrow that I make this acknowledgement, which nothing could have extorted from me but the strongest conviction of the mischievous and debasing tendencies of that wide-spread system, in which the works of Paley (his Sermons excepted) act not the less pernicious part, because the most decorous and plausible. The fallacious sophistry of the grounding principle in this whole system has been detected by Des Cartes, and Bishop Butler; and of late years, with great ability and originality, by Mr Hazlitt.

a 'And from this account of obligation it follows, that we are obliged to nothing but what we ourselves are to gain or lose something by; for nothing else can be a violent motive to us. As we should not be obliged to obey the laws or the magistrate, unless rewards or punishments, pleasure or pain, somehow or other, depended upon our obedience; so neither should we, without the same reason, be obliged to do what is right, to practise virtue, or to obey the commands of God.' – Paley, Moral and Polit. Phil. B.II. c. 2. *et passim.*

properly better as other men, whom therefore the world could not but hate, as aliens. Its own native growth, to whatever height it had been improved by cultivation (whether through the agency of blind sympathies, or of an intelligent self-interest, the two best guides to the loftiest points to which the worldly life can ascend) the world has always been ready and willing to acknowledge and admire. *They are of the world: therefore speak they out of the heart of the world* (ἐκ τοῦ κόσμου) *and the world heareth them.* (1 John, iv.)

To abstain from acts of wrong and violence, to be moreover industrious, useful, and of seemly bearing, are qualities presupposed in the Gospel code, as the preliminary conditions, rather than the proper and peculiar effects, of Christianity. But they are likewise qualities so palpably indispensable to the temporal interests of mankind that, if we except the brief frenzies of revolutionary riot, there never was a time, in which the world did not profess to reverence them: nor can we state any period, in which a more than ordinary character for assiduity, regularity, and charitableness did not secure the world's praise and favour, and were not calculated to advance the individual's own worldly interests: provided only, that his manners and professed tenets were those of some known and allowed body of men.

I ask then, what is the fact? We are – and, till its good purposes, which are many, have been all achieved, and we can become something better, long may we continue such – a busy, enterprising, and commercial nation. The habits attached to this character must, if there exist no adequate counterpoise, inevitably lead us, under the specious names of utility, practical knowledge, and so forth, to look at all things through the *medium* of the market, and to estimate the worth of all pursuits and attainments by their marketable value. In this does the spirit of trade consist. Now would the general experience bear us out in the assertion, that amid the absence or declension of all other antagonist forces, there is found in the very circle of the trading and opulent themselves, in the increase, namely, of religious professors among them, a spring of resistance to the excess of the commercial *impetus*, from the impressive example of their unworthy feelings evidenced by their moderation in wordly pursuits? I fear, that we may anticipate the answer wherever the religious zeal of such professors does not likewise manifest itself by the glad devotion of as large a portion of their time and industry, as the duty of providing a fair competence for themselves and their families leaves at their own disposal, to the comprehension of those inspired writings and the evolution of those pregnant truths, which are proposed for our earnest sedulous research, in order that by occupying our understandings they may more and more assimilate our affections. I fear that the inquiring traveller would more often hear of zealous religionists who have read (and as a duty too and with all due acquiescence) the prophetic *Woe to them that join house to house and lay field to field, that they may be alone in the land!* – and yet find no object deform the beauty of the prospect from their window or even from their castle turrets so annoyingly, as a meadow not their own, or a field under ploughing with the beam-end of the plough in the hands of its humble owner! I fear that he must too often make report of men lawful in their dealings, Scriptural in their language, almsgivers, and patrons of Sunday schools, who are yet resistless and overawing bidders at all land auctions in their neighbourhood, who live in the centre of farms without leases, and tenants without attachments! Or if his way should be through our great towns and manufacturing districts, instances would grow cheap with him of wealthy religious practitioners who never travel for orders without cards of edification in prose and verse, and small tracts of admonition and instruction, all 'plain and easy, and suited to the meanest capacities;' who pray daily, as the first act of the morning and as the last of the evening, *Lead us not into temptation; but deliver us from evil!* and employ all the interval with an edge of appetite keen as the scythe of death in the pursuit of yet more and yet more of a temptation so perilous, that (as they have full often read, and heard read, without the least questioning, or whisper of doubt) no power short of omnipotence could make their deliverance from it credible or conceivable. Of all denominations of Christians, there is not one in existence or on record whose whole scheme of faith and worship was so expressly framed for the one purpose of spiritualising the mind and of abstracting it from the vanities of the world, as the Society of Friends, not one, in which the members are connected, and their professed principles enforced by so effective and wonderful a form of discipline. But in the zeal of their founders and first proselytes for perfect spirituality they excluded from their system all ministers especially trained and educated for the ministry, with all professional theologians: and they omitted to provide for the raising up among themselves any other established class of learned men, as teachers and schoolmasters for instance, in their stead. Even at this day, though the Quakers are in general remarkably shrewd and intelligent in all worldly concerns, yet learning, and more particularly theological learning, is more rare among them in proportion to their wealth and rank in life, and holden in less value, than among any other known sect of Christians. What has been the result? If the occasion permitted, I could dilate with pleasure on their decent manners and decorous morals, as individuals, and their exemplary and truly illustrious philanthropic efforts as a Society. From all the gay and tinsel vanities of the world their discipline has preserved them, and the English character owes to their example some part of its manly plainness in externals. But my argument is confined to the question, whether religion in its present state and under the present conceptions of its demands and purposes does, even among the most religious, exert any efficient force of control over the commercial spirit, the excess of which we have attributed not to the extent and magnitude of the commerce itself, but to the absence or imperfection of its appointed checks and counter-agents. Now as the system of the Friends in its first intention is of all others most hostile to wordly-mindedness on the one hand; and as, on the other, the adherents of this system both in confession and practice confine Christianity to feelings and motives; they may be selected as representatives of the strict, but unstudied and uninquiring, religionists of every denomination. Their characteristic propensities will supply, therefore, no unfair test for the degree of resistance, which our present Christianity is capable of opposing to the cupidity of a trading people. That species of Christianity I mean, which, as far as knowledge and the faculties of thought are concerned, – which, as far as the growth and grandeur of the intellectual man is in question – is to be learnt *ex tempore*! A Christianity poured in on the *catechumen* all and all at once, as from a shower-bath: and which, whatever it may be in the heart, yet for the understanding and reason is from boyhood onward a thing past and perfected. If the almost universal opinion be tolerably correct, the question is answered. But I by no means appropriate the remark to the wealthy Quakers, or even apply it to them in any particular or eminent sense, when I say, that often as the motley reflexes of my experience move in long procession of manifold groups before me, the distinguished and world-honoured company of Christian Mammonists appears to the eye of my imagination as a drove of camels heavily laden, yet all at full speed, and each in the confident expectation of passing through the *eye of the needle*, without stop or halt, both beast and baggage.

Not without an uneasy reluctance have I ventured to tell the truth on this subject, lest I should be charged with the indulgence of a satirical mood and an uncharitable spleen. But my conscience bears me witness, and I know myself too near the grave to trifle with its name, that I am solely actuated by a sense of the exceeding importance of the subject at the present moment. I feel it an awful duty to exercise the honest liberty of free utterance in so dear a concernment as that of preparing my country for a change in its external relations, which must come sooner or later; which I believe to have already commenced; and that it will depend on the presence or absence of a corresponding change in the mind of the nation, and above all in the aims and ruling opinions of our gentry and moneyed men, whether it is to cast down our strength and prosperity, or to fix them on a firmer and more august basis. 'Surely to every good and peaceable man it must in nature needs be a hateful thing to be the displeaser and molester of thousands;*** but when God commands to take the trumpet and blow a dolorous or a jarring blast, it lies not in man's will what he shall say and what he shall conceal.'[1]

Thus, then, of the three most approved antagonists to the spirit of barter, and the accompanying disposition to overvalue riches with all the means and tokens thereof – of the three fittest and most likely checks to this tendency, namely, the feeling of ancient birth and the respect paid to it by the community at large; a genuine intellectual philosophy with an accredited, learned, and philosophic class; and lastly religion; we have found the first declining, the second not existing, and the third efficient, indeed, in many respects and to many excellent purposes, only not in this particular direction: the religion here spoken of, having long since parted company with that inquisitive and bookish theology which tends to defraud the student of his wordly wisdom, inasmuch as it diverts his mind from the accumulation of wealth by preoccupying his thoughts in the acquisition of knowledge. For the religion of best repute among us holds all the truths of Scripture and all the doctrines of Christianity so very transcendant, or so very easy, as to make study and research either vain or needless. It professes, therefore, to hunger and thirst after righteousness alone, and the rewards of the righteous; and thus habitually taking for granted all truths of spiritual import leaves the understanding vacant and at leisure for a thorough insight into present and temporal interests: which, doubtless, is the true reason why its followers are in general such shrewd, knowing, wary, well-informed, thrifty and thriving men of business. But this is likewise the reason, why it neither does nor can check or circumscribe the spirit of barter; and to the consequent

1 Milton. Reason of Church Government, B.II. Introd. – *Ed.*

monopoly which this commercial spirit possesses, must its over-balance be attributed, not the extent or magnitude of the commerce itself.

Before I enter on the result assigned by me as the chief ultimate cause of the present state of the country, and as the main ground on which the immediate occasions of the general distress have worked, I must en-treat my readers to reflect that the spirit of trade has been a thing of insensible growth; that whether it be enough, or more or less than enough, is a matter of relative, rather than of positive, determination; that it depends on the degree in which it is aided or resisted by all the other tendencies that co-exist with it; and that in the best of times this spirit may be said to live on a narrow *isthmus*, between a sterile desert and a stormy sea, still threatened and encroached on either by the too much or the too little. As the argument does not depend on any precise accuracy in the dates, I shall assume it to have commenced as an influencing part of the national character, with the institution of the public funds in the reign of William III, and from the peace of Aix-la-Chapelle in 1748, to have been hurrying onward to its *maximum*, which it seems to have attained during the late war. The short interruptions may be well represented as a few steps backward, that it might leap forward with an additional *momentum*. The words, old and modern, then and now are applied by me, the former to the interval between the Reformation and the Revolution; and the latter to the whole period since the Revolution: the one from 1460 to 1680, the other from 1680 to the present time.

Having premised this explanation, I can now return an intelligible answer to a question, that will have risen in the reader's mind during his perusal of the last three or four pages. How, it will be objected, does all this apply to the present times in particular? When was the industrious part of mankind not attached to the pursuits most likely to reward their industry? Was the wish to make a fortune, or, if you prefer an invidious phrase, the lust of lucre, less natural to our fore-fathers than to their descendants? If you say that though a not less frequent, nor less powerful passion with them than with us, it yet met with a more frequent and more powerful check, a stronger and a more advanced boundary-line in the religion of old times, and in the faith, fashion, habits, and authority of the religious: in what did this difference consist; and in what way did these points of difference act? If indeed the antidote in question once possessed virtues which it no longer possesses, or not in the same degree, what is the ingredient, either added, omitted, or diminished since that time, which can have rendered it less efficacious now than then?

Well! (I might reply) grant all this: and let both the profession and the professors of a spiritual principle, as a counterpoise to the wordly weights at the other end of the balance, be supposed much the same in one age as in the other. Assume for a moment, that I can establish neither the fact of its present lesser efficiency, nor any points of difference capable of accounting for it. Yet it might still be a sufficient answer to this objection, that as the commerce of the country, and with it the spirit of commerce, has increased fifty-fold since the commencement of the latter period, it is not enough that the counterweight should be as great as it was in the former period: to remain the same in its effect, it ought to have become very much greater. But though this be a consideration not less important than it is obvious, yet I do not purpose to rest in it. I affirm that a difference may be shown, and of no trifling importance as to that one point, to which my present argument is confined. For let it be remembered that it is not to any extraordinary influences of the religious principle that I am referring, not to voluntary poverty, or sequestration from social and active life, or schemes of mortification. I speak of religion merely as I should of any wordly object, which, as far as it employs and interests a man, leaves less room in his mind for other pursuits: except that this must be more especially the case in the instance of religion, because beyond all other interests it is calculated to occupy the whole mind, and employ successively all the faculties of man; and because the objects which it presents to the imagination as well as to the intellect cannot be actually contemplated, much less can they be the subject of frequent meditation, without dimming the lustre and blunting the rays of all rival attractions. It is well known, and has been observed of old, that poetry tends to render its devotees[1] careless of money and outward appearances, while philosophy inspires a contempt of both as objects of desire or admiration. But religion is the poetry and philosophy of all mankind; unites in itself whatever is most excellent in either, and while it at one

---

[1] *Hic error tamen et levis hæc insania quantas*
Virtutes habeat, sic collige: vatis avarus
Non temere est animus; versus amat, hoc studet unum;
Detrimenta, fungas servorum, incendia ridet;
Non fraudem socio, puerove incogitat ullam
Pupillo; vivit siliquis et pane secundo:
Militiæ quanquan piger et malus, utilis urbi.
HORAT. EPIST. II. I. 118.

46

and the same time calls into action and supplies with the noblest materials both the imaginative and the intellective faculties, superadds the interests of the most substantial and home-felt reality to both, to the poetic vision and the philosophic idea. But in order to produce a similar effect it must act in a similar way; it must reign in the thoughts of a man and in the powers akin to thought, as well as exercise an admitted influence over his hopes and fears, and through these on his deliberate and individual acts.

Now as my first presumptive proof of a difference (I might almost have said, of a contrast) between the religious character of the period since the Revolution, and that of the period from the accession of Edward VI to the abdication of James II, I refer to the sermons and to the theological works generally of the latter period. It is my full conviction that in any half dozen sermons of Donne, or Taylor, there are more thoughts, more facts and images, more excitements to inquiry and intellectual effort, than are presented to the congregations of the present day in as many churches or meetings during twice as many months. Yet both these were the most popular preachers of their times, were heard with enthusiasm by crowded and promiscuous audiences, and the effect produced by their eloquence was holden in reverential and affectionate remembrance by many attendants on their ministry, who, like the pious Isaac Walton, were not themselves men of much learning or education. In addition to this fact, think likewise on the large and numerous editions of massy, closely printed folios: the impressions so large and the editions so numerous, that all the industry of destruction for the last hundred years has but of late sufficed to make them rare. From the long list select those works alone, which we know to have been the most current and favourite works of their day: and of these again no more than may well be supposed to have had a place in the scantiest libraries, or perhaps with the Bible and Common Prayer Book to have formed the library of their owner. Yet on the single shelf so filled we should find almost every possible question, that could interest or instruct a reader whose whole heart was in his religion, discussed with a command of intellect that seems to exhaust all the learning and logic, all the historical and moral relations, of each several subject. The very length of the discourses, with which these rich souls of wit and knowledge fixed the eyes, ears, and hearts of their crowded congregations, are a source of wonder now-a-days, and (we may add) of self-congratulation, to many a sober Christian, who forgets with what delight he himself has listened to a two hours' harangue on a loan or tax, or at the trial of some remarkable cause or culprit. The transfer of the interest makes and explains the whole difference. For though much may be fairly charged on the Revolution in the mode of preaching as well as in the matter, since the fresh morning and fervent noon of the Reformation, when there was no need to visit the conventicles of fanaticism in order to

> See God's ambassador in pulpit stand,
> Where they could take notes from his look and hand;
> And from his speaking action bear away
> More sermon than our preachers use to say;

yet this too must be referred to the same change in the habits of men's minds, a change that involves both the shepherd and the flock: though like many other effects, it tends to reproduce and strengthen its own cause.

The last point, to which I shall appeal, is the warmth and frequency of the religious controversies during the former of the two periods; the deep interest excited by them among all but the lowest and most ignorant classes; the importance attached to them by the very highest; the number, and in many instances the transcendant merit, of the controversial publications – in short, the rank and value assigned to polemic divinity. The subjects of the controversies may or may not have been trifling; the warmth with which they were conducted, may have been disproportionate and indecorous; and we may have reason to congratulate ourselves that the age in which *we* live, is grown more indulgent and less captious. The fact is introduced not for its own sake, but as a symptom of the general state of men's feelings, and as an evidence of the direction and main channel, in which the thoughts and interests of men were then flowing. We all know that lovers are apt to take offence and wrangle with each other on occasions that perhaps are but trifles and which assuredly would appear such to those who had never been under the influence of a similar passion. These quarrels may be no proofs of wisdom; but still in the imperfect state of our nature the entire absence of the same, and this too on far more serious provocations, would excite a strong suspicion of a comparative indifference in the feelings of the parties towards each other, who can love so coolly where they profess to love so well. I shall believe our present religious tolerancy to proceed from the abundance of our charity and good sense, when I can see proofs that we are equally cool and forbearing as litigators and political partisans. And I must again intreat my reader to recollect that the present argument is exclusively

---

concerned with the requisite correctives of the commercial spirit, and with religion therefore no otherwise than as a counter-charm to the sorcery of wealth: and my main position is, that neither by reasons drawn from the nature of the human mind, nor by facts of actual experience, are we justified in expecting this from a religion which does not employ and actuate the understanding of men, and combine their affections with it as a system of truth gradually and progressively manifesting itself to the intellect; no less than as a system of motives and moral commands learnt as soon as heard, and containing nothing but what is plain and easy to the lowest capacities.

CHURCH AND STATE

CHAPTER V. Of the Church of England, or National Clergy, according to the Constitution; its characteristic ends, purposes and functions; and of the persons comprehended under the Clergy, or the functionaries of the National Church

AFTER these introductory preparations, I can have no difficulty in setting forth the right idea of a national Church as in the language of Queen Elizabeth the third great venerable estate of the realm; the first being the estate of the land-owners or possessors of fixed property, consisting of the two classes of the Barons and the Franklins; and the second comprising the merchants, the manufacturers, free artizans, and the distributive class. To comprehend, therefore, the true character of this third estate, in which the reserved Nationality was vested, we must first ascertain the end or national purpose, for which such reservation was made.

Now, as in the first estate the permanency of the nation was provided for; and in the second estate its progressiveness and personal freedom; while in the king the cohesion by interdependence, and the unity of the country, were established; there remains for the third estate only that interest which is the ground, the necessary antecedent condition, of both the former. These depend on a continuing and progressive civilization. But civilization is itself but a mixed good, if not far more a corrupting influence, the hectic of disease, not the bloom of health, and a nation so distinguished more fitly to be called a varnished than a polished people, where this civilization is not grounded in cultivation, in the harmonious developement of those qualities and faculties that characterize our humanity. We must be men in order to be citizens.

The Nationalty, therefore, was reserved for the support and maintenance of a permanent class or order with the following duties. A certain smaller number were to remain at the fountain heads of the humanities, in cultivating and enlarging the knowledge already possessed, and in watching over the interests of physical and moral science; being, likewise, the instructors of such as constituted, or were to constitute, the remaining more numerous classes of the order. The members of this latter and far more numerous body were to be distributed throughout the country, so as not to leave even the smallest integral part or division without a resident guide, guardian, and instructor; the objects and final intention of the whole order being these – to preserve the stores and to guard the treasures of past civilization, and thus to bind the present with the past; to perfect and add to the same, and thus to connect the present with the future; but especially to diffuse through the whole community and to every native entitled to its laws and rights that quantity and quality of knowledge which was indispensable both for the understanding of those rights, and for the performance of the duties correspondent: finally, to secure for the nation, if not a superiority over the neighbouring states, yet an equality at least, in that character of general civilization, which equally with, or rather more than, fleets, armies, and revenue, forms the ground of its defensive and offensive power. The object of the two former estates of the realm, which conjointly form the State, was to reconcile the interests of permanence with that of progression – law with liberty. The object of the national Church, the third remaining estate of the realm, was to secure and improve that civilization, without which the nation could be neither permanent nor progressive.

That, in all ages, individuals who have directed their meditations and their studies to the nobler characters of our nature, to the cultivation of those powers and instincts which constitute the man, at least separate him from the animal, and distinguish the nobler from the animal part of his own being, will be led by the supernatural in themselves to the contemplation of a power which is likewise superhuman; that science, and especially moral science, will lead to religion, and remain blended with it, – this, I say, will in all ages be the course of things. That in the earlier ages, and in the dawn of civility, there will be a twilight in which science and religion give light, but a light refracted through the dense and the dark, a superstition; – this is what we learn from history,

and what philosophy would have taught us to expect. But I affirm that
in the spiritual purpose of the word, and as understood in reference to a
future state, and to the abiding essential interest of the individual as a
person, and not as the citizen, neighbour, or subject, religion may be an
indispensable ally, but is not the essential constitutive end, of that
national institute, which is unfortunately, at least improperly, styled
the Church; a name which in its best sense is exclusively appropriate to
the Church of Christ. If this latter be *ecclesia*, the communion of such as
are called out of the world, that is, in reference to the especial ends and
purposes of that communion; this other might more expressively have
been entitled *enclesia*, or an order of men chosen in and of the realm,
and constituting an estate of that realm. And in fact, such was the
original and proper sense of the more appropriately named clergy. It
comprehended the learned of all names, and the clerk was the synonyme
of the man of learning. Nor can any fact more strikingly illustrate the
conviction entertained by our ancestors respecting the intimate connexion of this clergy with the peace and weal of the nation, than the
privilege formerly recognized by our laws, in the well-known phrase,
'benefit of clergy.'

Deeply do I feel, for clearly do I see, the importance of my theme.
And had I equal confidence in my ability to awaken the same interest in
the minds of others, I should dismiss as affronting to my readers all
apprehension of being charged with prolixity, while I am labouring to
compress in two or three brief chapters the principal sides and aspects
of a subject so large and multilateral as to require a volume for its full
exposition; – with what success will be seen in what follows, commencing with the Churchmen, or (a far apter and less objectionable designation), the national Clerisy.

The Clerisy of the nation, or national Church, in its primary accepta-
tion and original intention, comprehended the learned of all denominations, the sages and professors of the law and jurisprudence, of medicine and physiology, of music, of military and civil architecture, of the
physical sciences, with the mathematical as the common organ of the
preceding; in short, all the so called liberal arts and sciences, the possession and application of which constitute the civilization of a country,
as well as the theological. The last was, indeed, placed at the head of
all; and of good right did it claim the precedence. But why? Because
under the name of theology or divinity were contained the interpretation of languages, the conservation and tradition of past events,
the momentous epochs and revolutions of the race and nation, the

continuation of the records, logic, ethics, and the determination of ethical science, in application to the rights and duties of men in all their various relations, social and civil; and lastly, the ground-knowledge, the *prima scientia* as it was named, – philosophy, or the doctrine and discipline of ideas.[1]

Theology formed only a part of the objects, the theologians formed only a portion of the clerks or clergy, of the national Church. The theological order had precedency indeed, and deservedly; but not because its members were priests, whose office was to conciliate the invisible powers, and to superintend the interests that survive the grave; nor as being exclusively, or even principally, sacerdotal or templar, which, when it did occur, is to be considered as an accident of the age, a mis-growth of ignorance and oppression, a falsification of the constitutive principle, not a constituent part of the same. No, the theologians took the lead, because the science of theology was the root and the trunk of the knowledges that civilized man, because it gave unity and the circulating sap of life to all other sciences, by virtue of which alone they could be contemplated as forming, collectively, the living tree of knowledge. It had the precedency because, under the name theology, were comprised all the main aids, instruments, and materials of national education, the *nisus formativus* of the body politic, the shaping and informing spirit, which, educing or eliciting the latent man in all the natives of the soil, trains them up to be citizens of the country, free subjects of the realm. And lastly, because to divinity belong those fundamental truths, which are the common ground-work of our civil and our religious duties, not less indispensable to a right view of our temporal concerns, than to a rational faith respecting our

1 That is, of knowledges immediate, yet real, and herein distinguished in kind from logical and mathematical truths, which express not realities, but only the necessary forms of conceiving and perceiving, and are therefore named the formal or abstract sciences. Ideas, on the other hand, or the truths of philosophy, properly so called, correspond to substantial beings, to objects the actual subsistence of which is implied in their idea, though only by the idea revealable. To adopt the language of the great philosophic Apostle, they are *spiritual realities that can only spiritually be discerned*, and the inherent aptitude and moral preconfiguration to which constitutes what we mean by ideas, and by the presence of ideal truth and of ideal power, in the human being. They in fact, constitute his humanity. For try to conceive a man without the ideas of God, eternity, freedom, will, absolute truth, of the good, the true, the beautiful, the infinite. An animal endowed with a memory of appearances and of facts might remain. But the man will have vanished, and you have instead a creature, *more subtle than any beast of the field*, but likewise *cursed above every beast of the field; upon the belly must it go and dust must it eat all the days of its life*. But I recal myself from a train of thoughts little likely to find favour in this age of sense and selfishness.

immortal well-being. Not without celestial observations can even terrestrial charts be accurately constructed. And of especial importance is it to the objects here contemplated, that only by the vital warmth diffused by these truths throughout the many, and by the guiding light from the philosophy, which is the basis of divinity, possessed by the few, can either the community or its rulers fully comprehend, or rightly appreciate, the permanent distinction and the occasional contrast between cultivation and civilization; or be made to understand this most valuable of the lessons taught by history, and exemplified alike in her oldest and her most recent records – that a nation can never be a too cultivated, but may easily become an over-civilized, race.

CHAPTER VI. Secessions or offsets from the National Clerisy. Usurpations and abuses previous to the Reformation. Henry VIII. What he might and should have done. The main end and final cause of the Nationalty; and the duties, which the State may demand of the National Clerisy. A question, and the answer to it

As a natural consequence of the full developement and expansion of the mercantile and commercial order, which in the earlier epochs of the constitution only existed, as it were, potentially and in the bud; the students and possessors of those sciences, and those sorts of learning, the use and necessity of which were indeed constant and perpetual to the nation, but only accidental and occasional to individuals, gradually detached themselves from the Nationalty and the national clergy, and passed to the order, with the growth and thriving condition of which their emoluments were found to increase in equal proportion. Rather, perhaps, it should be said that under the common name of professional, the learned in the departments of law, medicine, and the like, formed an intermediate link between the established clergy and the burgesses.

This circumstance, however, can in no way affect the principle, nor alter the tenure, nor annul the rights, of those who remained, and who, as members of the permanent learned class, were planted throughout the realm, each in his appointed place, as the immediate agents and instruments in the great and indispensable work of perpetuating, promoting, and increasing the civilization of the nation, and who thus fulfilling the purposes for which the determinate portion of the total wealth from the land had been reserved, are entitled to remain its trustees and usufructuary proprietors. But I do not assert that the proceeds from the Nationalty cannot be rightfully vested, except in what we now mean by clergymen and the established clergy. I have every where implied the contrary. But I do assert, that the Nationalty cannot rightfully, and that without foul wrong to the nation it never has been, alienated from its original purposes. I assert that those who, being duly elected and appointed thereto, exercise the functions, and perform the duties, attached to the Nationalty possess collectively an inalienable, indefeasible, title to the same; and this by a *jus divinum*, to which the thunders from Mount Sinai might give additional authority, but not additional evidence.

COROLLARY. – During the dark times, when the *incubus* of superstition lay heavy across the breast of the living and the dying; and when all the familiar tricksy spirits in the service of an alien, self-expatriated and anti-national priesthood were at work in all forms and in all directions to aggrandize and enrich a *kingdom of this world;* large masses were alienated from the heritable proprieties of the realm, and confounded with the Nationalty under the common name of Church property. Had every rood, every pepper-corn, every stone, brick, and beam been re-transferred and made heritable at the Reformation, no right would have been invaded, no principle of justice violated. What that State by law – that is, by the collective will of its functionaries at any one time assembled – can do or suffer to be done; that the State by law can undo or inhibit. And in principle, such bequests and donations were vicious *ab initio*, implying in the donor an absolute property in land, unknown to the constitution of the realm, and in defeasance of that immutable reason which, in the name of the nation and the national majesty, proclaims: 'The land is not yours; it was vested in your lineage in trust for the nation.' And though, in change of times and circumstances, the interest of progression, with the means and motives for the same – hope, industry, enterprise – may render it the wisdom of the State to facilitate the transfer from line to line, still it must be within the same scale and with preservation of the balance. The most honest of our English historians, and with no superior in industry and research, Mr Sharon Turner, has labored successfully in detaching from the portrait of our first Protestant king the layers of soot and blood, with which pseudo-Catholic hate and pseudo-Protestant candour had coated it. But the name of Henry VIII would have outshone that of Alfred, and with a splendor which not even the ominous shadow of his declining life would have eclipsed, had he retained the will and possessed the power of effecting, what in part he promised and proposed to do; that is, if he had availed himself of the wealth and landed masses that had been unconstitutionally alienated from the State, namely, transferred from the scale of heritable lands and revenues, to purchase and win back whatever had been alienated from the opposite scale of the Nationalty; – wrongfully alienated; for it was a possession, in which every free subject in the nation has a living interest, a permanent, and likewise a possible personal and reversionary, interest; – sacrilegiously alienated; for it had been consecrated τῷ θεῷ οἰκείῳ, to the potential divinity in every man, which is the ground and condition of his civil existence, that without which a man can be neither free nor obliged, and by which alone, therefore, he is capable of being a free subject or a citizen: and if, I say, having thus righted the balance on both sides, Henry had then directed the Nationalty to its true national purposes, (in order to which, however, a different division and sub-division of the kingdom must have superseded the present barbarism, which forms an obstacle to the improvement of the country, of much greater magnitude than men are generally aware); and the Nationalty had been distributed in proportionate channels to the maintenance; 1, of the universities and great schools of liberal learning; 2, of a pastor, presbyter, or parson[1] in every parish; 3, of a schoolmaster in every parish, who in due time, and under condition of a faithful performance of his arduous duties, should succeed to the pastorate; so that both should be labourers in different compartments of the same field, workmen engaged in different stages of the same process, with such difference of rank, as might be suggested in the names pastor and sub-pastor, or as now exists between rector and curate, elder and deacon. Both alike, I say, being members and ministers of the national Clerisy or Church, working to the same end, and determined in the choice of their means and the direction of their labours by one and the same object – namely, the production and reproduction, the preservation, continuance, and

---

[1] *Persona κατ' ἐξοχήν; persona exemplaris;* the representative and exemplar of the personal character of the community or parish; of their duties and rights, of their hopes, privileges and requisite qualifications, as moral persons, and not merely living things. But this the pastoral clergy cannot be other than imperfectly; they cannot be that which it is the paramount end and object of their establishment and distribution throughout the country that they should be – each in his sphere the germ and *nucleus* of the progressive civilization – unless they are in the rule married men and heads of families. This, however, is adduced only as an accessory to the great principle stated in a following page, as an instance of its beneficial consequences, not as the grounds of its validity.

perfection, of the necessary sources and conditions of national civilization; this being itself an indispensable condition of national safety, power and welfare, the strongest security and the surest provision, both for the permanence and the progressive advance of whatever as laws, institutions, tenures, rights, privileges, freedoms, obligations, and the like, constitutes the public weal: these parochial clerks being the great majority of the national clergy, the comparatively small remainder being principally[1] *in ordine ad hos, Cleri doctores ut Clerus populi.*

I may be allowed, therefore, to express the final cause of the whole by the office and purpose of the greater part; and this is, to form and train up the people of the country to be obedient, free, useful, organizable subjects, citizens, and patriots, living to the benefit of the State, and prepared to die for its defence. The proper object and end of the national Church is civilization with freedom; and the duty of its ministers, could they be contemplated merely and exclusively as officiaries of the national Church, would be fulfilled in the communication of that degree and kind of knowledge to all, the possession of which is necessary for all in order to their civility. By civility I mean all the qualities essential to a citizen, and devoid of which no people or class of the people can be calculated on by the rulers and leaders of the State for the conservation or promotion of its essential interests.

It follows, therefore, that in regard to the grounds and principles of action and conduct, the State has a right to demand of the national Church that its instructions should be fitted to diffuse throughout the people legality, that is, the obligations of a well calculated self-interest, under the conditions of a common interest determined by common laws. At least, whatever of higher origin and nobler and wider aim the ministers of the national Church, in some other capacity, and in the performance of other duties, might labour to implant and cultivate in the minds and hearts of their congregations and seminaries, should include the practical consequences of the legality above mentioned. The State requires that the basin should be kept full, and that the stream which supplies the hamlet and turns the mill, and waters the meadow-fields, should be fed and kept flowing. If this be done the State is content, indifferent for the rest, whether the basin be filled by the spring in

---

[1] Considered, I mean, in their national relations, and in that which forms their ordinary, their most conspicuous purpose and utility; for God forbid, I should deny or forget that the sciences, and not only the sciences both abstract and experimental, but the *literæ humaniores,* the products of genial power, of whatever name, have an immediate and positive value even in their bearings on the national interests.

its first ascent, and rising but a hand's-breadth above the bed; or whether drawn from a more elevated source, shooting aloft in a stately column, that reflects the light of heaven from its shaft, and bears the *Iris, cœli decus, promissumque Jovis lucidum* on its spray, it fills the basin in its descent.

'In what relation then do you place Christianity to the national Church?' Though unwilling to anticipate what belongs to a part of my subject yet to come, namely, the idea of the Catholic or Christian Church, I am still more averse to leave this question, even for a moment, unanswered. And this is my answer.

In relation to the national Church, Christianity, or the Church of Christ, is a blessed accident,[1] a providential boon, a grace of God, a mighty and faithful friend, the envoy indeed and liege subject of another State, but which can neither administer the laws nor promote the ends of this other State, which is not of the world, without advantage, direct and indirect, to the true interests of the States, the aggregate of which is what we mean by the world, that is, the civilized world. As the olive tree is said in its growth to fertilize the surrounding soil, to invigorate the roots of the vines in its immediate neighbourhood, and to improve the strength and flavour of the wines; such is the relation of the Christian and the national Church. But as the olive is not the same plant with the vine, or with the elm or poplar, (that is, the State) with which the vine is wedded; and as the vine with its prop may exist, though in less perfection, without the olive, or previously to its implantation; – even so is Christianity, and *a fortiori* any particular scheme of theology derived and supposed by its partizans to be deduced from Christianity, no essential part of the being of the national Church, however conducive or even indispensable it may be to its well being. And even so a national Church might exist, and has existed, without, because before the institution of, the Christian Church; – as the Levitical Church in the Hebrew constitution, and the Druidical in the Keltic, would suffice to prove.

But here I earnestly entreat that two things may be remembered – first, that it is my object to present the Idea of a national Church, as the only safe criterion by which the judgment can decide on the existing state of things; for when we are in full and clear possession of the ultimate aim of an institution, it is comparatively easy to ascertain in

[1] Let not the religious reader be offended with this phrase. I mean only that Christianity is an aid and instrument which no State or realm could have produced out of its own elements, which no State had a right to expect. It was, most awefully, a GOD-SEND!

what respects this aim has been attained in other ways arising out of the growth of the nation, and the gradual and successive expansion of its germs; in what respects the aim has been frustrated by errors and diseases in the body politic; and in what respects the existing institution still answers the original purpose, and continues to be a mean to necessary or most important ends, for which no adequate substitute can be found. First, I say, let it be borne in mind that my object has been to present the idea of a national Church, not the history of the Church established in this nation. Secondly, that two distinct functions do not necessarily imply or require two different functionaries: nay, the perfection of each may require the union of both in the same person. And in the instance now in question, great and grievous errors have arisen from confounding the functions; and fearfully great and grievous will be the evils from the success of an attempt to separate them – an attempt long and passionately pursued, in many forms, and through many various channels, by a numerous party which has already the ascendancy in the State; and which, unless far other minds and far other principles than those which the opponents of this party have hitherto allied with their cause, are called into action, will obtain the ascendancy in the nation.

I have already said that the subjects, which lie right and left of my road, or even jut into it, are so many and so important that I offer these pages but as a catalogue of texts and theses, which will have answered their purpose if they excite a certain class of readers to desire or to supply the commentary. But there will not be wanting among my readers men who are no strangers to the ways in which my thoughts travel: and the jointless sentences that make up the following chapter or inventory of regrets and apprehensions will suffice to possess them of the chief points that press on my mind.

The commanding knowledge, the power of truth, given or obtained by contemplating the subject in the fontal mirror of the idea, is in Scripture ordinarily expressed by *vision:* and no dissimilar gift, if not rather in its essential characters the same, does a great living poet speak of, as

The vision and the faculty divine.

Indeed of the many political ground-truths contained in the Old Testament, I cannot recall one more worthy to be selected as the moral and *l'envoy* of a Universal History, than the text in Proverbs,[1] *Where no vision is, the people perisheth.*

[1] xxix. 18.

3

'Tracts for the Times': Nos. I, XI, and from No. XC, the sections on Justification by Faith, the Sacraments, Masses and the Papacy, together with Conclusion

Tract No. I, written by Newman *ad clerum* (to the clergy), was published at 1*d*. in 1833. Short and simple as it is, it is perhaps the most important of all the Tracts. For it drove a sharp wedge of division between two sets of facts and ideas which had formerly been considered as closely allied. It distinguished between the constitutional position of the Church, its wealth and aristocratic connections, on the one hand, and its essential spiritual authority on the other.

A passage which is particularly revealing is: 'Now every one of us believes this. I know that some will at first deny they do; still they believe it.' In Newman's eyes the idea of Apostolic Succession was so clearly stated in the Ordination Service that every sincere clergyman must admit that he held it, when his attention was drawn to it. But he was writing because he knew very well that in practice the majority of clergymen never gave it a thought. He was attempting to awaken their minds to what was really implied by their profession of belief.

In the background of this pamphlet, and exerting a strong influence on it, though never mentioned, are the Reform Bill riots, and the extreme unpopularity of some of the bishops. Newman meant that the true ground of the Church's authority would now have to be asserted because the false, the support of the State, and of a conservative society might soon fail to be effective.

No. XI, also by Newman in 1833, requires little comment. But it is interesting to note how Scriptural is the argument for the Church. The Bible was generally supposed to have a Protestant tendency. 'The Bible and the Bible only is the religion of Protestants' is an aphorism which reflected the deep conviction of millions. To some extent it was

E

felt that Bible and Church were alternatives. Newman argued that you could not really have one without the other, because the plain sense of the Bible pointed to the authority of the Church.

Tract XC is a document of great importance, and it is a matter of regret that its length makes it impracticable to include it in entirety. Published early in 1841, it was Newman's last attempt to reconcile his developing Catholic views with loyalty to Anglicanism.

It had always been felt that two different theological spirits informed Prayer Book and Articles; the High Church party had always tended to appeal to the first, and the Low Church to the second. But just as the two parties had co-existed in more or less uneasy unity, so, on the intellectual level, the felt opposition between Prayer Book and Articles had never been analysed.

Many people were sincerely scandalized by the methods used in this tract. Mere log-chopping, however brilliant, seemed a subversive method of dealing with religious problems, and Newman was freely accused both of dishonesty and irreverence. It is necessary to give the closest attention to the last page or so of the extracts quoted here (which is also the last page of the complete tract) to understand how Newman justified himself against these charges. Newman had far too much religious feeling to deal in this way with a creed or a prayer or a passage in the Gospel. The key point is *that he did not consider the Articles as a religious document at all*. The obligation to sign them was a legal one, determined by the actual historical situation of the Church in England, and not at all by the essential nature of the Catholic Church, which he still wished to be able to believe to be represented in England by the Established Church. This was the only consistent view possible to an Anglo-Catholic, because it is an essential part of the Anglo-Catholic case that the Reformation, in so far as it affected the Church of England, brought a change of administration and not of essential faith. Now it was clear enough that the Articles had been drawn up by men, some at least of whom wished to make changes in faith. Therefore, it was essential for Anglo-Catholics to ignore intentions altogether. The key sentence in Newman's argument comes right at the end: 'What was an economy in the reformers is a protection to us.' The reformers, he meant, though preserving a thoroughly Protestant tone in the Articles, wished to allow Catholics to subscribe the Articles without denying their most cherished convictions. It is only fair that Catholics should make the most of this dishonest trick used by the other side.

It is, obviously, a very finely drawn position, reached under consider-able stress. It is not surprising that Newman felt unable to maintain it for very long. The condemnation which followed was only to be expected, but it is doubtful whether it actually hastened Newman's departure from the Anglican Church, which was delayed for four more years.

Advertisement to Volume I

THE following Tracts were published with the object of contribut-ing something towards the practical revival of doctrines which, although held by the great divines of our Church, at present have become obsolete with the majority of her members, and are withdrawn from public view even by the more learned and orthodox few who still adhere to them. The Apostolic succession, the Holy Catholic Church, were principles of action in the minds of our predecessors of the seventeenth century; but, in proportion as the maintenance of the Church has been secured by law, her ministers have been under the temptation of leaning on an arm of flesh instead of her own divinely-provided discipline, a temptation increased by political events and arrangements which need not here be more than alluded to. A lament-able increase of sectarianism has followed; being occasioned (in addi-tion to other more obvious causes), first, by the cold aspect which the new Church doctrines have presented to the religious sensibilities of the mind, next to their meagreness in suggesting motives to restrain it from seeking out a more influential discipline. Doubtless obedience to the law of the land, and the careful maintenance of 'decency and order' (the topics in usage among us), are plain duties of the Gospel, and a reasonable ground for keeping in communion with the Established Church; yet, if Providence has graciously provided for our weakness more interesting and constraining motives, it is a sin thanklessly to neglect them; just as it would be a mistake to rest the duties of tem-perance or justice on the mere law of natural religion, when they are mercifully sanctioned in the Gospel by the more winning authority of our Saviour Christ. Experience has shown the inefficacy of the mere injunctions of Church order, however scripturally enforced, in re-straining from schism the awakened and anxious sinner; who goes to a dissenting preacher 'because (as he expresses it) he gets good from him': and though he does not stand excused in God's sight for yielding to the temptation, surely the Ministers of the Church are not blameless if, by keeping back the more gracious and consoling truths provided for the little ones of Christ, they indirectly lead him into it. Had he been taught as a child, that the Sacraments, not preaching, are the sources of Divine Grace; that the Apostolical ministry had a virtue in it which went out over the whole Church, when sought by the prayer of faith; that fellowship with it was a gift and privilege, as well as a duty, we could not have had so many wanderers from our fold, nor so many cold hearts within it.

This instance may suggest many others of the superior *influence* of an apostolical over a mere secular method of teaching. The awakened mind knows its wants, but cannot provide for them; and in its hunger will feed upon ashes, if it cannot obtain the pure milk of the Word. Methodism and Popery are in different ways the refuge of those whom the Church stints of the gifts of grace; they are the foster-mothers of abandoned children. The neglect of the daily service, the desecration of festivals, the Eucharist scantily administered, insubordination permitted in all ranks of the Church, orders and offices imperfectly developed, the want of Societies for particular religious objects, and the like deficiencies, lead the feverish mind, desirous of a vent to its feelings, and a stricter rule of life, to the smaller religious Communities, to prayer and bible meetings, and ill-advised institutions and societies, on the one hand, – on the other, to the solemn and captivating services by which Popery gains its proselytes. Moreover, the multitude of men cannot teach or guide themselves; and an injunction given them to depend on their private judgment, cruel in itself, is doubly hurtful, as throwing them on such teachers as speak daringly and promise largely, and not only aid but supersede individual exertion.

These remarks may serve as a clue, for those who care to pursue it, to the views which have led to the publication of the following Tracts. The Church of Christ was intended to cope with human nature in all its forms, and surely the gifts vouchsafed it are adequate for that gracious purpose. There are zealous sons and servants of her English branch, who see with sorrow that she is defrauded of her full usefulness by particular theories and principles of the present age, which interfere with the execution of one portion of her commission; and while they consider that the revival of this portion of truth is especially adapted to break up existing parties in the Church, and to form instead a bond of union among all who love the Lord Jesus Christ in sincerity, they believe that nothing but these neglected doctrines, faithfully preached, will repress that extension of Popery for which the ever-multiplying divisions of the religious world are too clearly preparing the way.

Oxford, *The Feast of All Saints*, 1834.

TRACT I. Thoughts on the Ministerial Commission. Respectfully Addressed to the Clergy

I AM but one of yourselves, – a Presbyter; and therefore I conceal my name, lest I should take too much on myself by speaking in my own person. Yet speak I must; for the times are very evil, yet no one speaks against them.

Is not this so? Do not we 'look one upon another,' yet perform nothing? Do we not all confess the peril into which the Church is come, yet sit still each in his own retirement, as if mountains and seas cut off brother from brother? Therefore suffer me, while I try to draw you forth from those pleasant retreats which it has been our blessedness hitherto to enjoy, to contemplate the condition and prospects of our Holy Mother in a practical way; so that one and all may unlearn that idle habit, which has grown upon us, of owning the state of things to be bad, yet doing nothing to remedy it.

Consider a moment. Is it fair, is it dutiful, to suffer our Bishops to stand the brunt of the battle without doing our part to support them? Upon them comes 'the care of all the Churches.' This cannot be helped: indeed it is their glory. Not one of us would wish in the least to deprive them of the duties, the toils, the responsibilities of their high Office. And, black event as it would be for the country, yet (as far as they are concerned) we could not wish them a more blessed termination of their course than the spoiling of their goods, and martyrdom.

To them then we willingly and affectionately relinquish their high privileges and honours; we encroach not upon the rights of the successors of the Apostles; we touch not their sword and crosier. Yet surely we may be their shield-bearers in the battle without offence; and by our voice and deeds be to them what Luke and Timothy were to St Paul.

Now then let me come at once to the subject which leads me to address you. Should the Government and Country so far forget their God as to cast off the Church, to deprive it of its temporal honours and substance, *on what* will you rest the claim of respect and attention which you make upon your flocks? Hitherto you have been upheld by your birth, your education, your wealth, your connections; should these secular advantages cease, on what must Christ's Ministers depend? Is not this a serious practical question? We know how miserable is the state of religious bodies not supported by the State. Look at the Dissenters on all sides of you, and you will see at once that their Ministers, depending simply upon the people, become the *creatures* of the people. Are you content that this should be your case? Alas! can a greater evil befall Christians than for their teachers to be guided by them, instead of guiding? How can we 'hold fast the form of sound words,' and 'keep that which is committed to our trust,' if our influence is to depend simply on our popularity? Is it not our very office to *oppose* the world? can we then allow ourselves to *court* it? to preach smooth things and prophesy deceits? to make the way of life easy to the rich and indolent, and to bribe the humbler classes by excitements and strong intoxicating doctrine? Surely it must not be so; – and the question recurs, on *what* are we to rest our authority when the State deserts us?

Christ has not left His Church without claim of its own upon the attention of men. Surely not. Hard Master He cannot be, to bid us oppose the world, yet give us no credentials for so doing. There are some who rest their divine mission on their own unsupported assertion; others, who rest it upon their popularity; others, on their success; and others, who rest it upon their temporal distinctions. This last case has, perhaps, been too much our own; I fear we have neglected the real ground on which our authority is built, – our apostolical descent.

We have been born, not of blood, nor of the will of the flesh, nor of the will of man, but of God. The Lord Jesus Christ gave His Spirit to His Apostles; they in turn laid their hands on those who should succeed them; and these again on others; and so the sacred gift has been handed down to our present Bishops, who have appointed us as their assistants, and in some sense representatives.

Now every one of us believes this. I know that some will at first deny they do; still they do believe it. Only, it is not sufficiently practically impressed on their minds. They *do* believe it; for it is the doctrine of the Ordination Service, which they have recognised as truth in the most solemn season of their lives. In order, then, not to prove, but to remind and impress, I entreat your attention to the words used when you were made Ministers of Christ's Church.

The office of Deacon was thus committed to you: 'Take thou authority to execute the office of a Deacon in the Church of God committed unto thee: In the name,' etc.

And the priesthood thus:

'Receive the Holy Ghost for the office and work of a Priest in the Church of God, now committed unto thee by the imposition of our hands. Whose sins thou dost forgive, they are forgiven; and whose sins thou dost retain, they are retained. And be thou a faithful dispenser of the Word of God, and of His Holy Sacraments: In the name,' etc.

These, I say, were words spoken to us, and received by us, when we were brought nearer to God than at any other time of our lives. I know the grace of ordination is contained in the laying on of hands, not in any form of words; – yet in our own case (as has ever been usual in the Church) words of blessing have accompanied the act. Thus we have confessed before God our belief that through the Bishop who ordained us, we received the Holy Ghost, the power to bind and to lose, to administer the Sacraments, and to preach. Now *how* is he able to give these great gifts? *Whence* is his right? Are these words idle (which would be taking God's name in vain), or do they express merely a wish (which surely is very far below their meaning), or do they not rather indicate that the Speaker is conveying a gift? Surely they can mean nothing short of this. But whence, I ask, his right to do so? Has he any right, except as having received the power from those who consecrated him to be a Bishop? He could not give what he had never received. It is plain then that he but *transmits;* and that the Christian Ministry is a *succession.* And if we trace back the power of ordination from hand to hand, of course we shall come to the Apostles at last. We know we do, as a plain historical fact: and therefore all we, who have been ordained Clergy, in the very form of our ordination acknowledged the doctrine of the Apostolical Succession.

And for the same reason, we must necessarily consider none to be *really* ordained who have not *thus* been ordained. For if ordination is a divine ordinance, it must be necessary; and if it is not a divine ordinance, how dare we use it? Therefore all who use it, all of *us*, must consider it necessary. As well might we pretend the Sacraments are not necessary to Salvation, while we make use of the offices of the Liturgy; for when God appoints means of grace, they are *the* means.

I do not see how any one can escape from this plain view of the subject, except (as I have already hinted) by declaring that the words do not mean all that they say. But only reflect what a most unseemly time for random words is that in which Ministers are set apart for their office. Do we not adopt a Liturgy, *in order to* hinder inconsiderate idle language, and shall we, in the most sacred of all services, write down, subscribe, and use again and again forms of speech, which have not been weighed, and cannot be taken strictly?

Therefore, my dear Brethren, act up to your professions. Let it not be said that you have neglected a gift; for if you have the Spirit of the Apostles on you, surely this *is* a great gift. 'Stir up the gift of God which is in you.' Make much of it. Show your value of it. Keep it before your minds as an honourable badge, far higher than that secular respectability, or cultivation, or polish, or learning, or rank, which gives you a hearing with the many. Tell *them* of your gift. The times will soon drive you to do this, if you mean to be still any thing. But wait not for the times. Do not be compelled, by the world's forsaking you, to recur as if unwillingly to the high source of your authority. Speak out now, before you are forced, both as glorying in your privilege, and to ensure your rightful honour from your people. A notion has gone abroad that they can take away your power. They think they have given and can take it away. They think it lies in the Church property, and they know that they have politically the power to confiscate that property. They have been deluded into a notion that present palpable usefulness, produceable results, acceptableness to your flocks, that these and such-like are the tests of your Divine commission. Enlighten them in this matter. Exalt our Holy Fathers, the Bishops, as the Representatives of the Apostles, and the Angels of the Churches; and magnify your office, as being ordained by them to take part in their Ministry.

But if you will not adopt my view of the subject, which I offer to you, not doubtingly, yet (I hope) respectfully, at all events, choose your side. To *remain neuter much longer will be itself to take a part. Choose* your side; since side you shortly must with one or other party, even though you do nothing. Fear to be of those whose line is decided for them by chance circumstances, and who may perchance find themselves with the enemies of Christ, while they think but to remove themselves from worldly politics. Such abstinence is impossible in troublous times. 'He that is not with Me is against Me, and he that gathereth not with Me scattereth abroad.'

TRACT XI. The Visible Church (In Letters to a Friend) Part I

LETTER I. You wish to have my opinion on the doctrine of 'the Holy Catholic Church,' as contained in Scripture, and taught in the Creed. So I send you the following lines, which perhaps may serve through God's blessing to assist you in your search after the truth in this matter, even though they do no more; indeed no remarks however just, can be much more than an assistance to you. You must search for yourself, and God must teach you.

I think I partly enter into your present perplexity. You argue, that true *doctrine* is the important matter for which we must contend, and a *right state of the affections* is the test of vital religion in the heart: and you ask, 'Why may I not be satisfied if my Creed is correct, and my affections spiritual? Have I not in that case enough to evidence a renewed mind, and to constitute a basis of union with others like minded? The love of Christ is surely the one and only requisite for Christian communion here, and the joys of heaven hereafter.' Again you say, that —— and —— are constant in their prayers for the teaching of the Holy Spirit; so that if it be true that every one who asketh receiveth, surely they must receive, and are in a safe state.

Believe me, I do not think lightly of these arguments. They are very subtle ones; powerfully influencing the imagination, and difficult to answer. Still I believe them to be mere fallacies. Let me try them in a parallel case. You know the preacher at ——, and have heard of his flagrantly immoral life; yet it is notorious that he can and does speak in a moving way of the love of Christ, etc. It is very shocking to witness such a case, which (we will hope) is rare; but it has its use. Do you not think him in peril, in spite of his impressive and persuasive language? Why? You will say, his life is bad. True; it seems then that more is requisite for salvation than an orthodox creed, and keen sensibility – viz., consistent conduct. Very well then, we have come to an additional test of true faith, obedience to God's word, and plainly a scriptural test, according to St John's canon. 'He who *doeth* righteousness is righteous.' Do not you see then your argument is already proved to be unsound? It seems that true doctrine and warm feelings are not enough. How am I to know what is enough? you ask. I reply, *by searching Scripture*. It was your original fault that, instead of inquiring what God has told you is necessary for being a true Christian, you chose out of your own head to *argue* on the subject; – *e.g.* 'I can never believe that to be such and such is not enough for salvation,' etc. Now this is *worldly wisdom*.

Let us join issue then on this plain ground, whether or not the doctrine of 'the Church,' and the duty of obeying it, be laid down *in Scripture*. If so, it is no matter as regards our practice, whether the doctrine is primary or secondary, whether the duty is much or little insisted on. A Christian mind will aim at obeying the *whole* counsel and will of God; on the other hand, to those who are tempted arbitrarily to classify and select their duties, it is written, 'Whosoever shall break one of these least commandments, and shall teach men so, he shall be called the least in the kingdom of heaven.'

And here first, that you may clearly understand the ground I am taking, pray observe that I am not attempting to controvert any one of those high evangelical points, on which perhaps we do not altogether agree with each other. Perhaps you attribute less efficacy to the Sacrament of Baptism than I do; bring out into greater system and prominence the history of an individual's warfare with his spiritual enemies; fix more precisely and abruptly the date of his actual conversion from darkness to light; and consider that Divine Grace acts more arbitrarily against the corrupt human will, than I think is revealed in Scripture. Still, in spite of this difference of opinion, I see no reason why you should not accept, heartily the Scripture doctrine of 'the Church.' And this is the point I wish to press, not asking you at present to abandon your own opinions, but to *add to them* a practical belief in a tenet which the Creed teaches and Scripture has consecrated. And this surely is quite possible. The excellent Mr ——, of ——, who has lately left ——, was born a Calvinist and a strenuous High-Churchman.

You are in the practice of distinguishing between the Visible and Invisible Church. Of course I have no wish to maintain that those who shall be saved hereafter are exactly the same company that are under the means of grace here; still I must insist on it, that Scripture makes the existence of a Visible Church a condition of the existence of the Invisible. I mean, the *Sacraments* are evidently in the hands of the Church Visible; and these, we know, are generally necessary to salvation, as the Catechism says. Thus it is an undeniable fact, as true as that souls will be saved, that a Visible Church must exist as a means towards that end. That Sacraments are in the hands of the Clergy; this few will deny, or that their efficacy is independent of the personal character of the administrator. What then shall be thought of any attempts to weaken or exterminate that Community, or that Ministry, which is an appointed condition of the salvation of the elect? But every one who makes or encourages a schism, *must* weaken it. Thus it is plain, schism must be wrong in itself, even if Scripture did not in express terms forbid it, as it does.

But further than this: it is plain this Visible Church is a *standing* body.

Every one who is baptised, is baptised *into* an existing community. Our Service expresses this when it speaks of baptised infants being *incorporated* into God's holy Church. Thus the Visible Church is not a voluntary association of the day, but a continuation of one which existed in the age before us, and then again in the age before that; and so back till we come to the age of the Apostles. In the same sense, in which Corporations of the State's creating are perpetual, is this which Christ has founded. This is a matter of fact hitherto: and it necessarily will be so always, for is not the notion absurd of an unbaptised person baptising others? which is the only way in which the Christian community can have a new beginning.

Moreover, Scripture directly *insists* upon the doctrine of the Visible Church, as being of importance. *E.g.* St Paul says – 'There is *one body*, and one Spirit, even as ye are called in one hope of your calling; one Lord, one faith, one baptism, one God and Father of all' (Ephes. iv, 5, 6). Thus, as far as the Apostle's words go, it is false and unchristian (I do not mean in degree of guilt, but in its intrinsic sinfulness) to make more bodies than one, as to have many Lords, many Gods, many Creeds. Now, I wish to know, how it is possible for any one to fall into this sin, if Dissenters are clear of it? What *is* the sin, if separation from the Existing Church is not it?

I have shown that there is a divinely instituted Visible Church, and that it has been one and the same by successive incorporation of members from the beginning. Now I observe further, that the word Church, as used in Scripture, ordinarily means this actually existing visible body. The possible exception to this rule, out of about a hundred places in the New Testament where the word occurs, are four passages in the Epistle to the Ephesians; two in the Colossians; and one in the Hebrews (Eph. i. 22; iii. 10, 21; v. 23-32. Col. i. 18, 24. Heb. xii. 23). And in some of these exceptions the sense is at most but doubtful. Further, our Saviour uses the word twice, and in both times of the Visible Church. They are remarkable passages, and may here be introduced, in continuation of my argument.

Matt. xvi. 18: 'Upon this rock I will build My Church, and the gates of hell shall not prevail against it.' Now I am certain, any unprejudiced mind, who knew nothing of controversy, considering the Greek word ἐκκλησία means simply an *assembly*, would have no doubt at all that it meant in this passage a visible body. What right have we to disturb the plain sense? why do we impose a meaning, arising from some system of our own? And this view is altogether confirmed by the other occasion of our Lord's using it, where it can *only* denote the Visible Church. Matt. xviii. 17: 'If he (thy brother) shall neglect to hear them, tell it unto the Church; but if he neglect to hear the Church, let him be unto thee as a heathen man and a publican.'

Observe then what we gain by these two passages: the grant of *power* to the Church; and the promise of *permanence*. Now look at the fact. The body then begun has continued; and has always claimed and exercised the power of a corporation or society. Consider merely the article in the Creed, 'The Holy Catholic Church;' which embodies this notion. Do not Scripture and History illustrate each other?

I end this first draught of my argument with the text in 1 Tim. iii. 15, in which St Paul calls the Church 'the pillar and ground of the truth,' – which can refer to nothing but a Visible Body; else martyrs may be invisible, and preachers, and teachers, and the whole order of the Ministry.

My paper is exhausted. If you allow me, I will send you soon a second Letter; meanwhile I sum up what I have been proving from Scripture thus: that Almighty God might have left Christianity as a sort of sacred literature, as contained in the Bible, which each person was to take and use by himself; just as we read the works of any human philosopher or historian, from which we gain practical instruction, but the knowledge of which does not bind us to be Newtonians, or Aristotelians, etc., or to go out of our line of life in consequence of it. This, I say, He might have done; but, in matter of fact, He has ordained otherwise. He has actually set up a Society, which exists even this day all over the world, and which (as a general rule) Christians are bound to join; so that to believe in Christ is not a mere opinion or secret conviction, but a social or even a political principle, forcing one into what is often stigmatised as party strife, and quite inconsistent with the supercilious mood of those professed Christians of the day, who stand aloof, and designate their indifference as philosophy.

LETTER II. I am sometimes struck with the inconsistency of those who do not allow us to express the gratitude due to the Church, while they do not hesitate to declare their obligation to individuals who have benefited them. To avow that they owe their views of religion and their present hopes of salvation to this or that distinguished preacher, appears to them as harmless as it may be in itself true and becoming; but if a person ascribes his faith and knowledge to the

Church, he is thought to forget his peculiar and unspeakable debt to that Saviour who died for him. Surely, if our Lord makes man His instrument of good to man, and if it is possible to be grateful to man without forgetting the source of all grace and power, there is nothing wonderful in His having appointed a company of men as the especial medium of His instruction and spiritual gifts, and in consequence, of His having laid upon us the duty of gratitude to it. Now this is all I wish to maintain, what is most clearly (as I think) revealed in Scripture, that the blessings of redemption come to us through the Visible Church; so that, as we betake ourselves to a Dispensary for medicine, without attributing praise or intrinsic worth to the building or the immediate managers of its stores, in something of the like manner we are to come to that One Society, to which Christ has entrusted the office of stewardship in the distribution of gifts, of which He alone is the Author and real Dispenser.

In the letter I sent you the other day, I made some general remarks on this doctrine; now let me continue the subject.

First, the Sacraments, which are the ordinary means of grace, are clearly in possession of the Church. Baptism is an incorporation into a body; and invests with spiritual blessings, because it is the introduction so invested. In 1 Cor. xii. we are taught first, the Spirit's indwelling in the Visible Church or body; I do not say *in every member of it*, but generally *in* it; – next, we are told that the Spirit baptises individuals *into* that body. Again, the Lord's Supper carries evidence of its social nature even in its name; it is not a solitary individual act, it is a joint communion. Surely nothing is more alien to Christianity than the spirit of Independence; the peculiar Christian blessing, *i.e.* the presence of Christ, is upon *two or three* gathered together, not on mere individuals.

But this is not all. The Sacraments are committed, not into the hand of the Church Visible assembled together (though even this would be no unimportant doctrine practically), but into certain definite persons, who are selected from their brethren for that trust. I will not here determine who these are in each successive age, but will only point out how far this principle itself will carry us. The doctrine is implied in the original institution of the Lord's Supper, where Christ says to His Apostles, 'Do this.' Further, take that remarkable passage in Matt. xxiv. 45–51. Luke xii. 42–46: 'Who then is that faithful and wise Steward, whom his Lord shall make ruler over His household, to give them their portion of meat in due season? Blessed is that servant, whom his Lord, *when He cometh*, shall find so doing!' etc. Now I do not inquire *who* in every age are the stewards spoken of (though in my own mind I cannot doubt the line of Bishops is that Ministry, and consider the concluding verses fearfully prophetic of the Papal misuse of the gift; – by-the-by, at least it shows this, that bad men may nevertheless be the channels of grace to God's 'household'), I do not ask who are the stewards, but surely the words, *when He cometh*, imply that they are to continue till the end of the world. This reference is abundantly confirmed by our Lord's parting words to the eleven; in which, after giving them the baptismal commission, he adds, 'Lo! I am with you *always*, even unto the end of the world.' If then He was with the Apostles in a way in which He was not present with teachers who were strangers to their 'fellowship' (Acts ii. 42), which all will admit, so, in like manner, it cannot be a matter of indifference in *any* age, what teachers and fellowship a Christian selects; there must be those with whom Christ is present, who are His 'Stewards,' and whom it is our duty to obey.

As I have mentioned the question of faithfulness and unfaithfulness in Ministers, I may refer to the passage in 1 Cor. iv. where St Paul, after speaking of himself and others as '*Stewards* of the mysteries of God,' and noticing that 'it is required of Stewards, that a man be found faithful,' adds, 'With me it is a very small thing that I should be judged of you or of man's judgment . . . therefore *judge nothing before the time.*'

To proceed, consider the following passage: 'Obey them that have rule over you, and submit yourselves' (Heb. xiii, 17). Again, I do not ask *who* these are; but whether this is not a duty, however it is to be fulfilled, which multitudes *in no sense* fulfil. Consider the number of people, professing and doubtless in a manner really actuated by Christian principle, who yet wander about from church to church or from church to meeting, as sheep without a shepherd, or who choose a preacher merely because he pleases their taste, and whose first movement towards any clergyman they meet, is to examine and criticise his doctrine; what conceivable meaning do they put upon these words of the Apostle? Does any one *rule over* them? do they in any way *submit themselves?* Can these persons excuse their conduct, except on the deplorably profane plea (which yet I believe is in their hearts at the bottom of their disobedience), that it matters little to keep Christ's 'least commandments,' so that we embrace the peculiar doctrines of His Gospel?

72

Some time ago I drew up a sketch of the Scripture proof of the doctrine of the Visible Church; which with your leave I will here tran-
scribe. You will observe, I am not arguing for this or that form of
Polity, or for the Apostolical Succession, but simply the duties of order,
union, ecclesiastical gifts, and ecclesiastical obedience; I limit myself to
these points, as being persuaded that, when they are granted, the others
will eventually follow.

I. That there was a Visible Church in the Apostles' day.
    1. General texts: Matt. xvi. 18; xviii. 17. 1 Tim. iii. 15. Acts
       passim, etc.
    2. Organisation of the Church.
       (1.) Diversity of ranks: 1 Cor. xii. Eph. iv. 4–12. Rom. xii.
          4–8. 1 Pet. iv. 10, 11.
       (2.) Governors: Matt. xxviii. 19. Mark xvi. 15, 16. John xx. 22,
          23. Luke xxii. 19, 20. Gal. ii. 9, etc.
       (3.) Gifts: Luke xii. 42, 43. John xx. 22, 23. Matt. xviii. 18.
       (4.) Order: Acts viii. 5, 6, 12, 14, 15, 17; xi. 22, 23; xi. 2, 4; ix.
          27; xv. 2, 4, 6, 25; xvi. 4; xviii. 22; xxi. 17–19, conf. Gal. i.
          1, 12. 1 Cor. xiv. 40. 1 Thess. v. 14.
       (5.) Ordination: Acts vi. 6. 1 Tim. iv. 14; v. 22. 2 Tim. i. 6. Tit.
          i. 5. Acts xiii. 3, conf. Gal. i. 1, 12.
       (6.) Ecclesiastical obedience: 1 Thess. v. 12, 13. Heb. xiii. 17.
          1 Tim. v. 17.
       (7.) Rules and discipline: Matt. xxviii. 19. Matt. xviii. 17. 1 Cor.
          v. 4–7. Gal. v. 12, etc. 1 Cor. xvi. 1, 2. 1 Cor. xi. 2, 16, etc.
       (8.) Unity: Rom. xvi. 17. 1 Cor. i. 10; iii. 3; xiv. 26. Col. ii. 5.
          1 Thess. v. 14. 2 Thess. iii. 6.
II. That the Visible Church, thus instituted by the Apostles, was intended to continue.
    1. Why should it not? The *onus probandi* lies with those who deny
       this position. If the doctrines and precepts already cited are
       obsolete at this day, why should not the following texts? – *e.g.*
       1 Pet. ii. 13, or *e.g.* Matt. vii. 14. John iii. 3.
    2. Is it likely so elaborate a system should be framed, yet with no
       purpose of its continuing?
    3. The objects to be obtained by it are as necessary now as then.
       (1) Preservation of the faith. (2) Purity of doctrine. (3) Edifica-
       tion of Christians. (4) Unity of operation. *Vid.* Epistles to Tim.
       and Tit. *passim*.

4. If system were necessary in a time of miracles, much more is it now.

5. 2 Tim. ii. 2. Matt. xxviii. 20, etc.

Take these remarks, as they are meant, as mere suggestions for your private consideration.

TRACT XC

§ 2. Justification by Faith only

ARTICLE xi. 'That we are justified by Faith only, is a most wholesome doctrine.'

The Homilies add that Faith is the sole *means*, the sole *instrument* of justification. Now, to show briefly what such statements imply, and what they do not.

1. They do *not* imply a denial of *Baptism* as a means and an instrument of justification; which the Homilies elsewhere affirm, as will be shown incidentally in a later section.

The instrumental power of Faith cannot interfere with the instrumental power of Baptism; because Faith is the sole justifier, not in contrast to *all* means and agencies whatever (for it is not surely in contrast to our Lord's merits, or God's mercy), but to all other *graces*. Well, then, Faith is called the sole instrument, this means the sole *internal* instrument, not the sole instrument of any kind.

There is nothing inconsistent, then, in Faith being the sole instrument of justification, and yet Baptism also the sole instrument, and that at the same time, because in distinct senses; an inward instrument in no way interfering with an outward instrument, Baptism may be the hand of the giver, and Faith the hand of the receiver.

Nor does the sole instrumentality of Faith interfere with the doctrine of *Works* being a mean also. And that it is a mean, the Homily of Almsdeeds declares in the strongest language, as will also be quoted in Section 11.

An assent to the doctrine that Faith alone justifies, does not at all preclude the doctrine of Works justifying also. If, indeed, it were said that Works justify in *the same sense* as Faith only justifies, this would be a contradiction in terms; but Faith only may justify in one sense – Good Works in another – and this is all that is here maintained. After all, does not Christ only justify? How is it that the doctrine of Faith justifying does not interfere with our Lord's being the sole Justifier? It will, of course, be replied, that our Lord is the *meritorious cause*, and

74

Faith the *means*; that Faith justifies in a different and subordinate sense. As, then, Christ justifies *in the sense* in which He justifies alone, yet Faith also justifies in its own sense; so Works, whether moral or ritual, may justify us in their own respective senses, though in the sense in which Faith justifies, it only justifies. The only question is, *What* is that sense in which Works justify, so as not to interfere with faith only justifying? It may, indeed, turn out on inquiry that the sense alleged will not hold, either as being unscriptural, or for any other reason; but, whether so or not, at any rate the apparent inconsistency of language should not startle persons; nor should they so promptly condemn those who, though they do not use *their* language, use St James's. Indeed, is not this argument the very weapon of the Arians in their warfare against the Son of God? They said, Christ is not God, because the Father is called the '*Only God.*'

2. Next we have to inquire *in what sense* Faith only does justify. In a number of ways, of which here two only shall be mentioned.

First, it is the pleading or impetrating principle, or constitutes our *title* to justification; being analogous among the graces to Moses lifting up his hands on the Mount, or the Israelites eyeing the Brazen Serpent – actions which did not merit God's mercy, but *asked* for it. A number of means go to effect our justification. We are justified by Christ alone, in that He has purchased the gift; by Faith alone, in that Faith asks for it; by Baptism alone, for Baptism conveys it; and by newness of heart alone, for newness of heart is the life of it.

And secondly, Faith, as being the beginning of perfect or justifying righteousness, is taken from what it tends towards, or ultimately will be. It is said by anticipation to be that which it promises; just as one might pay a labourer his hire before he began his work. Faith working by love is the seed of divine graces, which in due time will be brought forth and flourish – partly in this world, fully in the next.

§ 3. *Works before and after Justification*

ARTICLES xii and xiii. 'Works done before the grace of Christ, and the inspiration of His Spirit ["before justification," *title of the Article*], are not pleasant to God (minimè Deo grata sunt); forasmuch as they spring not of Faith in Jesus Christ, neither do they make man meet to receive grace, or (as the school authors say) deserve grace of congruity (merentur gratiam de congruo); yea, rather for that they are not done as God hath willed and commanded them to be done, we doubt not but they have the nature of sin. Albeit good works, which are the fruits of faith, and follow after justification (justificatos sequuntur), cannot put away (expiare) our sins, and endure the severity of

God's judgment, yet are they pleasing and acceptable (grata et accepta) to God in Christ, and do spring out necessarily of a true and lively Faith.'

Two sorts of works are here mentioned – works before justification, and works after; and they are most strongly contrasted with each other.

1. Works before justification are done 'before the grace of Christ, and the inspiration of His Spirit.'

2. Works before 'do not spring of Faith in Jesus Christ'; works after are 'the fruits of Faith.'

3. Works before 'have the nature of sin'; works after are 'good works.'

4. Works before 'are not pleasant (grata) to God'; works after 'are pleasing and acceptable (grata et accepta) to God.'

Two propositions, mentioned in these Articles, remain, and deserve consideration. First, that works *before* justification do not make or dispose men to receive grace, or, as the school writers say, deserve grace of congruity; secondly, that works *after* 'cannot put away our sins, and endure the severity of God's judgment.'

1. As to the former statement – to deserve *de congruo*, or of congruity, is to move the divine regard, not from any claim upon it, but from a certain fitness or suitableness; as, for instance, it might be said that dry wood had a certain disposition or fitness towards heat which green wood had not. Now, the Article denies that works done before the grace of Christ, or in a mere state of nature, in this way dispose towards grace, or move God to grant grace. And it asserts, with or without reason (for it is a question of *historical fact*, which need not specially concern us), that certain schoolmen maintained the affirmative.

Now, that this is what it means is plain from the following passages of the Homilies, which in no respect have greater claims upon us than as comments upon the Articles:

Therefore they that teach repentance *without a lively faith* in our Saviour Jesus Christ, do teach none other but Judas's repentance, as all the schoolmen do, which do *only* allow these three parts of repentance – the contrition of the heart, the confession of the mouth, and the satisfaction of the work. But all these things we find in Judas's repentance, which, in outward appearance, did far exceed and pass the repentance of Peter . . . This was commonly the penance which Christ enjoined sinners, 'Go thy way, and sin no more'; which penance we shall never be able to fulfil, *without the special grace* of Him that doth say, 'Without Me, ye can do nothing.' – *On Repentance*, p. 460.

To take a passage which is still more clear:

As these examples are not brought to the end that we should thereby take a boldness to sin, presuming on the mercy and goodness of God, but to the end that if, through the frailness of our own flesh, and the temptation of the devil, we fall into the like sins, we should in nowise despair of the mercy and goodness of God: even so must we beware and take heed that we do in nowise think in our hearts, imagine, or believe *that we are able to repent aright or to turn effectually unto the Lord by our own might and strength.* – *Ibid.*, part i. fin.

The Article contemplates these two states – one of justifying grace, and one of the utter destitution of grace; and it says that those who are in utter destitution cannot do anything to gain justification; and, indeed, to assert the contrary would be Pelagianism. However, there is an intermediate state, of which the Article says nothing, but which must not be forgotten, as being an actually existing one. Men are not always either in light or in darkness, but are sometimes between the two; they are sometimes not in a state of Christian justification, yet not utterly deserted by God, but in a state something like that of Jews or of Heathen, turning to the thought of religion. They are not gifted with *habitual* grace, but they still are visited by divine influences, or by *actual* grace, or rather *aid;* and these influences are the first-fruits of the grace of justification going before it, and are intended to lead on to it, and to be perfected in it, as twilight leads to day. And since it is a Scripture maxim that 'he that is faithful in that which is least, is faithful also in much'; and 'to whosoever hath, to him shall be given'; therefore it is quite true that works done *with* divine aid, and in faith, *before* justification, *do* dispose men to receive the grace of justification; – such were Cornelius's alms, fastenings, and prayers, which led to his baptism. At the same time it must be borne in mind that, even in such cases, it is not the works themselves which make them meet, as some schoolmen seem to have said, but the secret aid of God, vouchsafed, equally with the 'grace and Spirit,' which is the portion of the baptised, for the merits of Christ's sacrifice.

[But it may be objected that the silence observed in the Article about a state between that of justification and grace, and that of neither, is a proof that there is none such. This argument, however, would prove too much; for in like manner there is a silence in the Sixth Article about a *judge* of the scripturalness of doctrine, yet a judge there must be. And, again, few, it is supposed, would deny that Cornelius, before the angel came to him, was in a more hopeful state than Simon Magus or Felix.

The difficulty then, if there be one, is common to persons of whatever school of opinion.]

2. If works *before* justification, when done by the influence of divine aid, gain grace, much more do works *after* justification. They are, according to the Article, 'grata,' 'pleasing to God'; and they are accepted, 'accepta'; which means that God rewards them, and that of course according to their degree of excellence. At the same time, as works before justification may nevertheless be done under a divine influence, so works after justification are still liable to the infection of original sin; and, as not being perfect, 'cannot expiate our sins,' or 'endure the severity of God's judgment.'

§ 7. The Sacraments

ART. xxv. 'Those five, commonly called Sacraments, that is to say, Confirmation, Penance, Orders, Matrimony, and Extreme Unction, are not to be counted for Sacraments of the Gospel, being such as have grown, partly of the corrupt following (pravâ imitatione) of the Apostles, partly from states of life allowed in the Scriptures; but yet have not like nature of sacraments (sacrementorum eandem rationem), with Baptism and the Lord's Supper, for that they have not any visible sign or ceremony ordained of God.'

This Article does not deny the five rites in question to be sacraments, but to be sacraments in *the sense* in which Baptism and the Lord's Supper are sacraments; 'sacraments of *the Gospel*,' sacraments *with an outward sign ordained of God.*

They are not sacraments in *any* sense, *unless* the Church has the power of dispensing grace through rites of its own appointing, or is endued with the gift of blessing and hallowing the 'rites or ceremonies' which, according to the twentieth article, it 'hath power to decree.' But we may well believe that the Church has this gift.

If, then, a sacrament be merely *an outward sign of an invisible grace given under it,* the five rites may be sacraments; but if it must be an outward sign *ordained by God or Christ,* then only Baptism and the Lord's Supper are sacraments.

Our Church acknowledges both definitions; in the article before us, *the stricter;* and again in the Catechism, where a sacrament is defined to be 'an outward visible sign of an inward spiritual grace, given unto us, *ordained by Christ himself.*' And this, it should be remarked, is a characteristic of our formularies in various places, not to deny the *truth* or *obligation* of certain doctrines or ordinances, but simply to deny (what no Roman opponent now can successfully maintain) that Christ for certain directly ordained them. For instance, in regard to the visible Church, it is sufficient that the ministration of the sacraments should be '*according to Christ's ordinance.*' Art. xix. And it is added, 'in all those things that *of necessity* are requisite to the same.' The question entertained is, what is *the least* that God requires of us. Again, 'the baptism of young children is to be retained, as most agreeable to *the institution of Christ.*' Art. xxvii. Again, 'the sacrament of the Lord's Supper was not by Christ's *ordinance* reserved, carried about, lifted up, or worshipped.' Art. xxviii. Who will maintain the paradox that what the Apostles 'set in order when they came' had been already done by Christ? Again, 'both parts of the Lord's sacrament, *by Christ's ordinance and commandment*, ought to be administered to all Christian men alike.' Art. xxx. Again, 'bishops, priests, and deacons *are not commanded by God's law* either to vow the estate of single life or to abstain from marriage.' Art. xxxii. [In making this distinction, however, it is not here insinuated, though the question is not entered on in these particular articles, that every one of these points, of which it is only said that they are not ordained by Christ, is justifiable on grounds short of His appointment.]

On the other hand, our Church takes the *wider* sense of the meaning of the word sacrament in the Homilies, observing –

> In the second Book against the Adversary of the Law and the Prophets, he [St Augustine] calleth sacraments *holy signs*. And writing to Bonifacius of the baptism of infants, he saith, 'If sacraments had not a certain similitude of those things whereof they be sacraments, they should be no sacraments at all. And of this similitude they do for the most part receive the names of the selfsame things they signify.' By these words of St Augustine it appeareth that he alloweth the common description of a sacrament, which is, that it is *a visible sign of an invisible grace;* that is to say, that setteth out to the eyes and other outward senses the inward working of God's free mercy, and doth, as it were, seal in our hearts the promises of God. – *Homily on Common Prayer and Sacraments,* pp. 296, 297.

Accordingly, starting with this definition of St Augustine's, the writer is necessarily carried on as follows:

> You shall hear how many sacraments there be that were instituted by our Saviour Christ, and are to be continued, and received of every Christian, in due time and order, and for such purposes as our Saviour Christ willed them to be received. And as for the number of them, if they should be considered according to the *exact* signification of a sacrament, namely, for visible signs

expressly commanded in the New Testament, whereunto is annexed the promise of free forgiveness of our sins, and of our holiness and joining in Christ, there be but two – namely, Baptism, and the Supper of the Lord. For although absolution hath the promise of forgiveness of sin; yet by the *express* word of the New Testament, it hath not this promise annexed and tied to the visible sign, which is imposition of hands. For this visible sign (I mean laying on of hands) is not *expressly* commanded in the New Testament to be used in absolution, as the visible signs in Baptism and the Lord's Supper are; and therefore absolution is no *such* sacrament as Baptism, and the Communion are. And though the ordering of ministers hath this visible sign and promise; yet it lacks the promise of remission of sin, as all other sacraments besides the two above named do. Therefore neither it, nor any *other* sacrament else, be *such* sacraments as Baptism and the Communion are. But in a general acception, the name of a sacrament may be attributed to anything, whereby a holy thing is signified. In which understanding of the word, the ancient writers have given this name, not only to the other five, commonly of late years taken and used for supplying the number of the seven sacraments; but also to divers and sundry other ceremonies, as to oil, washing of feet, and such like; not meaning thereby to repute them as sacraments, *in the same signification* that the two forenamed sacraments are. And therefore St Augustine, weighing the true signification and exact meaning of the word, writing to Januarius, and also in the third Book of Christian Doctrine, affirmeth that the sacraments of the Christians, as they are most excellent in signification, so are they most few in number, and in both places maketh mention expressly of two, the sacrament of Baptism, and the Supper of the Lord. And although there are retained by order of the Church of England, besides these two, certain other rites and ceremonies, about the institution of ministers in the Church, Matrimony, Confirmation of Children, by examining them of their knowledge in the Articles of the Faith, and joining thereto the prayers of the Church for them, and likewise for the Visitation of the Sick; yet no man ought to take these for sacraments, in such signification and meaning as the sacraments of Baptism and the Lord's Supper are; but either for godly states of life, necessary in Christ's Church, and therefore worthy to be set forth by public action and solemnity, by the ministry of the Church, or else judged to be such ordinances as may make for the instruction, comfort, and edification of Christ's Church – *Homily on Common Prayer and Sacraments*, pp. 298–300.

Another definition of the word sacrament, which equally succeeds in limiting it to the two principal rites of the Christian Church, is also contained in the Catechism, as well as alluded to in the above passage: 'Two only, as *generally necessary* to salvation, Baptism and the Supper of the Lord.' On this subject the following remark has been made:

The Roman Catholic considers that there are seven [sacraments]; we do not strictly determine the number. We define the word generally to be an 'outward sign of an inward grace,' without saying to how many ordinances this applies. However, what we do determine is, that Christ has ordained two special sacraments, as *generally necessary to salvation*. This, then, is the characteristic mark of those two, separating them from all other whatever; and this is nothing else but saying in other words, that they are the only *justifying* rites, or instruments of communicating the Atonement, which is the one thing necessary to us. Ordination, for instance, gives *power*, yet without making the soul *acceptable* to God; Confirmation gives *light and strength*, yet is the mere *completion* of Baptism; and Absolution may be viewed as a negative ordinance removing the *barrier* which sin has raised between us and that grace, which by inheritance is ours. But the two sacraments 'of the Gospel,' as they may be emphatically styled, are the instruments of inward *life*, according to our Lord's declaration, that Baptism is a new *birth*, and that in the Eucharist we eat the *living* bread.

§ 9. Masses

ARTICLE xxxi. 'The sacrifice (sacrificia) of Masses, in the which it was commonly said, that the priest did offer Christ for the quick and the dead, to have remission of pain or guilt, were blasphemous fables and dangerous deceits (perniciosæ imposturæ).'

Nothing can show more clearly than this passage that the Articles are not written against the creed of the Roman church, but against actual existing errors in it, whether taken into its system or not. Here the sacrifice of the *Mass* is not spoken of, in which the special question of doctrine would be introduced; but 'the sacrifice of *Masses*,' certain observances, for the most part private and solitary, which the writers of the Articles knew to have been in force in time past, and saw before their eyes, and which involved certain opinions and a certain teaching. Accordingly the passage proceeds, 'in which it *was commonly said*'; which surely is a strictly historical mode of speaking.

If any testimony is necessary in aid of what is so plain from the wording of the Article itself, it is found in the drift of the following passage from Burnet:

It were easy from all the rituals of the ancients to show, that they had none of these ideas that are now in the Roman Church. They had but one altar in a Church, and probably but one in a city: they had but one communion in a day at that altar; so far were they from the many altars in every church, and *the many masses* at every altar, that are now in the Roman Church. They did not know what *solitary masses* were, without a communion. All the liturgies and all the writings of ancients are as express in this matter as is possible. The whole constitution of their worship and discipline shows it. Their worship always concluded with the Eucharist: such as were not capable of it, as the catechumens, and those who were doing public penance for their sins, assisted at the more general parts of the worship; and so much of it was called their mass, because they were dismissed at the conclusion of it. When that was done, then the faithful stayed, and did partake of the Eucharist; and at the conclusion of it they were likewise dismissed, from whence it came to be called the mass of the faithful – *Burnet on the XXXIst Article*, p. 482.

These sacrifices are said to be 'blasphemous fables and pernicious impostures.' Now the 'blasphemous fable' is the teaching that there is a sacrifice for sin other than Christ's death, and that masses are that sacrifice. And the 'pernicious imposture' is the turning this belief into a means of filthy lucre.

1. That the 'blasphemous fable' is the teaching that masses are sacrifices for sin distinct from the sacrifice of Christ's death, is plain from the first sentence of the Article. 'The offering of Christ *once made*, is that perfect redemption, propitiation, and satisfaction for *all* the sins of the *whole world, both original and actual.* And *there is none other* satisfaction for sin, but *that alone. Wherefore* the sacrifice of masses, etc.' It is observable too that the heading of the Article runs, 'Of the one oblation of Christ finished upon the Cross,' which interprets the *drift* of the statement contained in it about masses.

Our Communion Service shows it also, in which the prayer of consecration commences pointedly with a declaration, which has the force of a protest, that Christ made on the cross, 'by His *one* oblation of Himself *once* offered, a *full, perfect,* and *sufficient* sacrifice, oblation, and *satisfaction* for the sins of the whole world.'

And again in the offering of the sacrifice:

We entirely desire thy fatherly goodness mercifully to accept our sacrifice of praise and thanksgiving, most humbly beseeching Thee to grant that *by the merits and death of Thy Son Jesus Christ,* and through faith in His blood, we and all Thy whole Church may obtain *remission of our sins* and all *other benefits* of His passion.

[And in the notice of the celebration:

I purpose, through God's assistance, to administer to all such as shall be religiously and devoutly disposed, the most comfortable Sacrament of the Body and Blood of Christ; to be by them received in remembrance of His meritorious Cross and Passion; *whereby alone* we obtain remission of our sins, and are made partakers of the kingdom of heaven.]

But the popular charge still urged against the Roman system, as introducing in the Mass a second or rather continually recurring atonement, is a sufficient illustration, without further quotations, of this part of the Article.

2. That the 'blasphemous and pernicious imposture' is the turning the Mass into a gain, is plain from such passages as the following:

With what earnestness, with what vehement zeal, did our Saviour Christ drive the buyers and sellers out of the temple of God, and hurled down the tables of the changers of money, and the seats of the dove-sellers, and could not abide that a man should carry a vessel through the temple. He told them, that they had made His Father's house a den of thieves, partly through their superstition, hypocrisy, false worship, false doctrine, and insatiable covetousness, and partly through contempt, abusing that place with walking and talking, with worldly matters, without all fear of God, and due reverence to that place. What dens of thieves the Churches of England have been made by the *blasphemous buying and selling the most precious body and blood of Christ in the Mass*, as the world was made to believe, at dirges, at months minds, at trentalls, in abbeys and chantries, besides other horrible abuses (God's holy name be blessed for ever), which we now see and understand. All these abominations they that supply the room of Christ have cleansed and purged the Churches of England of, taking away all such fulsomeness and filthiness, as through blind devotion and ignorance hath crept into the Church these many hundred years. – *On Repairing and Keeping Clean of Churches*, pp. 229–230.

Other passages are as follow:

Have not the Christians of late days, and even in our days also, in like manner provoked the displeasure and indignation of Almighty God; partly because they have profaned and defiled their Churches with heathenish and Jewish abuses, with images and idols, with numbers of altars, too superstitiously and intolerably abused, with gross abusing and filthy corrupting of the Lord's holy Supper, the blessed sacrament of His body and blood, with an infinite number of toys and trifles of their own devices, to make a goodly outward show, and to deface the homely, simple, and sincere religion of Christ Jesus; partly, they resort to the Church like hypocrites, full of all iniquity and sinful life, having a vain and dangerous fancy and persuasion, that if they come to the Church, besprinkle them with holy water, *hear a mass, and be blessed with a chalice*, though they understand not one word of the whole service, nor feel one motion of repentance in their heart, all is well, all is sure? – *On the Place and Time of Prayer*, p. 293.

Again –

What hath been the cause of this gross idolatry, but the ignorance here? What hath been the cause of this *mummish massing*, but the ignorance hereof? Yes, what hath been, and what is at this day the cause of this want of love and charity, but the ignorance hereof? Let us therefore so travel to understand the Lord's Supper, that we be no cause of the decay of God's worship, of no idolatry, of no *dumb massing*, of no hate and malice; so may we the bolder have access thither to our comfort – *Homily concerning the Sacrament*, pp. 377, 378.

To the same purpose is the following passage from Bishop Bull's Sermons:

It were easy to show how the whole frame of religion and doctrine of the Church of Rome, as it is distinguished from that Christianity which we hold in common with them, is evidently designed and contrived *to serve the interest and profit* of them that rule the Church, by the disservices, yea, and ruin of those souls that are under their government. . . . What can the doctrine of men's playing an aftergame for their salvation in purgatory be designed for, but to enhance *the price of the priest's masses* and dirges for the dead? Why must a *solitary mass, bought for a piece of money,* performed and participated by a priest alone, in a private corner of a church, be, not only against the sense of Scripture and the Primitive Church, but also against common sense and grammar, called a Communion, and be accounted useful to him that buys it, though he never himself receive the sacrament, or but once a year; but for this reason, that there is *great gain,* but no godliness at all, in this doctrine? – *Bp Bull's Sermons,* p. 10.

And Burnet says –

Without going far in tragical expressions, we cannot hold saying what our Saviour said upon another occasion, 'My house is a house of prayer, but ye have made it a den of thieves.' A trade was set up on this foundation. The world was made believe, that by the virtue of so many *masses, which were to be purchased by great endowments,* souls were redeemed out of purgatory, and scenes of visions and apparitions, sometimes of the tormented, and sometimes of the delivered souls, were published in all places: which had so wonderful an effect, that in two or three centuries, *endowments* increased to so vast a degree, that if the scandals of the clergy on the one hand, and the statutes of mortmain on the other, had not restrained the profuseness that the world was wrought up to on this account, it is not easy to imagine how far this might have gone; perhaps to an entire subjecting of the temporality to the spirituality. The practices by which this was managed, and the effects that followed on it, we can call by no other name than downright *impostures;* worse than the making or vending false coin: when the world was drawn in by such arts to plain bargains, to *redeem* their own souls, and the souls of their ancestors and posterity, *so many masses were to be said,* and forfeitures were to follow upon their not being said: thus the *masses were really the price* of the lands. – *On Article XXII,* pp. 303, 304.

The truth of these representations cannot be better shown than by extracting the following passage from the Session 22 of the Council of Trent:

Whereas many things appear to have crept in heretofore, whether by the fault of the times or by the neglect and wickedness of men, foreign to the dignity of so great a sacrifice, in order that it may regain its due honour and observance, to the glory of God and the edification of His faithful people, the Holy Council decrees that the bishops, ordinaries of each place, diligently take care and be bound to forbid and put an end to all these things, which either *avarice*, which is idolatry, or *irreverence*, which is scarcely separable from impiety, or *superstition*, the pretence of true piety, has introduced. And to say much in a few words, first of all, as to avarice, let them altogether forbid agreements, and bargains of *payment* of whatever kind, and *whatever is given for celebrating new masses*, moreover importunate and mean extortion, rather than petition of alms, and such-like practices, which border on simoniacal sin, certainly on *filthy lucre*. . . . And let them banish from the church those musical practices, *when with the organ or with the chant anything lascivious or impure is mingled*; also all secular practices, vain and therefore profane conversations, promenadings, bustle, glamour; so that the house of God may truly seem and be called the house of prayer. Lastly, lest any opening be given to superstition, let them provide by edict and punishments appointed, that the priests cele-brate it at no other than the due hours, nor use rites or ceremonies and prayers in the celebration of masses, other than those which have been approved by the Church, and received on frequent and laudable use. And let them altogether remove from the Church a *set number of certain masses and candles*, which has proceeded rather from *superstitious observance* than from true religion, and teach the people in what consists, and from whom, above all, proceeds the so precious and heavenly fruit of this most holy sacrifice. And let them admon-ish the same people to come frequently to their parish churches, at least on Sundays and the greater feasts, etc.

On the whole, then, it is conceived that the Article before us neither speaks against the Mass in itself, nor against its being [an offering, though commemorative] for the quick and the dead for the remission of sin [(especially since the decree of Trent says that 'the fruits of the Bloody Oblation are through this most abundantly obtained; so far is the latter from detracting in any way from the former')]; but against its being viewed, on the one hand, as independent of or distinct from the Sacrifice on the Cross, which is blasphemy; and, on the other, its being directed to the emolument of those to whom it pertains to celebrate it, which is imposture in addition.

§ 12. *The Bishop of Rome*

ARTICLE xxxviii. 'The Bishop of Rome hath no jurisdiction in this realm of England.'

By 'hath' is meant 'ought to have,' as the Article in the 36th Canon and the Oath of Supremacy show, in which the same doctrine is drawn out more at length. 'No foreign prince, person, *prelate*, state, or poten-tate hath, *or ought to have*, any jurisdiction, power, superiority, pre-eminence, or authority, ecclesiastical or spiritual, within this realm.'

This is the profession which every one must in consistency make, who does not join the Roman Church. If the Bishop of Rome has jurisdiction and authority here, why do we not acknowledge it, and submit to him? To say then the above words, is nothing more or less than to say 'I am not a Roman Catholic'; and whatever reasons there are against saying them, are so far reasons against remaining in the English Church. They are a mere enunciation of the principle of Anglicanism.

Anglicans maintain that the supremacy of the Pope is not directly from revelation, but an event in Providence. All things may be undone by the agents and causes by which they are done. What revelation gives, revelation takes away; what Providence gives, Providence takes away. God ordained by miracle, He reversed by miracle, the Jewish election; He promoted in the way of Providence, and He cast down by the same way the Roman Empire. 'The powers that be, are ordained of God,' *while* they be, and have a claim on our obedience. When they cease to be, they cease to have a claim. They cease to be, when God removes them. He may be considered to remove them when He un-does what He had done. The Jewish election did not cease to be, when the Jews went into captivity; this was an event in Providence; and what miracle had ordained, it was miracle that annulled. But the Roman power ceased to be when the barbarians overthrew it; for it rose by the sword, and it therefore perished by the sword. The Gospel Ministry began in Christ and His Apostles; and what they began, they only can end. The Papacy began in the exertions and passions of man; and what man can make, man can destroy. Its jurisdiction, while it lasted, was 'ordained of God'; when it ceased to be, it ceased to claim our obedience; and it ceased to be at the Reformation. The Reformers, who could not destroy a Ministry which the Apostles began, could destroy a Dominion which the Popes founded.

Perhaps the following passage will throw additional light upon this point:

The Anglican view of the Church has ever been this: that its portions need not otherwise have been united together for their essential completeness, than as being descended from one original. They are like a number of colonies sent out from a mother-country. . . . Each Church is independent of all the rest, and is to act on the principle of what may be called Episcopal independence, except, indeed, so far as the civil power unites any number of them together. . . . Each diocese is a perfect independent Church, sufficient for itself; and the communion of Christians one with another, and the unity of them altogether, lie, not in a mutual understanding, intercourse, and combination, not in what they do in common, but in what they are and have in common, in their possession of the Succession, their Episcopal form, their Apostolical faith, and the use of the Sacraments. . . . Mutual intercourse is but an *accident* of the Church, not of its essence. . . . Intercommunion is a duty, as other duties, but is not the tenure or instrument of the communion between the unseen world and this; and much more the confederacy of sees and churches, the metropolitan, patriarchal, and papal systems, are matters of expedience or of natural duty from long custom, or of propriety from gratitude and reverence, or of necessity from voluntary oaths and engagements, or of ecclesiastical force from the canons of Councils, but not necessary in order to the conveyance of grace, or for fulfilment of the ceremonial law, as it may be called, of unity. Bishop is superior to bishop only in rank, not in real power; and the Bishop of Rome, the head of the Catholic world, is not the centre of unity, except as having a primacy of order. Accordingly, even granting for argument's sake that the English Church violated a duty in the sixteenth century, in releasing itself from the Roman supremacy, still it did not thereby commit that special sin which cuts off from it the fountains of grace, and is called schism. It was essentially complete without Rome, and naturally independent of it; it had, in the course of years, whether by usurpation or not, come under the supremacy of Rome; and now, whether by rebellion or not, it is free from it: and as it did not enter into the Church invisible by joining Rome, so it was not cast out of it by breaking from Rome. These were accidents in its history, involving, indeed, sin in individuals, but not affecting the Church as a Church.

Accordingly, the Oath of Supremacy declares 'that no foreign prelate hath or ought to have any jurisdiction, power, pre-eminence, or authority within this realm.' In other words, there is nothing in the Apostolic system which gives an authority to the Pope over the Church, such as it does not give to a Bishop. It is altogether an ecclesiastical arrangement; not a point *de fide*, but of expedience, custom, or piety, which cannot be claimed as if the Pope *ought* to have it, any more than, on the other hand, the King could of Divine right claim the supremacy; the claim of both one and the other resting, not on duty or revelation, but on specific engagement. We find ourselves, as a Church, under the King now, and we obey him; we were under the Pope formerly, and we obeyed him. 'Ought' does not, in any degree, come into the question.

Conclusion

One remark may be made in conclusion. It may be objected that the tenor of the above explanations is anti-Protestant, whereas it is notorious that the Articles were drawn up by Protestants, and intended for the establishment of Protestantism; accordingly, that it is an evasion of their meaning to give them any other than a Protestant drift, possible as it may be to do so grammatically, or in each separate part.

But the answer is simple:

1. In the first place, it is a *duty* which we owe both to the Catholic Church and to our own, to take our reformed confessions in the most

Catholic sense they will admit; we have no duties towards their framers. [Nor do we receive the Articles from the original framers, but from several successive convocations after their times; in the last instance, from that of 1662.]

2. In giving the Articles a Catholic interpretation, we bring them into harmony with the Book of Common Prayer, an object of the most serious moment to those who have given their assent to both formularies.

3. Whatever be the authority of the [Declaration] prefixed to the Articles, so far as it has any weight at all, it sanctions the mode of interpreting them above given. For its injoining the 'literal and grammatical sense,' relieves us from the necessity of making the known opinions of their framers a comment upon their text; and its forbidding any person to 'affix any *new* sense to any Article,' was promulgated at a time when the leading men of our Church were especially noted for those Catholic views which have been here advocated.

4. It may be remarked, moreover, that such an interpretation is in accordance with the well-known general leaning of Melancthon, from whose writings our Articles are principally drawn, and whose Catholic tendencies gained for him that same reproach of popery which has ever been so freely bestowed upon members of our own reformed Church.

Melancthon was of opinion [says Moshein] that, for the sake of peace and concord, many things might be given up and tolerated in the Church of Rome which Luther considered could by no means be endured. . . . In the class of matters indifferent, this great man and his associates placed many things which had appeared of the highest importance to Luther, and could not of consequence be considered as indifferent by his true disciples. For he regarded as such the doctrine of justification by faith alone; the necessity of good works to eternal salvation; the number of the sacraments, the jurisdiction claimed by the Pope and the Bishops; extreme unction; the observation of certain religious festivals, and several superstitious rites and ceremonies. – *Cent. XVI*, § 3, part 2, 27, 28.

5. Further: the Articles are evidently framed on the principle of leaving open large questions, on which the controversy hinges. They state broadly extreme truths, and are silent about their adjustment. For instance, they say that all necessary faith must be proved from Scripture, but do not say *who* is to prove it. They say that the Church has authority in controversies, they do not say *what* authority. They say that it may enforce nothing beyond Scripture, but do not say *where* the remedy lies when it does. They say that works *before* grace *and* justification are worthless and worse, and that works *after* grace *and* justification are acceptable, but they do not speak at all of works *with*

God's aid, *before* justification. They say that men are lawfully called and sent to minister and preach, who are chosen and called by men who have public authority *given* them in the congregation to call and send; but they do not add *by whom* the authority is to be given. They say that councils called *by princes* may err; they do not determine whether councils called *in the name of Christ* will err.

[6. The variety of doctrinal views contained in the Homilies, as above shown, views which cannot be brought under Protestantism itself, in its widest comprehension of opinions, is an additional proof, considering the connection of the Articles with the Homilies, that the Articles are not framed on the principle of excluding those who prefer the theology of the early ages to that of the Reformation; or rather since both Homilies and Articles appeal to the Fathers and Catholic antiquity, let it be considered whether, in interpreting them by these, we are not going to the very authority to which they profess to submit themselves.]

7. Lastly, their framers constructed them in such a way as best to comprehend those who did not go so far in Protestantism as themselves. Anglo-Catholics then are but the successors and representatives of those moderate reformers; and their case has been directly anticipated in the wording of the Articles. It follows that they are not perverting, they are using them, for an express purpose for which among others their authors framed them. The interpretation they take was intended to be admissible; though not that which their authors took themselves. Had it not been provided for, possibly the Articles never would have been accepted by our Church at all. If, then, their framers have gained their side of the compact in effecting the reception of the Articles, let Catholics have theirs too in retaining their own Catholic interpretation of them.

An illustration of this occurs in the history of the 28th Article. In the beginning of Elizabeth's reign a paragraph formed part of it, much like that which is now appended to the Communion Service, but in which the Real Presence was *denied in words*. It was adopted by the clergy at the first convocation, but not published. Burnet observes on it thus:

When these Articles were first prepared by the convocation in Queen Elizabeth's reign, this paragraph was made a part of them; for the original subscription by both houses of convocation, yet extant, shows this. But the *design of the government* was at that time much turned to *the drawing over the body of the nation to the Reformation*, in whom the old leaven had gone deep; and no part of it deeper than the belief of the corporeal presence of Christ in the Sacrament; therefore it was *thought not expedient* to *offend* them by so particular a definition in this matter; in which the very word Real Presence was rejected. It might, perhaps, be also suggested that here a definition was made that went too much upon the principles of natural philosophy; which, how true soever, they might not be the proper subject of an article of religion. Therefore it was thought fit to suppress this paragraph; though it was a part of the Article that was subscribed, yet it was not published, but the paragraph that follows, 'The Body of Christ,' etc., was put in its stead, and was received and published by the next convocation; which upon the matter was a full explanation of the way of Christ's presence in this Sacrament; that 'He is present in a heavenly and spiritual manner, and that faith is the mean by which He is received.' This seemed to be more theological; and it does indeed amount to the same thing. But howsoever we see what was the sense of the first convocation in Queen Elizabeth's reign, it differed in nothing from that in King Edward's time; and therefore though this paragraph is now no part of our Articles, yet we are certain that the clergy at that time did not at all doubt of the truth of it; we are sure it was their opinion; since they subscribed it, though *they did not think fit* to publish it at first; and though it was afterwards changed for another, that was the same in sense. – *Burnet on Article XXVIII*, p. 416.

What has lately taken place in the political world will afford an illustration in point. A French minister, desirous of war, nevertheless, as a matter of policy, draws up his state papers in such moderate language that his successor, who is for peace, can act up to them without compromising his own principles. The world, observing this, has considered it a circumstance for congratulation; as if the former minister, who acted a double part, had been caught in his own snare. It is neither decorous, nor necessary, nor altogether fair, to urge the parallel rigidly; but it will explain what it is here meant to convey. The Protestant Confession was drawn up with the purpose of including Catholics; and Catholics now will not be excluded. What was an economy in the reformers, is a protection to us. What would have been a perplexity to us then is a perplexity to Protestants now. We could not then have found fault with their words; they cannot now repudiate our meaning.

OXFORD, *The Feast of the Conversion of St Paul* [*January 25th*], 1841

4

THOMAS ARNOLD: *Two Sermons on the Interpretation of Prophecy*

Arnold's importance does not derive primarily from the power of his thought but from the earnestness of his feelings and the over-powering strength of his personality. Appointed headmaster of Rugby in 1828, he died in 1842, when he was not quite forty-seven. There is something surprising in these simple facts. It is hard to believe that he had time to be such an influential teacher; and hard also to believe that he died so early in the new Queen's reign, for in his earnestness, his emotionalism, his seriousness about education and his touches of naivety and unwordliness, he can be seen as the first Victorian.

Theologically, he was Erastian, believing the Church to be the State in its religious aspect, and was in some ways near to the type later distinguished as Liberal Protestant. But the most interesting feature of his writings is his combination of theological breadth and vagueness with a burning certainty about all moral questions. In the two essays given here he transposes the whole idea of prophecy into moral terms; 'we see clearly enough why its promises are not fulfilled to the letter; the promises were for the righteous and we are not righteous'. And he sees the conflict of tribes described in the Old Testament as essentially a moral conflict.

Perhaps, however, his writings fail to suggest the full effect of his personality in life. His pupils never forgot him; and among those most strongly influenced were Stanley, who wrote his life, and Clough. But perhaps the most striking tribute to his influence is the poem *Rugby Chapel* written by his son Matthew, a man even more gifted than himself. Matthew, cool, ironical and confident, is the last person one would expect to worship a long-dead father. It is easy to infer from this what must have been his impact on weaker spirits.

SERMON I

Numbers xxiii. 9. Lo, the people shall dwell alone, and shall not be reckoned among the nations.

IT is a striking thing to observe, as we turn over the records of past times, what various subjects have at different periods occupied the attention of mankind. But it is no less striking to notice what falls actually within our own experience, how many various subjects engage the attention of different persons in the same generation and the same country. How different are the objects of general interest at a university, for instance, from those most regarded in a great commercial city; how different again are the views most familiar to different classes or sects of persons within the very same town. Following this up still further, and if we come even to subjects connected with Christianity itself, what different degrees of interest are awakened by the same points in different minds. Some dwell principally on the doctrines of Christianity, others on its practical lessons; with some the success of missions is the point nearest their heart; with others it is the unity of the Church, and the customs and opinions of Christian antiquity; while others again turn with especial fondness to the question of Prophecy, and endeavour to trace out what has actually been fulfilled, and what still, as they think, remains to be so. Now it is not an evil, but a great good, that all these subjects should be studied; neither is it to be regretted, much less to be blamed, that some of them should be peculiarly followed by some persons, and others by others. But it is to be regretted, that men should ever follow any one of these so peculiarly, as to forget the claims of the rest; for then their view and their spirit become narrow, and they understand their own favourite subject the worse, because they look at it in one light only.

Of all these divisions to which I have been alluding, the class of persons who bestow their peculiar attention on the subject of Prophecy, receive perhaps in general the least sympathy from the rest. They themselves regard their subject indeed with intense interest, but they cannot prevail on many others to study it. But there is this peculiarity in the subject of Prophecy, that where it has not been studied, men's notions respecting it are even more than commonly vague. They may have snatches of notions respecting it here and there, yet even to themselves they are conscious of their unsatisfactoriness. They talk about the evidence of Prophecy, yet I believe it is very rare indeed to meet with any one whose faith rests much upon that evidence, or indeed who has ever really tried its validity.

The subject of Prophecy, however, is one which ought, I do not say to be predominantly, far less exclusively, studied, but certainly not to be altogether neglected. If it were only for the sake of the many appeals made to it by our Lord and his Apostles, it would have a just claim on our attention. Besides, the Prophets form no inconsiderable portion of the volume of the Scriptures, and the prophetic parts of Scripture are often, as in the first Lesson of this morning's Service, read publicly in the Service of the Church. It is well, therefore, even if we do not follow up the subject minutely, that the ideas which we have respecting it should be clear and edifying.

Now first of all, it is a very misleading notion of Prophecy, if we regard it as an anticipation of History. History, in our common sense of the term, is busy with particular nations, times, places, actions, and even persons. If in this sense Prophecy were a history written before-hand, it would alter the very condition of humanity, by removing from us our uncertainty as to the future; it would make us acquainted with those times and seasons which the Father hath put in His own power. It is anticipated History, not in our common sense of the word, but in another and far higher sense. Common History, amid a vast number of particular facts and persons, can hardly trace the general principles which are to be deduced from them. Nay, the imperfection of the characters with which History deals, naturally embarrasses its general conclusions: we can trace the rise and fall of such a nation or such a city; but this is not the rise or fall of any one principle, either good or evil; but of many principles which are partly good and partly evil. Our sympathy with the prosperity and adversity of any one people must be qualified; there is an evil about them, which triumphs in their triumph; there is good about them, which suffers in their overthrow.

Now what History does not and cannot do, that Prophecy does; and for that very reason it is very different from History. Prophecy fixes our attention on principles, on good and evil, on truth and false-hood, on God and on His enemy. Here, there is no division of feeling, no qualified sympathy; the one are deserving of our entire devotion and love, the other of our unmixed abhorrence.

Prophecy then is God's voice, speaking to us respecting the issue in all times of that great struggle which is the real interest of human life, the struggle between good and evil. Beset as we are by evil within us and without, it is the natural and earnest question of the human mind, What shall be the end at last? And the answer is given by Prophecy, that it shall be well at last; that there shall be a time when good shall perfectly triumph. But the answer declares also, that the struggle shall be long and hard; that there will be much to suffer before the victory be complete. The seed of the woman shall bruise the serpent's head, but the serpent notwithstanding shall first bruise his heel. So completely is the earliest prophecy recorded in Scripture, the sum and substance so to speak of the whole language of Prophecy, how diversified soever in its particular forms.

History, we have said, is busied with particular nations, persons, and events; and from the study of these, extracts, as well as it can, some general principles. Prophecy is busy with general principles; and inasmuch as particular nations, persons, and events represent these principles up to a certain point, so far it is concerned also with them. But their mixed character, as it embarrasses and qualifies the judgment of the historian, so it must necessarily lower and qualify the promises and threatenings of the prophet. The full bliss which he delights to contemplate, because his eye is fixed chiefly upon God and perfect goodness, is not equally suited to the most imperfect goodness of God's servants. The utter extremity of suffering which belongs to God's enemy, must be mitigated for those earthly evildoers, whom God till the last great day has not yet wholly ceased to regard as His creatures.

Now then, to take examples of this both ways; Israel, the people of Israel, their kings, and their prophets, stand forth in the History and in the Prophecy of Scripture as the representatives, so to speak, of the cause of God and of goodness. But the History shows that they were very imperfect representatives of it, and therefore they can only be imperfectly the subject of the promises of Prophecy. So far as they belonged to God, the blessing is theirs; so far as they fell short of what God's servants should be, the blessing is not theirs; for they are not the real subjects of the Prophecy. For it is History, and not Prophecy, which deals with the twelve tribes of the land of Canaan, their good and evil kings, their fallings away, and final rejection of Christ their Saviour: the Israel of Prophecy is God's Israel really and truly, who walk with Him faithfully, and abide with Him to the end.

Thus, as in the text, Balak king of the Moabites calls upon Balaam the prophet to curse Israel. This is the History; on the one hand there was one people, on the other there was another; Moab was not all evil, Israel was not all good. But mere History can find no difficulty in determining, that so opposed to one another in that wilderness between

Egypt and Palestine, the highest good to unborn generations of the human race was involved in the preservation of Israel. It is this comparative good and evil which History can discern in the two nations, which determines their respective characters as the representatives, at that time and place, of that real good and evil whose contest is the enduring subject of Prophecy. They are their representatives, but only imperfectly; signs of ideas, which Prophecy uses, as Revelation avails itself of human language; a shadow of the reality, but not its substance.

Was it indeed that murmuring rebellious people, rebellious against God from the time when Moses brought them out of Egypt, of whom Prophecy declared, that God had not beheld iniquity, nor seen perverseness? Or that camp, in which every man did that which was right in his own eyes, that camp pitched amid the sands of the wilderness, beside such a narrow strip of green watered country as is all that can be found by the traveller in the desert, – did it really contain the goodly tents and tabernacles which Prophecy saw spread forth as gardens by the river side, as cedar trees beside the waters? Was it the Israel of History, whose short term of greatness in the days of David and Solomon was so soon overcast by internal division and external invasion, sinking down gradually into long centuries of subjection, humiliation, or exile, that was to rise up as a great lion, and lift up himself as a young lion, not to lie down till he should eat of the prey and drink the blood of the slain; from which the Star should come and the Sceptre arise, that should smite all the corners of Moab, and destroy all the children of Sheth? Prophecy spoke without reserve of the triumph of God and God's servants; if Israel belonged to God only imperfectly, her share in the triumphs of God must in that same proportion be imperfect also.

But, on the other hand, the Israel of History was comparatively with other people, the chosen of God; and for that very reason she was appointed to the honour of representing God's true people in the language of Prophecy. As far as she represented them imperfectly, the language of Prophecy belongs not to her; but so far as she did represent them, she received their blessing; and if there was a triumph too high for her to obtain because of her imperfections, there must be also a blessing upon her for the sake of Him whose name she bears, and whose cause she is permitted to represent before the world. And so we shall find it; 'The people shall dwell alone, and shall not be reckoned among the nations.' Nor have they been. For where is Moab now, or Amalek, or Ammon, or Babylon? They are vanished out of History. Not as if the places were accursed for ever: or as if the language of utter vengeance, which we find in Prophecy, was really applicable to the soil of Mesopotamia or Edom; but the people, the race, the language, the institutions, the religion, all that constitutes national personality, if I may so speak, are passed away from the earth. And if Mesopotamia were to be civilized and fertilized to-morrow, and Babylon again re-built, yet it could not be the old Babylon, for that has become extinct for ever.

So with Egypt, which now is flourishing as a country: it is not the Egypt of old times; there is a chasm not to be filled up, between the people who built the pyramids, and engraved their hieroglyphics on the obelisks, and the new nation that may occupy their land. So it is even with Greece. Christian Athens is divided, and must be, by one deep and impassable barrier, from the heathen Athens of old. But Israel exists still unchanged; still God's people in every land carry back their sympathies unbroken to the age of the first father of the faithful; the patriarchs and prophets are the spiritual ancestors of the Apostles and of ourselves; their prayers are ours, their cause was ours, for their God was ours.

And if Israel after the flesh were to return unto the Lord, what has she lost of her old identity? Place does not make a nation, but the sameness of sympathies; and in this respect there is nothing of Israel in the earliest times, which would be dead to Israel now. This can be said of no other nation upon earth: and thus has Israel endured, because she was, though imperfectly, the representative of the cause of that God who alone endureth for ever.

SERMON II

St Matthew iv. 6. If thou be the Son of God, cast thyself down: for it is written, He shall give his angels charge concerning thee; and in their hands they shall bear thee up, lest at any time thou dash thy foot against a stone.

IN what I said last Sunday on the subject of Prophecy, I endeavoured to lay down what appeared to be its general object and character; namely, to assure man amidst the existing evils of the world, that the cause of good would be finally and entirely triumphant. And this being so, as it is most certain that no people on earth has ever either perfectly served the cause of good, or utterly opposed it, so it follows, that no people can, if I may so speak, fully satisfy the mind of Prophecy; because no people purely represents those unmixed principles of good and evil, with which Prophecy is alone properly concerned. And thus it has happened, that those who have attempted to trace an historical fulfilment of the language of Prophecy with regard to various nations, have never done their work satisfactorily; nor on their system was it possible to do it. For the language of Prophecy on these subjects could not be literally accomplished for two reasons; first, because, as I have said before, it was not properly applicable to any earthly nation, from the imperfection of all human things; and, secondly, because even that character of imperfect good or evil which made certain nations the representatives, so to speak, of the principles of good and evil themselves, was not and could not be perpetual; there are in the course of generations changes in the character of every people, both for the better and for the worse. Now where such a change took place either for good or for evil, there the prophecy could not be fulfilled at all; as in the case of Jonah's prophecy of the destruction of Nineveh; and they who under such circumstances would require the fulfilment, in order to save, as it were, the honour of the prophecy, are rebuked beforehand in the language addressed to Jonah, when he indulged a similar feeling. God's prophecies are not against Nineveh, but against sin; if Nineveh turns from her sin, she is no longer the subject of any prophecy of vengeance. Thus there may be cases where no historical fulfilment of national prophecies is to be found at all; but in all cases, the fulfilment will fall short of the full strength of the language, because, to say it once again, the language in its proper scope and force was aimed at a more unmixed good and evil than have ever been exhibited in the character of any earthly people.

And here then, arrived at this view of Prophecy, and seeing on the one hand the largeness of its promises, and on the other the necessary incompleteness of their fulfilment, – how shall the truth of God's word be reconciled with the laws of His moral government? Must He stint for our sin's sake the abundance of His mercy, or impair for His promises' sake the perfection of His justice? Surely here too, as in other respects, the creation was groaning and travailing in pain together; the children were come to the birth, but there was not strength to bring forth: hope and disappointment were struggling together; the promise was still of blessing, but the experience was of sin, – and therefore not of blessing, but of judgment.

And look around even now, and does it fare better with the historical interpretation of Prophecy than it did in times past? Does the Christian Israel answer more worthily to the expectations of Prophecy, than the Israel after the flesh answered to them of old? Grant that Rome in later times is in some sense and in some degree the Babylon of Christian Prophecy, yet who that knows the history of the Roman Church from first to last, can pretend that its character is of such unmixed or such intense evil, as to answer to the features of the mystic Babylon of the Revelation? As truly might it be pretended that any historical Church, protestant or primitive, was a faithful image of the heavenly Jerusalem.

But where then is the consolation of Prophecy to the heart of man? What becomes of the assurance that it shall be well, infinitely well, with God's people, if no such people are to be found? Prophecy may be true in the abstract, true, it may be, for other worlds; but how to us and to this world can the magnificence of its promises of blessing be more than the exact measure of the extent of our enemy's triumph? It shows us of how great things sin has deprived us.

Thus there is a mass of prophetical language, which, according to the view we have now taken, may seem to be indefinitely waiting for its fulfilment. And so it is, and must be according to the view which we have taken, for it was not and is not in man to be the worthy subject of God's Prophecy. Not in man merely: but what shall we say, if there was one who was man truly, – man in His temptations, man in His sufferings, but who was God in His holiness, God in His strength and power! Then there is one who is the true subject of Prophecy; then there is victory for man final and complete; then the cause of good must infinitely triumph as far as this earth is concerned, or else indeed there can be no truth in Prophecy.

We see, then, how that our Lord Jesus Christ is the real subject of all Prophecy for good. We see how His resurrection and ascension into heaven are its entire fulfilment. All the promises of God in Him are yea, and in Him Amen.

For now what is the case before us? Our experience of life tells us, that it has many troubles; that good, such as we see it, has constantly its portion of affliction. This Prophecy recognised; there are pictures of suffering frequently joined to the most exalted pictures of triumph. And so it was with Christ. He bore the troubles which are the portion of man: He turned not back even from that death which seems most to prove the enemy's conquest over us. When He was taken down from the cross and laid in the sepulchre, – He in whose life there had been no sin, He who, speaking of His human nature merely, had been so truly the child of God; – when His disciples in the sorrow of their hearts said, 'We trusted that it had been He who should have redeemed Israel;' we did trust so once, but behold our hope is buried in His

grave; – then was there, if I may so speak, the trial moment, the agony
of Prophecy: what could be any more hoped from its promises, if evil
and death had triumphed even over Him, in whom there was no sin?
And so, when the third morning came, and death's triumph was broken,
and He rose from the dead to die no more, then was there the justification of all Prophecy; for it was well at last with the righteous, well
infinitely, well eternally; all power was given to Him in heaven and in
earth; all things were put under his feet; death was swallowed up in
victory.

And now we see that it was not arbitrarily or capriciously that so
many passages in Scripture are applied to our Lord by Himself and by
His Apostles; passages which, according to the undoubted evidence of
their context, were historically and literally spoken of some imperfect
prophet, or king, or priest, or people, in whom they had found, and
could find, no adequate fulfilment. For God had provided some better
thing for us than their imperfect righteousness and imperfect blessings.
Look at the 91st Psalm, from which the words of the text are taken.
How largely does the Prophet speak of the security and happiness of
the children of God! Our ears are familiar with its words of promise,
'There shall no evil befal thee, neither shall any plague come nigh thy
dwelling; thou shalt tread upon the lion and adder, the young lion and
the dragon shalt thou trample under feet. God shall give his angels
charge over thee, to keep thee in all thy ways; they shall bear thee up
in their hands, lest thou dash thy foot against a stone.' Nor may we rob
God's servants in every age of their share in these promises: Moses and
Aaron stood unhurt amidst the plague; Paul shook off the adder from
his hand, and felt no harm; chariots and horseman of fire watched round
the hill of Dothan to guard the prophet Elisha. But their full and entire
fulfilment was in Him, and in Him alone, who had truly made the
Most High His habitation even from the beginning; over whom all evil
at all times was powerless, save so far as for our sakes He vouchsafed to
bear it; who said to the sea, Peace, be still; and who, even in yielding
to death, laid down His life of Himself, which none could have taken
from Him, who had power to lay it down, and had power to take it
again.

See also how in Him, and in Him alone, were fulfilled those remarkable promises to David, which otherwise seem incapable of fulfilment,
without a violation of God's laws of righteous government. God
declared to David that his house and his kingdom should be established
for ever: that even though his sons should sin, yet His mercy should not

99

finally depart from them. What then, shall God clear the guilty, and shall He prolong the line of any one man for ever, though it is sure that in the course of many generations it will become unworthy to continue any more? No. God has punished the guilty; David's posterity did sin, and were cut off. It was said by the prophet Jeremiah of the last king, Coniah or Jehoiachin, 'Write ye this man childless, a man that shall not prosper in his days; for no man of his seed shall prosper sitting upon the throne of David, and ruling any more in Judah.' But yet God's promise to David has stood sure: the Son of David has reigned for more than eighteen hundred years, owned over all the earth as King and Lord; and of His kingdom there shall be no end.

Christ is thus the true and complete fulfilment of Prophecy: no promise of exultation to the good is expressed in higher language than has been, and is, and will continue for ever to be, in Him accomplished. We can turn as our fathers have done, to Christ's resurrection, and say, There is our warrant for the truth of Prophecy; good has triumphed over evil.

But still we see not yet all things put under Christ; the last enemy is not yet destroyed; the state of Israel now, no less than of Israel of old, is no state of perfect peace, and love, and joy. It is not that we need be concerned for the honour of Prophecy; we see clearly enough, conscience tells us too plainly, why its promises are not fulfilled amongst us to the letter; the promises were for the righteous, and we are not righteous. But for ourselves there is great need of our being concerned, lest Christ's triumph extend not to us, and lest we, like the Israel of old, should in the last great day be found not to be amongst His people. He wills that those whom God has given Him shall be with Him where He is; that He and His redeemed shall for all eternity fulfil the promises of Prophecy, and prove that there is indeed a glory for the righteous. We need not fear for the truth of this: God is able of the stones to raise up children unto Abraham: there will be guests enough found to sit down at the marriage-supper of the Lamb. Twice has God willed to mark out these guests here; that all who belonged to His Church on earth, all who were circumcised, all who were baptized, should be the heirs of the promises of Prophecy. But twice has man's sin rendered this impossible: the seal of Baptism has proved no surer a mark than the seal of Circumcision; again have the people whom He brought out of Egypt corrupted themselves. Still there is, and ever has been, a remnant; still there are those whom Christ owns now, and will own for ever. Theirs are the promises in all their fulness; not that their own righteousness is proportioned to such blessings, but because they are Christ's, and Christ in God's. In us there is still as in times past the same incapability of answering to the language of Prophecy; but the kingdom which Christ has gained, is for His sake given to His true people. It is given to those whom at the last great day, when He shall judge to whom all hearts are open, He shall acknowledge to be His.

So then the promises and the consolations of Prophecy may all be ours. Christ's triumph is not for Himself alone; we may all partake in it; to us all may, through Him, be given the full extent of blessing which the 91st Psalm and other similar passages contain. Those passages may be a dead letter to us; but they may also be life and reality. If, looking on the world as God looks on it, we feel keenly the struggle which is going on between good and evil, and fain would take our part in it to the death under Christ's banner; then, along with all the anxieties and the sufferings of the contest, we have our portion besides in the hopes of the final issue. Then, as we become more deeply interested in it, the language of Prophecy becomes more welcome; the pledge of its truth, the fact of Christ's resurrection, becomes more unspeakably precious. With such anxieties, such efforts, and such hopes, we have the Christian's sure seal; not that outward seal of baptism, which is too often broken, but the seal of God's Spirit, that as Christ was, so are we in this world. Blessed are they, in whom the hopes and fears, which are the common portion of us all, are directed to those objects which Christ's true people hope for and fear; to whom Prophecy is no empty language about matters of other days or other persons, but the answer given by God to the earnest questionings of their nature, 'Has God cast me off for ever, or shall it be a blessing to me to have been born?'

5

From HENRY CHRISTMAS: *A Concise History of the Hampden Controversy*

As a theologian Hampden was comparatively unimportant. A muddled and inconsistent thinker, he frequently leaves his meaning obscure. His general tendency is to exalt Scripture as the infallible word of God, but to leave it uncertain whether any particular doctrine is actually contained in Scripture. His Bampton Lectures of 1832 led to suspicions about his orthodoxy, and when Lord Melbourne appointed him Regius Professor of Divinity in 1836, the University of Oxford declared its lack of confidence in him as a teacher of theology, and absolved students from the duty of attending his lectures.

The controversy that followed his nomination by Lord John Russell as bishop of Hereford in 1847 can be studied in the following letters. The interesting point today is not theological but administrative. The bleak, sarcastic flavour of Russell's last letter shows that he regarded the Church as a Department of State, and the Dean who conscientiously voted against a Crown appointment as analogous to a mutinous soldier. Russell saw the contest as a party struggle between Tractarian and Protestant, and he thought it his duty as a good Englishman to take the Protestant side. The Tractarians must have felt that the Royal Supremacy in practice meant that the judge from whose decision there was no appeal was frankly partisan. Hampden's supporters, however, felt that the Royal Supremacy alone guaranteed the Church's national and Protestant character, and that without this safeguard, the Church would become an inward-looking, donnish and semi-Popish sect. The weak point in the case of Hampden's supporters was that they were ready to give absolute power in Church matters to a man who might know nothing of theology, might be at most tepidly Christian, and might be seeking nothing more elevated than political advantage in the exercise of his choice.

The weak point of the anti-Hampden case was that they were com-

mitted by the constitution of the Church of England itself to belief in
the Royal Supremacy in some sense. If they were simply opposed to the
way it was being used in a particular case, they were bound to submit
when the case went against them, as to an umpire's bad decision. But
if they were utterly opposed to the Royal Supremacy in principle, they
could hardly maintain that they were truly Anglicans at all.

[Protest of thirteen bishops]

My Lord, – We, the undersigned Bishops of the Church of
England, feel it duty to represent to your lordship, as head of her
Majesty's Government, the apprehension and alarm which have been
excited in the minds of the clergy by the rumoured nomination to the
See of Hereford of Dr Hampden, in the soundness of whose doctrine
the University of Oxford has affirmed, by a solemn decree, its want of
confidence.

We are persuaded that your lordship does not know how deep and
general a feeling prevails on this subject, and we consider ourselves to
be acting only in the discharge of our bounden duty both to the crown
and to the church, when we respectfully but earnestly express to your
lordship our conviction, that if this appointment be completed, there
is the greatest danger both of the interruption of the peace of the church,
and of the disturbance of the confidence which it is most desirable that
the clergy and laity of the church should feel in every exercise of the
royal supremacy, especially as regards that very delicate and important
particular, the nomination to vacant Sees.

We have the honour to be, my lord,
Your lordship's obedient faithful servants,

C. J. London	J. H. Gloucester and Bristol
C. Winton	H. Exeter
J. Lincoln	E. Sarum
Chr. Bangor	A. T. Chichester
Hugh. Carlisle	J. Ely Saml. Oxon
G. Rochester	Rich. Bath and Wells

[The Bishop of Norwich's Letter explaining reasons for not protesting]

Palace, Norwich, Dec. 1, 1847.

My dear Lord, – On maturely considering the memorial which
has been forwarded to me against the appointment of Dr Hampden to

the See of Hereford – not on the ground of any general unfitness for the office, or on any specific charge of heterodoxy – but because the 'University of Oxford has affirmed, by a solemn decree, its want of confidence in the soundness of his doctrines,' I feel I cannot conscientiously sign it for the following reasons:

'1. Because I conceive that by such proceeding we are giving to an university censure an authority which in no way belongs to it, and which many of its most devoted friends have disclaimed. And further, that I can attach little weight to a decision emanating from Oxford on that occasion, bearing in mind that the movement against Dr Hampden originated with a party suspected (how justly subsequent events fully proved) of entertaining a strong leaning towards the Church of Rome. That the opinions, moreover, of many of those members of Convocation who opposed Dr Hampden were manifested with a bitterness of party spirit little creditable to them as members of a Christian community and a calm deliberative assembly; and that there is good reason for believing that the majority was obtained by votes given by many individuals who came up expressly for the purpose, though it was notorious that they had never read the works which they professed to condemn.

2. That even if the censure of 1836 were deserving attention, it was virtually repealed by a statute in the early part of 1842, which expressly appointed Dr Hampden to the office of Examiner in the new Theological Examination, and which was, by several influential members of the University understood to cancel the previous censure; and that in the summer of 1842, an attempt was actually made to repeal the censure of 1836, which very nearly succeeded, supported, as it was, by some of the most distinguished members of the University; amongst others, I believe, by no less than fifteen out of seventeen of the heads of colleges, and that it was opposed by a large portion of those well known for their Tractarian tendencies.

3. Because I believe Dr Hampden to have been very unfairly treated, judged as he was by extracts separated from their context, and many of them obscurely worded, on points involving deep metaphysical reasoning, requiring unprejudiced and dispassionate investigations to decide upon.

4. Because I consider that on other occasions, more especially in his Inaugural Lecture, he has shown clearly and unequivocally, and beyond all controversy, that his sentiments on those particular topics on which

he was supposed to be unsound were in accordance with the formularies of our Church and with the Holy Scriptures.'

Such are the reasons for inducing me to withhold my signature to the memorial proposed to be presented by my right rev. brethren, expressive of their disapprobation of Dr Hampden's appointment to the vacant See of Hereford.

I have only to add, though, indeed, I consider it scarcely necessary, that did I suspect Dr Hampden in the slightest degree of holding opinions impugning the doctrines of the Trinity or the Atonement, I should not have hesitated a single moment in requesting that my name might be affixed to the memorial with my fullest concurrence and approbation of its object.

I remain, yours very truly,

E. NORWICH.

[*Lord John Russell's reply to the thirteen bishops*]

Chesham Place, Dec. 8, 1847.

MY LORDS, – I have had the honour to receive a representation signed by your lordships on the subject of the nomination of Dr Hampden to the See of Hereford.

I observe that your lordships do not state any want of confidence on your part in the soundness of Dr Hampden's doctrine. Your lordships refer me to a decree of the University of Oxford passed eleven years ago, and founded upon lectures delivered fifteen years ago.

Since the date of that decree Dr Hampden has acted as Regius Professor of Divinity in the University of Oxford; and many bishops, as I am told, have required certificates or attendance on his lectures before they proceeded to ordain candidates who had received their education at Oxford. He has likewise preached sermons for which he has been honoured with the approbation of several prelates of our Church.

Several months before I named Dr Hampden to the Queen for the See of Hereford, I signified my intention to the Archbishop of Canterbury, and did not receive from him any discouragement.

In these circumstances, it appears to me that should I withdraw my recommendation of Dr Hampden, which has been sanctioned by the Queen, I should virtually assent to the doctrine that a decree of the University of Oxford is a perpetual ban of exclusion against a clergyman of eminent learning and irreproachable life; and that, in fact, the supremacy which is now by law vested in the Crown is to be transferred to a majority of the members of one of our universities.

Nor should it be forgotten, that many of the most prominent among that majority have since joined the communion of the Church of Rome.

I deeply regret the feeling that is said to be common among the clergy on this subject. But I cannot sacrifice the reputation of Dr Hampden, the rights of the Crown, and what I believe to be the true interests of the Church, to a feeling which I believe to be founded on misapprehension and fomented by prejudice.

At the same time I thank your lordships for an interposition which I believe to be intended for the public benefit.

I have, &c.

J. RUSSELL.

[The Dean of Hereford's Letter to Lord John Russell]

MY LORD, – I have had the honour to receive your lordship's letter, announcing that you had received my memorial to the Queen, and that you had transmitted it to Sir G. Grey for presentation to her Majesty; and by the same post I also receive the information that Sir G. Grey had laid the same before the Queen, and that 'he was to inform me that her Majesty has not been pleased to issue any commands thereupon.' Under these circumstances I feel compelled once more to trouble your lordship with a few remarks.

Throughout the correspondence in which I have had the honour to be engaged with your lordship, as well as in the interview which you were pleased to afford me on the subject of the appointment to the see of Hereford, it has been my object frankly and faithfully to declare to you the facts which have come to my knowledge, and the honest conviction of my mind. I desire still to act upon the same principle, and to submit to your lordship finally, and as briefly as possible, the following considerations, upon which I feel constrained to adopt a course which, however I may apprehend it will not be entirely congenial to your lordship's wishes, will, under the circumstances in which I am placed, obtain from your lordship's candour the admission that it is the only course which I could pursue.

I crave your lordship's indulgence whilst I enumerate the special obligations to which I am bound, and I state them in the order of their occurrence.

When matriculated to the University of Oxford, of which I am still a member, the following oath was administered to me, as well as on taking each of my degrees: 'Tu dabis fidem ad observandum omnia statuta, privilegia, et consuetudines hujus Universitatis; ita Deus te adjuvet tactis sacrosanctis Christi Evangeliis.'

Again – when I was admitted to the sacred orders of priest in the Church of God, a part of my ordination vow was expressed in these words – that I would 'banish and drive away all erroneous and strange doctrine contrary to God's word.'

Again – when I was inducted, on occasion of the installation to the office which I hold in the cathedral church of Hereford, as I stepped over the threshold of the fabric, the restoration of which, for the due honour of Almighty God, it has been my pride and anxious endeavour to promote, I was required to charge my soul with this responsibility: 'Ego, Joannes Merewether, Decanus Herefordensis, ab hâc horâ in antea, fidelis ero huic sacrosanctæ Herefordensi ecclesiæ, necnon jura, libertates, privilegia, et consuetudines ejusdem, pro viribus observabo et ea manutenebo et defendam pro posse meo; sic me Deus adjuvet, et hæc sancta Evangelia.'

My lord, I cannot divest my mind of the awful sense of the stringency of those engagements at the present exigency. Let me entreat your lordship's patience whilst I endeavour to explain my apprehension of them.

In my letter of the 1st of December, in reply to the second which your lordship was pleased to address to me – and to which correspondence I trust your lordship will permit me publicly to refer in vindication of my conduct, should need require it – I observed, 'In regard to Dr Hampden's tenets, I would abstain from any opinion upon them till I had again fairly and attentively read his writings.' That act of justice I have carefully performed, and I will add with an earnest desire to discover grounds upon which, in case of Dr Hampden's ever occupying the high station for which he has been selected by your lordship, my mind might be relieved from all distrust, and I might be enabled as cordially as possible to render that service which the relative duties of diocesan and dean and chapter involve.

It is painful in the extreme to feel obliged to declare that I discover in those writings many *assertions* – not merely references to theories or impressions of others – but *assertions*, which to my calm and deliberate appreciation appear to be heterodoxical, I believe I may say heretical, and very, very much, which is most dangerous, most objectionable, calculated to weaken the hold which the religion we possess as yet obtains, and ought to obtain always, upon the minds of its professors. I feel certain that the perusal of several of these works by any of that class who, 'by reason of use' (in cautious examination of such productions) 'have not their senses exercised to discern both good and evil,' would produce a doubt and distrust in the teaching of our church, in her creeds, – her formularies, – her liturgy; would rob them of the inestimable joy and peace in believing, and be highly detrimental to the spread of true religion.

Such being my conviction, I would ask your lordship how it must affect my conscience in reference to those solemn obligations which I have already detailed? I have sworn that I will observe all the statutes of the University of which I am still a member. The statute of that University touching this matter stands in the following words, at this moment uncancelled, unrepealed: 'Quin ab universitate commissum fuerit, S. Theologiæ Professori Regio, ut unus sit ex eorum numero a quibus designantur selecti concionatores, secundum Tit. XVI, 58 (Addend. p. 150), necnon ut ejus concilium adhibeatur si quis concionator coram Vice-Cancellario in questionem vocatur, secundum Tit., XVI s. 11 (Addend. p. 151), quum vero qui nunc Professor est *scriptis suis publici juris factis, ita res theologicas tractaverit, ut in hâc parte nullam ejus fiduciam habeat Universitas*; statutum est, quod munerum prædictorum expers sit S. Theologiæ Professor Regius, donec aliter Universitati placuerit, ne vero quid detrimenti capiat interea Universitas, Professoris ejusdem vicibus fungantur alii, scilicet, in concionatores selectos designando senior inter Vice-Cancellarii deputatos, vel eo absente, aut ipsius Vice-Cancellarii locum tenente, proximus ex ordine deputatus (proviso semper quod sacros ordines susceperit) et in consilio de concionibus habendo, Prælector Dominæ Margarettæ Comitissæ Richmondiæ.' Should I not be guilty of deliberate perjury, if in direct defiance of such a decree I did any act which should place the object of it in such a position as to be not only the judge of the soundness of the theological opinions and preaching of a whole diocese, but of those whom, from time to time, he must admit to cure of souls, and even to the sacred orders of the ministry?

I have sworn, at the most awful moment of my life, that I will 'banish and drive away all erroneous and strange doctrines contrary to God's word.' It may be replied, that this engagement applies to the ministrations in the care of souls, inherent only in parochial functions; but the statutes of our cathedral church constitute me one of the guardians of the soundness of the doctrine which may be preached in that sacred edifice: 'Si quid a quopiam pro concione properatur, quod cum verbo Dei, articulis Religionæ, aut Liturgiæ Anglicanæ consentire non videtur, eâ de re, Decanus atque Residentiarii, quotquot audierunt, Dominum Episcopum sine morâ per literas suas monebunt.' With what confidence, or what hope of the desired end, should I communicate such a case to a bishop whose own soundness of theological teaching was more than suspected? Should I not be guilty of a breach of my ordination vows if I did not protest against the admission of such a person to such a responsible post, and endeavour to 'banish and drive away,' by all lawful means, that person of the 18,000 clergy of this land on whom the censure and deprivation of one of the most learned and renowned seminaries of religious teaching in the world is yet in its full operation and effect, one who is already designated thereby as a setter forth of erroneous and strange doctrines? Again, I have sworn to be FAITHFUL to the cathedral church of Hereford. Faithful I could not be, either as to the maintenance of the doctrine, or the discipline of the Church in those respects already alluded to, or the welfare and unity of that Church, either in the cathedral body itself or in the diocese at large, under existing circumstances, if by any act of mine I promoted Dr Hampden's elevation to the episcopal throne of that church and diocese. Faithful I have laboured to be in the restoration and the saving of its material and venerable fabric. Faithful by God's help, I will strive to be, in obtaining for it that oblation of sound and holy doctrine which should ascend, together with the incense of prayer and praise, 'in the beauty of holiness,' untainted and unalloyed by any tincture of 'philosophy and vain deceit, after the tradition of men, after the rudiments of the world, and not after Christ.'

But your lordship may reply, there is another oath by which I have bound myself, which I have as yet overlooked: not so, my lord. Of my sentiments on the royal prerogative I have already put your lordship in possession. When I warned you of the consequences of your appointment, of the tendency which it would produce to weaken the existing relations between Church and State, I fully recognised the just prerogative of the Crown; and when I thought I had not sufficiently dwelt upon it, I wrote a second time to make myself distinctly understood.

Nor is it only the sense of legal obligation which would constrain me to a dutiful regard to such observance. Few men have a greater cause to feel their duty in this respect, warmed by the sense of kindness and condescension from those of royal station, than myself. The memory of one who anxiously contemplated the future happiness and *true* glory of his successor, fixed indelibly those sentiments upon my heart. And, if for his sake only, who could to a long course of almost parental kindness add, in an affecting injunction, the expression of his wishes for my good upon his deathbed, I should never be found forgetful – even although I may never have taken in the present reign the oath of allegiance – of that loyalty and devotion to my Sovereign which is not less a duty of religion than the grateful and constitutional homage of an English heart. Forgive me, my lord, for the reflection on that deathbed injunction, if I say, that had it been observed, – as but for party and political influence it would have been – your lordship, the Church, and the nation, would have been spared this most unhappy trial, the results of which, as I have already again and again foreboded to your lordship, it is impossible to foresee. Nor, under any circumstances, is it likely that the obligation of the oath of allegiance in my person will be infringed upon; its terms are, that 'I will be faithful and bear *true* allegiance;' and, accordingly, the *conge d'élire* has these expressions, 'requiring and commanding you, by the faith and allegiance by which you stand bound to us, to elect such a person for your bishop and pastor as may *be devoted to God*, and USEFUL *and faithful to us* and *our* KINGDOM.' Would it be any proof of fidelity or *true* allegiance, my lord, to elect a person as 'MEET TO BE ELECTED' who was the contrary to those requirements? And can it be possible that in the *course of divine service* in the *Chief Sanctuary* of *Almighty God* in the diocese, however *named* and *recommended*, a person should be 'UNANIMOUSLY CHOSEN *and* ELECTED' in the awful falsification of these words, IN THE PRESENCE OF GOD, *against the consciences of the unhappy* electors, simply because the adviser of the Crown (for 'the Crown can do no wrong') has in his short-sightedness and ignorance of facts (to say the least), thought fit to name an objectionable person, the one of all the clergy in the land so disqualified; and, when warned of the consequences by the voices of the Primate, of thirteen bishops, and hosts of priests and deacons, clergy and laity by hundreds, of all shades of opinions in the Church, persisted in the reckless determination?

In the words of an eminent writer of our Church, 'All power is given unto edification, none to the overthrow and destruction of the Church,' *Hooker's Ecclesiastical Polity*, book viii, chap. 7; and the matter is perhaps placed in the true light and position by the learned author of *Vindiciæ Ecclesiæ Anglicanæ* – Francis Mason; the whole of which is well worthy of your lordship's notice. I venture to supply a brief extract, book iv, chap. 13, 1625:

'Philodoxus. – You pretended to treat of Kings electing bishops and conferring of bishoprics, and now you ascribe not the election to Kings, but to the clergy, and claim only nomination for Kings?

'Orthodoxus. – The King's nomination is, with us, a fair beginning to the election. Therefore, when he nominates any person he elects him, and gives, as I may say, the first vote for him.

'Philodoxus. – What kind of elections are those of your deans and chapters? 'Tis certain they can't be called free elections, since nothing is to be done without the King's previous authority.

'Orthodoxus. – The freedom of election doth not exclude the King's sacred authority, but *force and tyranny* only. If any unworthy person should be forced upon them against their will, or the clergy should be constrained to give their voices by force and threatening, such an election cannot be said to be free. But if the King do nominate a worthy person, according to the laws, as our Kings have used to do, and give them authority to choose him, there is no reason why this may not be called a free election; for here is no force or violence used.

'Philodoxus. – But if the King, deceived by *undeserved recommendations*, should happen to propose to the clergy a person unlearned, or of ill morals, or otherwise manifestly unworthy of that function, what's to be done then?

'Orthodoxus. – Our Kings are wont to proceed in these cases maturely and cautiously – I mean with the utmost care and prudence; and hence it comes to pass that the Church of England is at this time in such a flourishing condition.

'Philodoxus. – Since they are but men they are liable to human weakness; and therefore what's to be done, if such a case should happen?

'Orthodoxus. – If the electors could make sufficient proof of such crimes or incapacities, I think it were becoming them *to represent the same to the King, with all due humility, modesty, and duty, humbly* beseeching his Majesty, out of his known clemency, to take care of the interest of the widowed church; and our Princes are so famous for their piety and condescension, that I doubt not that his Majesty would graciously answer their pious petition, and nominate another unexceptionable person, agreeable to all their wishes. Thus a mutual affection would be kept up between the bishop and his church.'

Nor is this a mere supposition, but there are instances in the history of this kingdom of such judicious reconsideration of an undesirable appointment. I will cite but one from *Burnett's History of his own Times*, A.D. 1693, vol. iv. p. 209. London, 1733:

'The state of Ireland leads me to insert here a very particular instance of the Queen's pious care in disposing of bishoprics. Lord Sydney was so far engaged in the interest of a great family in Ireland, that he was too easily wrought on to recommend a branch of it to a vacant See. The representation was made with an undue character of the person; so the Queen granted it. But when she understood that he lay under a very bad character, she wrote a letter in her own hand to Lord Sydney, letting him know what she had heard, and ordered him to call for six Irish bishops, whom she named to him, and to require them to certify to her their opinion of that person. They all agreed that he laboured under an ill fame, and till that examined into they did not think proper to promote him; so that matter was let fall. I do not name the person, for I intend not to leave a blemish on him, but set this down as an example fit to be imitated by Christian Princes.'

But, alas! remonstrance seems unheeded, and if our venerable Primate and thirteen bishops have raised their united voice of warning and entreaty to no purpose, it is no marvel that my humble supplication should have pleaded in vain, for time – for investigation – for some regard to our consciences – some consideration for our painful and delicate position.

The time draws near – on Tuesday next the *semblance* of an election is to be exhibited. I ventured to assure your lordship that I could not undertake to say that it would be an unanimous election; I was bold enough to affirm that it would not be unanimous; and I, in my turn, received the intimation and the caution – I will not say *the threat* – that the law must be vindicated. Already have I assured your lordship that the principle on which this painful affair is regarded, is that of the most solemn religious responsibility; thousands regard it in this light. I have already told you, my lord, that the watchword of such is this – 'Whether it be right in the sight of God to hearken unto you more than unto God, judge ye.' I have anxiously implored your lordship to pause – to avert the blow. I have long since told you the truth. I have endeavoured to prevent, by every means in my power, the commotion which has arisen, and the necessity of the performance of a painful duty. I hoped the *congé d'élire* would not be issued *until a fair inquiry and investigation had been instituted*. A suit has been commenced in the ecclesiastical courts – why not have awaited its issue? When the *congé d'élire* did appear, I at once presumed, humbly but faithfully, though

I stood alone, to petition the Crown; and now, when I am officially informed, that 'her Majesty has not been pleased to issue any commands thereupon,' I feel it to be my bounden duty, after a full and calm deliberation on the whole subject, having counted the cost, but remembering the words of Him whose most unworthy servant I am – 'He that loveth house or lands more than me is not worthy of me' – loving my children dearly, and ardently desiring to complete the noble work which I have for seven years laboured to promote, yet not forgetting that there is an 'hour of death and a day of judgment,' when I trust, through the merits of my Redeemer, to be allowed to look up with hope, that I may be considered by the intercessions of mercy and pity to have been faithful in the hour of trial, to have 'fought the good fight, to have kept the faith, to have finished *my* course,' – believing that I risk much, and shall incur your lordship's heavy displeasure, who may, if you will, direct the sword of power against me and mine – being certain that I preclude myself from that which might otherwise have been my lot, and expecting that I shall bring down upon myself the abuse and blame of some – I say, my lord, having fully counted the cost, having weighed *the sense of bounden duty* in the one scale against the consequences in the other, I have come to the deliberate resolve, that on Tuesday next no earthly consideration shall induce me to give my vote in the chapter of Hereford cathedral for Dr Hampden's elevation to the see of Hereford.

I have the honour to be, my lord,
Your lordship's faithful humble servant,
JOHN MEREWETHER, Dean of Hereford.
Hereford, Dec. 22.

[*Lord John Russell's reply to the Dean of Hereford*]

Woburn Abbey, Dec. 25.
SIR, – I have had the honour to receive your letter of the 22nd instant, in which you intimate to me your intention of violating the law.

I have the honour to be your obedient servant,
J. RUSSELL.

[*Account of the Dean of Hereford's protest at election of new bishop*]

The DEAN of HEREFORD rose amidst breathless silence, and spoke to the following effect: 'I am standing in the sanctuary of the Most

High God, and, together with my brethren, the ordained ministers of our Lord and Master Jesus Christ, am called upon in the name of the Sovereign of this land to choose and elect such a person as may be meet to be the bishop and pastor of this diocese. I solemnly declare here, in the divine presence, that it is my earnest and hearty desire to be faithful and bear true allegiance, to pay all humble duty and submissive obedience to her most excellent Majesty, the Queen of these dominions, who, I feel assured on her part, "knowing whose minister she is, will above all things seek His honour and glory who is the King of kings and Lord of lords," to whom above all I owe my first allegiance. And whereas by the exercise of that civil privilege which gives to the first minister of the Crown the power of recommending to the Sovereign for nomination to vacant bishoprics, the Rev. Renn Dickson Hampden, D.D., has been so nominated and to us recommended by the official instruments this day laid before us, to the bishopric of Hereford – and whereas we the Dean and Chapter of this cathedral church are forbidden under heavy penalties to elect any other person into the said bishopric except the said Renn Dickson Hampden, – and whereas, the University of Oxford in full and lawful convention did decree that the said Renn Dickson Hampden should be deprived of certain functions and offices in the said University, because in his writings he had so treated theological subjects, that in this respect the Church and University had no confidence in him, and that the Convocation afterwards, within five years last past, after full debate refused to rescind the said decree and deprivation; and whereas the said Renn Dickson Hampden is now under the effect of the said decree of the University of Oxford in convocation assembled, and from the careful and attentive perusal of the said writings, I do believe their decree to be just, those writings unsound in doctrine, and dangerous in their tendency; and whereas, taking the premises solemnly and anxiously into consideration, I preferred a humble petition to her most excellent Majesty, dated the 17th December instant, praying a postponement of the election until due investigation had been made, and a sufficient removal of the censure and deprivation of the Rev. Dr Renn Dickson Hampden had been effected by a just and competent tribunal; and, moreover, further pleaded to her Majesty's prime minister the entire circumstances of the case, together with the awful and constraining obligations by which we are bound; and whereas the primate of all England, with thirteen bishops or more, have preferred their objections to the said appointment, and great numbers of clergy and laity throughout the land, of every shade of religious opinion tolerated by the church, have by the most solemn appeals entreated us to exert ourselves in staying such election until such time as the aforesaid objections should be removed or another unobjectionable person substituted – on taking all the aforesaid circumstances into my most serious consideration, I did most humbly and imploringly supplicate that her Majesty might even yet be pleased to reconsider this earnest and disinterested prayer, to correct and amend the errors and misfortunes which have arisen, and still more seriously threaten us from the ill-considered advice of a misinformed minister, as on other occasions her Majesty's royal predecessors have done, and so avert the injury which must otherwise be inflicted on the Church, and pacify the outraged feelings of her members. And here, in the sight of God, in the midst of his temple, and in the performance of the priestly office, I solemnly protest that it is no deficiency in the smallest degree of loyalty and humble devotion to our Sovereign, or of implicit respect and deference to the laws of this realm, which impels me to make this declaration; it is the dictate of my conscience, the conviction of my mind, which constrains me thus to act in arresting the progress of infidelity, mockery of religion, and profaneness. Upon these grounds I cannot vote for the election of Dr Renn Dickson Hampden as bishop of the vacant See of Hereford, and pastor of the cathedral Church of which I am dean. And I do hereby protest against this proceeding to-day, inasmuch as many persons have voted who are merely honorary prebendaries, and have not complied with the statutes of this Church which I have declared I will observe; and I protest also against the majority which will be claimed, inasmuch as it is necessary for giving validity to a vote that the majority should include the dean and three canons residentiary. This protest I shall forward to the Crown, the bishop elect (Dr Hampden), and the Archbishop of Canterbury.'

6

A. H. CLOUGH: *Notes on the Religious Tradition*

Clough belonged to a very rare type. He was really able to consider the possibility that his instinct for truth might be mistaken, and that those who were 'obviously wrong' might be right. The open mind, which so many people claim to possess, generally means no more than putting trust in traditions and prejudices rather than in doctrines. Clough's statement is perfectly clear and speaks for itself. But I wish to draw attention particularly to his distinction between doctrinal truth and intellectual and spiritual richness, or what he calls 'treasures of pure religious tradition'. Clough realized what most of his contemporaries forgot, that a doctrine was more than a historical or philosophical or legal statement (though it might be any or all of these). It was also an outward expression of the corporate experience of a given religious tradition. He realized too that liturgy and traditions of public worship could be as influential as doctrines.

I T is impossible for any scholar to have read, and studied, and reflected without forming a strong impression of the entire uncertainty of history in general, and of the history of Christianity in particular.

It is equally impossible for any man to live, act, and reflect without feeling the significance and depth of the moral and religious teaching which passes amongst us by the name of Christianity.

The more a man feels the value, the true import of this, the more will he hesitate to base it upon those foundations which as a scholar he feels to be unstable. Manuscripts are doubtful, records may be unauthentic, criticism is feeble, historical facts must be left uncertain.

Even in like manner my own personal experience is most limited, perhaps even most delusive: what have I seen, what do I know? Nor is my personal judgment a thing which I feel any great satisfaction in trusting. My reasoning powers are weak; my memory doubtful and confused; my conscience, it may be, callous or vitiated.

I see not how it is possible for a man disinclined to adopt arbitrarily the watchword of a party to the sacrifice of truth – indisposed to set up for himself, and vehemently urge some one point – I see not what other alternative any sane and humble-minded man can have but to throw himself upon the great religious tradition.

But I see not either how any upright and strict dealer with himself – how any man not merely a slave to spiritual appetites, affections, and wants – any man of intellectual as well as moral honesty – and without the former the latter is but a vain thing – I see not how any one who will not tell lies to himself, can dare to affirm that the narrative of the four Gospels is an essential integral part of that tradition. I do not see that it is a great and noble thing, a very needful or very worthy service, to go about proclaiming that Mark is inconsistent with Luke, that the first Gospel is not really Matthew's, nor the last with any certainty John's, that Paul is not Jesus, &c. &c. &c. It is at the utmost a commendable piece of honesty; but it is no new gospel to tell us that the old one is of dubious authenticity.

I do not see either, on the other hand, that it can be lawful for me, for the sake of the moral guidance and the spiritual comfort, to ignore all scientific or historic doubts, or if pressed with them to the utmost, to take refuge in Romish infallibility, and, to avoid sacrificing the four Gospels, consent to accept the legends of the saints and the tales of modern miracles.

I believe that I may without any such perversion of my reason, without any such mortal sin against my own soul, which is identical with reason, and against the Supreme Giver of that soul and reason, still abide by the real religious tradition.

It is indeed just conceivable that the Divine Orderer of the universe, and Father of our spirits, should have so created these and ordered that, as that the one should be directly contradictory to the other. It may be that the facts which we, by the best force of our intellects, discern, are by His ordinance delusions, intended of a set purpose to tempt us from our highest path, that of His love and the worship of Him. It is conceivable that he has subtly arranged that two and two should be four (by delusion) everywhere, that our faith (the one reality) may be tried when we propose to harmonise it with this fallacy. It is possible that as our senses and appetites would make us believe bad things, because pleasant, therefore good, so also our reason may cheat us to believe wrong things, because reasonable, therefore right. The rule which He has placed to measure all things by, and bid us trust in them implicitly, may be, by His special purpose, false for the highest things. What in our solemn courts of justice we should call false witness, may be in the Church to decide our verdict; what in the exchange would be imposture, may be in the sanctuary pure truth. I say, this thing is conceivable, yet it is conceivable also that sense and mind, that intellect and religion, things without and things within, are in harmony with each other. If it is conceivable that the earth in the natural world goes round the sun, delusively to tempt us from the revealed act of the supernatural world that the sun goes round the earth, it is also conceivable that the heavens, as astronomically discerned, declare the glory of God, and the firmament showeth His handywork.

It is conceivable that religious truths of the highest import may grow up naturally, and appear before us involved in uncertain traditions, with every sort of mere accessory legend and story attached to them and entangled with them.

It may be true that as the physical bread has to be digested and the nutritive portion separated from the innutritive, so may it also be with the spiritual. It may be true that man has fallen, though Adam and Eve are legendary. It may be a divine fact that God is a person, and not a sort of natural force; and it may have happened that the tales of His personal appearance to Abraham, Isaac, and Jacob, were the means of sustaining and conveying down to posterity that belief, and yet that He never sat in the tent on the plains of Mamre, nor wrestled with Jacob by night, nor spoke with Moses in the mount.

Where then, since neither in Rationalism nor in Rome is our refuge, where then shall we seek for the Religious Tradition?

Everywhere; but above all in our own work: in life, in action, in submission, so far as action goes, in service, in experience, in patience, and in confidence. I would scarcely have any man dare to say that he has found it, till that moment when death removes his power of telling it. Let no young man presume to talk to us vainly and confidently about it. Ignorant, as said Aristotle, of the real actions of life, and ready to follow all impressions and passions, he is hardly fitted as yet even to listen to practical directions couched in the language of religion. But this apart – everywhere.

The Religious Tradition – as found everywhere – as found not only among clergymen and religious people, but among all who have really tried to order their lives by the highest action of the reasonable and spiritual will. I will go to Johnson; I will go to Hume, as well as to Bishop Butler. The precepts with which our parents often startle our religious instincts, and our companions revolt our young moral convictions, these also are in some sense to be considered in the religious and moral tradition. Every rule of conduct, every maxim, every usage of life and society, must be admitted, like Ecclesiastes of old in the Old Testament, so in each new age to each new age's Bible.

Everywhere – to India, if you will, and the ancient Bhagvad Gita and the laws of Menu; to Persia and Hafiz; to China and Confucius; to the Vedas and the Shasters; to the Koran; to pagan Greece and Rome; to Homer; to Socrates and Plato; to Lucretius, to Virgil, to Tacitus. Try all things, I do not imagine that any spiritual doctrine or precept of life found in all that travel from east to west and north to south will disqualify us to return to what *prima facie* does appear to be, not indeed the religion of the majority of mankind, but the religion of the best, so far as we can judge in past history, and despite of professed infidelity of the most enlightened of our own time.

Whether Christ died upon the Cross, I cannot tell; yet I am prepared to find some spiritual truth in the doctrine of the Atonement. Purgatory is not in the Bible; I do not therefore think it incredible.

There is only one theory or precept which must be noticed ere I end. It is said that each of us is born with a peculiar nature of his own, a constitution as it were for one form of truth to the exclusion of others; that we must each look for what will suit us, and not be over-solicitous for wide and comprehensive attainments. What is one man's food is another's poison. Climate, parentage, and other circumstances are too strong for us; it is impossible for the Italian to be Protestant, or for the sons of New England Puritans to turn Roman Catholics to any great extent.

I do not doubt that the Protestant has excluded himself (necessary perhaps it was that he should so do) from large religious experience which the Roman Catholic preserves. I am convinced again that the Unitarian is morally and religiously only half educated compared with the Episcopalian. Modern Unitarianism is, I conceive, unfortunate on the one hand in refusing to allow its legitimate force to the exercise of reason and criticism; on the other hand, in having by its past exercise of reason and criticism thrown aside treasures of pure religious tradition because of their dogmatic exterior.

7

H. L. MANSEL: *Limits of Religious Thought*

Bampton Lectures *1858*, Lecture VI

Mansel is perhaps the only man to appear in this selection whose approach to Christianity is mainly philosophical. Born in 1820, he pursued an academic and scholarly career and became Dean of St Paul's in 1868; but he had little time to make his mark there, for he died in 1871. A disciple of the great Anglican theologian of the previous century, Bishop Butler, he maintained that a true understanding of the limitations of the human mind would tend to disarm all the rational objections usually made against Christian theology. He took as his great principle and quoted on the title-page of his Bampton Lectures the words of Sir William Hamilton: 'No difficulty emerges in theology, which had not previously emerged in philosophy'. Mansel is a distinguished member of that school of Christian thinkers, of whom Tertullian and Pascal are perhaps the most famous examples, who achieve faith by going all the way on the road of scepticism.

I Corinthians ii. 11. For what man knoweth the things of a man, save the spirit of man which is in him? even so the things of God knoweth no man, but the Spirit of God.

THE conclusion to be drawn from our previous inquiries is, that the doctrines of Revealed Religion, like all other objects of human thought, have a relation to the constitution of the thinker to whom they are addressed; within which relation their practical application and significance is confined. At the same time, this very relation indicates the existence of a higher form of the same truths, beyond the range of human intelligence, and therefore not capable of representation in any positive mode of thought. Religious ideas, in short, like all other objects of man's consciousness, are composed of two distinct elements, – a Matter, furnished from without, and a Form, imposed from within

by the laws of the mind itself. The latter element is common to all
objects of thought as such: the former is the peculiar and distinguishing
feature, by which the doctrines of Revelation are distinguished from
other religious representations, derived from natural sources; or by
which, in more remote comparison, religious ideas in general may be
distinguished from those relating to other objects. Now it is indispensable, before we can rightly estimate the value of the various objections
which are adduced against this or that representation of Christian doctrine, to ascertain which of these elements it is, against which the force
of the objection really makes itself felt. There may be objections whose
force, such as it is, tells against the revealed doctrine alone, and which
are harmless when directed against any other mode of religious representation. And there may also be objections which are applicable to the
form which revealed religion shares in common with other modes of
human thinking, and whose force, if they have any, is in reality directed,
not against Revelation in particular, but against all Religion, and indeed
against all Philosophy also. Now if, upon examination, it should
appear that the principal objections which are raised on the side of
Rationalism properly so called, – those, namely, which turn on a supposed incompatibility between the doctrines of Scripture and the
deductions of human reason, – are of the latter kind, and not of the
former, Christianity is at least so far secure from any apprehension of
danger from the side of rational philosophy. For the weapon with
which she is assailed exhibits its own weakness in the very act of
assailing. If there is error or imperfection in the essential forms of human
thought, it must adhere to the thought criticizing, no less than to the
thought criticized; and the result admits of but two legitimate alternatives. Either we must abandon ourselves to an absolute Scepticism,
which believes nothing and disbelieves nothing, and which thereby
destroys itself in believing that nothing is to be believed; or we must
confess that reason, in thus criticizing, has transcended its legitimate
province: that it has failed, not through its inherent weakness, but
through being misdirected in its aim. We must then shift the inquiry to
another field, and allow our belief to be determined, not solely by the
internal character of the doctrines themselves, as reasonable or unreasonable, but partly at least, by the evidence which can be produced
in favour of their asserted origin as a fact. The reasonable believer, in
short, must abstain from pronouncing judgment on the nature of the
message, until he has fairly examined the credentials of the messenger.

There are two methods by which such an examination of objections may be conducted. We may commence by an analysis of thought in general, distinguishing the Form, or permanent element, from the Matter, or variable element; and then, by applying the results of that analysis to special instances, we may shew, upon deductive grounds, the formal or material character of this or that class of objections. Or we may reverse the process, commencing by an examination of the objections themselves; and, by exhibiting them in their relation to other doctrines besides those of Revelation, we may arrive at the same conclusion as to their general or special applicability. The former method is perhaps the most searching and complete, but could hardly be adequately carried out within my present limits, nor without the employment of a language more technical than would be suitable on this occasion. In selecting the latter method, as the more appropriate, I must request my hearers to bear in mind the general principles which it is proposed to exhibit in one or two special instances. These are, first, that there is no rational difficulty in Christian Theology which has not its corresponding difficulty in human Philosophy; and, secondly, that therefore we may reasonably conclude that the stumbling-blocks which the rationalist professes to find in the doctrines of revealed religion arise, not from defects peculiar to revelation, but from the laws and limits of human thought in general, and are thus inherent in the method of rationalism itself, not in the objects which it pretends to criticize.

But, before applying this method to the peculiar doctrines of the Christian revelation, it will be desirable to say a few words on a preliminary condition, on which our belief in the possibility of any revelation at all is dependent. We must justify, in the first instance, the limitations which have been assigned to human reason in relation to the great foundation of all religious belief whatsoever: we must shew how far the same method warrants the assertion which has been already made on other grounds; namely, that we may and ought to believe in the existence of a God whose nature we are unable to comprehend; that we are bound to believe *that* God exists; and to acknowledge Him as our Sustainer and our Moral Governor: though we are wholly unable to declare *what* He is in His own Absolute Essence.

Many philosophical theologians, who are far from rejecting any of the essential doctrines of revelation, are yet unwilling to ground their acceptance of them on the duty of believing in the inconceivable.

The doctrine of the incognizability of the Divine essence [says the learned and deep-thinking Julius Müller], with the intention of exalting God to the highest, deprives Him of the realities, without which, as it is itself obliged to confess, we cannot really think of Him. That this negative result, just as decidedly as the assumption of an absolute knowledge of God, contradicts the Holy Scriptures, which especially teach that God becomes revealed in Christ, as it does that of the simple Christian consciousness, may be too easily shewn for it to be requisite that we should here enter upon the same: it is also of itself clear into what a strange position theology must fall by the renunciation of the knowledge of its essential object.

As regards the former part of this objection, I endeavoured, in my last Lecture, to shew that a full belief in God, as revealed in Christ, is not incompatible with a speculative inability to apprehend the Divine Essence. As regards the latter part, it is important to observe the exact parallel which in this respect exists between the fundamental conception of Theology and that of Philosophy. The Principle of Causality, the father, as it has been called, of metaphysical science, is to the philosopher what the belief in the existence of God is to the theologian. Both are principles inherent in our nature, exhibiting, whatever may be their origin, those characteristics of universality and certainty which mark them as part of the inalienable inheritance of the human mind. Neither can be reduced to a mere logical inference from the facts of a limited and contingent experience. Both are equally indispensable to their respective sciences: without Causation, there can be no Philosophy; as without God there can be no Theology. Yet to this day, while enunciating now, as ever, the fundamental axiom, that for every event there must be *a Cause*, Philosophy has never been able to determine what Causation is; to analyse the elements which the causal nexus involves; or to shew by what law she is justified in assuming the universal postulate upon which all her reasonings depend. The Principle of Causality has ever been, and probably ever will be, the battle ground on which, from generation to generation, Philosophy has struggled for her very existence in the death-gripe of Scepticism; and at every pause in the contest, the answer has been still the same: 'We *cannot* explain it, but we *must* believe it.' Causation is not the mere invariable association of antecedent and consequent: we feel that it implies something more than this. Yet, beyond the little sphere of our own volitions, what more can we discover? and within that sphere, what do we discover that we can explain? The unknown something, call it by what name you will, – power, effort, tendency, – still remains absolutely concealed, yet is still conceived as absolutely indispensable. Of Causality, as of Deity, we may almost say, in the emphatic language of Augustine, 'Cujus nulla scientia est in anima, nisi scire quomodo eum nesciat.' We can speak out boldly and clearly of each, if we are asked, what it is not: we are silent only when we asked, what it is. The eloquent words of the same great father are as applicable to human as to divine Philosophy:

Deus ineffabilis est: facilius dicimus quid non sit, quam quid sit. Terram cogitas; non est hoc Deus: mare cogitas; non est hoc Deus: omnia quæ sunt in terra, homines et animalia; non est hoc Deus: omnia quæ sunt in mari, quæ volant per aerem; non est hoc Deus: quidquid lucet in cœlo, stellæ, sol et luna; non est hoc Deus: ipsum cœlum; non est hoc Deus. Angelos cogita, Virtutes, Potestates, Archangelos, Thronos, Sedes, Dominationes; non est hoc Deus. Et quid est? Hoc solum potui dicere, quid non sit.

From the fundamental doctrine of Religion in general, let us pass on to that of Christianity in particular. 'The Catholic Faith is this: that we worship one God in Trinity, and Trinity in Unity.' How, asks the objector, can the One be Many, or the Many One? or how is a distinction of Persons compatible with their perfect equality? It is not a contradiction to say, that we are compelled by the Christian Verity to acknowledge every Person by Himself to be God and Lord; and yet are forbidden by the Catholic Religion to say, There be three Gods, or three Lords.

To exhibit the philosophical value of this objection, we need only make a slight change in the language of the doctrine criticized. Instead of a Plurality of Persons in the Divine Unity, we have only to speak of a Plurality of Attributes in the Divine Essence. How can there be a variety of Attributes, each infinite in its kind, and yet all together constituting but one Infinite? or how, on the other hand, can the Infinite be conceived as existing without diversity at all? We know, indeed, that various attributes exist in man, constituting in their plurality one and the same conscious self. Even here, there is a mystery which we cannot explain; but the fact is one which we are compelled, by the direct testimony of consciousness, to accept without explanation. But in admitting, as we are compelled to do, the coexistence of many attributes in one person, we can conceive those attributes only as distinct from each other, and as limiting each other. Each mental attribute is manifested as a separate and determinate mode of consciousness, marked off and limited, by the very fact of its manifestation as such. Each is developed in activities and operations from which the others are excluded. But this type of conscious existence fails us altogether, when we attempt to transfer it to the region of the Infinite. That there can be but one Infinite, appears to be a necessary conclusion of reason; for diversity is itself a limitation: yet here we have many Infinites, each distinct from the other, yet all constituting one Infinite, which is neither identical with them nor distinguishable from them. If Reason, thus baffled, falls back on the conception of a simple Infinite Nature, composed of no attributes, her case is still more hopeless. That which has no attributes is nothing conceivable; for things are conceived by their attributes. Strip the Infinite of the Attributes by which it is distinguished as infinite, and the Finite of those by which it is distinguished as finite; and the residue is neither the Infinite as such, nor the Finite as such, nor any one being as distinguished from any other being. It is the vague and empty conception of Being in general, which is no being in particular: a shape,

> If Shape it might be called, that shape had none
> Distinguishable in member, joint, or limb,
> Or Substance might be called, that Shadow seemed,
> For each seemed either.

The objection, 'How can the One be Many, or the Many One?' is thus so far from telling with peculiar force against the Catholic doctrine of the Holy Trinity, that it has precisely the same power, or want of power, and may be urged with precisely the same effect, or want of effect, against any conception, theological or philosophical, in which we may attempt to represent the Divine Nature and Attributes as infinite, or, indeed, to exhibit the Infinite at all. The same argument applies with equal force to the conception of the Absolute. If the Divine Nature is conceived as being nothing more than the sum of the Divine Attributes, it is not Absolute; for the existence of the whole will be dependent on the existence of its several parts. If, on the other hand, it is something distinct from the Attributes, and capable of existing without them, it becomes, in its absolute essence, an absolute void, – an existence manifested by no characteristic features, – a conception constituted by nothing conceivable.

The same principle may be also applied to another portion of this great fundamental truth. The doctrine of the Son of God, begotten of the Father, and yet coeternal with the Father, is in no wise more or less comprehensible by human reason, than the relation between the Divine Essence and its Attributes. In the order of Thought, or of Nature, the substance to which attributes belong has a logical priority to the attributes which exist in relation to it. The Attributes are attributes *of a Substance*. The former are conceived as the dependent and derived; the latter as the independent and original existence. Yet in the order of Time, (and to the order of Time all human thought is limited), it is as impossible to conceive the Substance existing before its Attributes, as the Attributes before the Substance. We cannot conceive a being originally simple, developing itself in the course of time into a complexity of attributes; for absolute simplicity cannot be conceived as containing within itself a principle of development, nor as differently related to different periods of time, so as to commence its development at any particular moment. Nor yet can we conceive the attributes as existing prior to the substance; for the very conception of an attribute implies relation to a substance. Yet the third hypothesis, that of their coexistence in all time, is equally incomprehensible; for this is to merge the Absolute and Infinite in an eternal relation and difference. We cannot conceive God as first existing, and then as creating His own attributes; for the creative power must then itself be created. Nor yet can we conceive the Divine Essence as constituted by the eternal coexistence of attributes; for then we have many Infinites, with no bond of unity between them. The mystery of the Many and the One, which has baffled philosophy ever since philosophy began, meets it here, as every where, with its eternal riddle. Reason gains nothing by repudiating Revelation; for the mystery of Revelation is the mystery of Reason also.

I should not for an instant dream of adducing this metaphysical parallel as offering the slight approach to a *proof* of the Christian doctrine of the Trinity in Unity. What it really illustrates is, not God's Nature, but man's ignorance. Without an Absolute Knowing there can be no comprehension of Absolute Being. The position of human reason, with regard to the ideas of the Absolute and the Infinite, is such as equally to exclude the Dogmatism which would demonstrate Christian Doctrine from philosophical premises, and the Rationalism which rejects it on the ground of philosophical difficulties, as well as that monstrous combination of both, which distorts it in pretending to systematize it. The Infinite is known to human reason, merely as the negation of the Finite: we know what it is not; and that is all. The conviction, *that* an Infinite Being exists, seems forced upon us by the manifest incompleteness of our finite knowledge; but we have no rational means whatever of determining *what* is the nature of that Being. The mind is thus perfectly blank with regard to any speculative representation of the Divine Essence; and for that very reason, Philosophy is not entitled, on internal evidence, to accept any, or to reject any. The only question which we are reasonably at liberty to ask in this matter, relates to the evidences of the Revelation as a fact. If there is sufficient evidence, on other grounds, to shew that the Scripture, in which this doctrine is contained, is a Revelation from God, the doctrine itself must be unconditionally received, not as reasonable, nor as unreasonable, but as scriptural. If there is not such evidence, the doctrine itself will lack its proper support; but the Reason which rejects it is utterly incompetent to substitute any other representation in its place.

Let us pass on to the second great doctrine of the Catholic Faith, – that which asserts the union of two Natures in the Person of Christ. 'The right Faith is, that we believe and confess, that our Lord Jesus Christ, the Son of God, is God and Man: God of the Substance of the Father, begotten before the worlds; and Man, of the Substance of His Mother, born in the world'.

Our former parallel was drawn from the impossibility of conceiving, in any form, a relation between the Infinite and the Infinite. Our present parallel may be found in the equal impossibility of conceiving, by the natural reason, a relation between the Infinite and the Finite; – an impossibility equally insurmountable, whether the two natures are conceived as existing in one Being, or in divers. Let us attempt, if we can, to conceive, at any moment of time, a finite world coming into existence by the fiat of an Infinite Creator. Can we conceive that the amount of existence is thereby increased, – that the Infinite and the Finite together contain more reality than formerly existed in the Infinite alone? The supposition annihilates itself; for it represents Infinite Existence as capable of becoming greater still. But, on the other hand, can we have recourse to the opposite alternative, and conceive the Creator as evolving the world out of His own Essence; the amount of Being remaining as before, yet the Infinite and the Finite both existing? This supposition also annihilates itself; for if the Infinite suffers diminution by that portion of it which becomes the Finite, it is infinite no longer; and if it suffers no diminution, the two together are but equal to the Infinite alone, and the Finite is reduced to absolute nonentity. In any mode whatever of human thought, the coexistence of the Infinite and the Finite is inconceivable; and yet the non-existence of either is, by the same laws of consciousness, equally inconceivable. If Reason is to be the supreme Judge of Divine Truths, it will not be sufficient to follow its guidance up to a certain point, and to stop when it is inconvenient to proceed further. There is no logical break in the chain of consequences, from Socinianism to Pantheism, and from Pantheism to Atheism, and from Atheism to Pyrrhonism; and Pyrrhonism is but the suicide of Reason itself. 'Nature', says Pascal, 'confounds the Pyrrhonists, and reason confounds the Dogmatists. What then becomes of man, if he seeks to discover his true condition by his natural reason? He cannot avoid one of these sects, and he cannot subsist in either.'

Let Religion begin where it will, it must begin with that which is above Reason. What then do we gain by that parsimony of belief, which strives to deal out the Infinite in infinitesimal fragments, and to erect the largest possible superstructure of deduction upon the smallest possible foundation of faith? We gain just this: that we forsake an incomprehensible doctrine, which rests upon the word of God, for one equally incomprehensible, which rests upon the word of man. Religion, to be a relation between God and man at all, must rest on a belief in the Infinite, and also on a belief in the Finite; for if we deny the first, there is no God; and if we deny the second, there is no Man. But the co-existence of the Infinite and the Finite, in any manner whatever, is inconceivable by reason; and the only ground that can be taken for accepting one representation of it, rather than another, is that one is revealed, and another is not revealed. We may seek as we will for a 'Religion within the limits of the bare Reason'; and we shall not find it; simply because no such thing exists; and if we dream for a moment that it does exist, it is only because we are unable or unwilling to pursue reason to its final consequences. But if we do not, others will; and the system which we have raised on the shifting basis of our arbitrary resting-place, waits only till the wind of controversy blows against it, and the flood of unbelief descends upon it, to manifest itself as the work of the 'foolish man which built his house upon the sand'.[1]

Having thus endeavoured to exhibit the limits of human reason in relation to those doctrines of Holy Scripture which reveal to us the nature of God, I shall next attempt briefly to apply the same argument to those representations which more directly declare His relation to the world.

The course of Divine Providence, in the government of the world, is represented in Scripture under the twofold aspect of *General Law* and *Special Interposition*. Not only is God the Author of the universe, and of those regular laws by which the periodical recurrence of its natural phenomena is determined;[2] but He is also exhibited as standing in a special relation to mankind; as the direct cause of events by which their

1 St Matthew vii. 26.
2 Genesis i. 14; viii. 22; Job xxxviii, xxxix; Psalm xix. 1–6; lxxiv. 17; civ. 5–31; cxxxv. 7; cxlviii. 6.

temporal or spiritual welfare is affected; as accessible to the prayers of
His servants; as to be praised for His special mercies towards each of us
in particular.[1] But this scriptural representation has been discovered by
Philosophy to be irrational. God is unchangeable; and therefore He
cannot be moved by man's entreaty. He is infinitely wise and good;
and therefore He ought not to deviate from the perfection of His
Eternal Counsels.

The religious man [says a writer of the present day], who believes that all
events, mental as well as physical, are pre-ordered and arranged according to
the decrees of infinite wisdom, and the philosopher, who knows that, by the
wise and eternal laws of the universe, cause and effect are indissolubly chained
together, and that one follows the other in inevitable succession – equally feel
that this ordination – this chain – cannot be changeable at the cry of man,
. . . If the purposes of God were not wise, they would not be formed: if wise,
they cannot be changed, for then they would become unwise. . . . The devout
philosopher, trained to the investigation of universal system – the serene
astronomer, fresh from the study of the changeless laws which govern innumer-
able worlds – shrinks from the monstrous irrationality of asking the great
Architect and Governor of all to work a miracle in his behalf – to interfere, for
the sake of *his* convenience or *his* plans, with the sublime order conceived by
the Ancient of Days in the far Eternity of the Past; for what is a special providence but an interference with established laws? and what is such interference
but a miracle?

Now here, as in the objections previously noticed, the rationalist
mistakes a general difficulty of all human thought for a special difficulty
of Christian belief. The really insoluble problem is, how to conceive
God as acting at all; not how to conceive Him as acting in this way,
rather than in that. The creation of the world at *any* period of time; –
the establishment, at *any* moment, of immutable laws for the future
government of that world; – this is the real mystery which Reason is
unable to fathom: this is the representation which seems to contradict
our conceptions of the Divine Perfection. To that pretentious perversion of the finite which philosophy dignifies with the name of the
Infinite, it is a contradiction to suppose that any change can take place
at any moment; – that any thing can begin to exist, which was not from
all eternity. To conceive the Infinite Creator, at any moment of time,
calling into existence a finite world, is, in the human point of view, to
suppose an imperfection, either before the act, or after it. It is to suppose the development of a power hitherto unexercised, or the limiting
to a determinate act that which was before general and indeterminate.

[1] Psalm lxv. 2; cii. 17, 18; ciii. 1, 3; cxliii. 1, 2; cxlv. 19.

May we not then repeat our author's objection in another form? How can a Being of Infinite Wisdom and Goodness, without an act of self-deterioration, change the laws which have governed His own solitary existence in the far Eternity when the world was not? Or rather, may we not ask what these very phrases of 'changeless laws' and 'far Eternity' really mean? Do they not represent God's existence as manifested under the conditions of duration and succession, – conditions which necessarily involve the conception of the imperfect and the finite? They have not emancipated the Deity from the law of Time: they have only placed Him in a different relation to it. They have merely substituted, for the revealed representation of the God who from time to time vouchsafes His aid to the needs of His creatures, the rationalizing representation of the God who, throughout all time, steadfastly refuses to do so.

If then the condition of Time is inseparable from all human conceptions of the Divine Nature, what advantage do we gain, even in philosophy, by substituting the supposition of immutable order in time for that of special interposition in time? Both of these representations are doubtless *speculatively* imperfect: both depict the Infinite God under finite symbols. But for the *regulative* purposes of human conduct in this life, each is equally necessary: and who may dare, from the depths of his own ignorance, to say that each may not have its prototype in the ineffable Being of God? We are sometimes told that it gives us a more elevated idea of the Divine Wisdom and Power, to regard the Creator as having finished His work once for all, and then abandoned it to its own unerring laws, than to represent Him as interfering, from time to time, by the way of direct personal superintendence: just as it implies higher mechanical skill to make an engine which shall go on perpetually by its own motion, than one which requires to be continually regulated by the hand of its maker. This ingenious simile fails only in the important particular, that both its terms are utterly unlike the objects which they profess to represent. The world is not a machine; and God is not a mechanic. The world is not a machine; for it consists, not merely of wheels of brass, and springs of steel, and the fixed properties of inanimate matter; but of living and intelligent and free-acting persons, capable of personal relations to a living and intelligent and free-acting Ruler. And God is not a mechanic; for the mechanic is separated from his machine by the whole diameter of being; as mind, giving birth to material results; as the conscious workman, who meets with no reciprocal consciousness in his work. It may be a higher evidence of mechanical skill, to abandon brute matter once for all to its own laws; but to take this as the analogy of God's dealings with His living creatures – as well tell us that the highest image of parental love and forethought is that of the ostrich, 'which leaveth her eggs in the earth, and warmeth them in dust'.[1]

But if such conclusions are not justified by our *a priori* knowledge of the Divine nature, are they borne out empirically by the actual constitution of the world? Is there any truth in the assertion, so often put forth as an undeniable discovery of modern science, 'that cause and effect are indissolubly chained together, and that one follows the other in inevitable succession'? There is just that amount of half-truth which makes an error dangerous; and there is no more. Experience is of two kinds, and Philosophy is of two kinds; – that of the world of matter, and that of the world of mind, – that of physical succession, and that of moral action. In the material world, if it be true that the researches of science *tend towards* (though who can say that they will ever reach?) the establishment of a system of fixed and orderly recurrence; in the mental world, we are no less confronted, at every instant, by the presence of contingency and free will. In the one we are conscious of a chain of phenomenal effects; in the other of *self*, as an acting and originating cause. Nay the very conception of the immutability of the law of cause and effect, is not so much derived from the positive evidence of the former, as from the negative evidence of the latter. We believe the succession to be necessary, because nothing but mind can be conceived as interfering with the successions of matter; and, where mind is excluded, we are unable to imagine contingence. But what right has this so-called philosophy to build a theory of the universe on material principles alone, and to neglect what experience daily and hourly forces upon our notice, – the perpetual interchange of the relations of matter and mind? In passing from the material to the moral world, we pass at once from the phenomenal to the real; from the successive to the continuous; from the many to the one; from an endless chain of mutual dependence to an originating and self-determining source of power. That mysterious, yet unquestionable presence of *Will*: that agent, uncompelled, yet not uninfluenced, whose continuous existence and productive energy are summed up in the word *Myself*: that perpetual struggle of good with evil: those warnings and promptings of a Spirit, striving with our spirit, commanding, yet not compelling; acting upon us, yet leaving us free to act for ourselves: that twofold consciousness of infirmity and

[1] Job xxxix. 14.

strength in the hour of temptation: that grand ideal of what we ought to be, so little, alas! to be gathered from the observation of what we are: that overwhelming conviction of Sin in the sight of One higher and holier than we: that irresistible impulse to Prayer, which bids us pour out our sorrows and make our wants known to One who hears and will answer us: that indefinable yet inextinguishable consciousness of a direct intercourse and communion of man with God, of God's influence upon man, yea, and (with reverence be it spoken), of man's influence upon God: these are facts of experience, to the full as real and as certain as the laws of planetary motions and chemical affinities; – facts which Philosophy is bound to take into account, or to stand convicted as shallow and one-sided; – facts which can deceive us, only if our whole Consciousness is a liar, and the boasted voice of Reason itself but an echo of the universal lie.

Even within the domain of Physical Science, however much analogy may lead us to conjecture the universal prevalence of law and orderly sequence, it has been acutely remarked, that the phenomena which are most immediately important to the life and welfare of man, are precisely those which he never has been, and probably never will be, able to reduce to a scientific calculation. The astronomer, who can predict the exact position of a planet in the heavens a thousand years hence, knows not what may be his own state of health to-morrow, nor how the wind which blows upon him will vary from day to day. May we not be permitted to conclude, with a distinguished Christian philosopher of the present day, that there is a Divine Purpose in this arrangement of nature; that, while enough is displayed to stimulate the intellectual and practical energies of man, enough is still concealed to make him feel his dependence upon God?

For man's training in this life, the conceptions of General Law and of Special Providence are both equally necessary; the one, that he may labour for God's blessings, and the other, that he may pray for them. He sows, and reaps, and gathers in his produce, to meet the different seasons, as they roll their unchanging course: he acknowledges also that 'neither is he that planteth any thing, neither he that watereth; but God that giveth the increase'.[1] He labours in the moral training of himself and others, in obedience to the general laws of means and ends, of motives and influences; while he asks, at the same time, for wisdom from above to guide his course aright, and for grace to enable him to follow that guidance. Necessary alike during this our state of trial, it

[1] 1 Corinthians iii. 7.

may be that both conceptions alike are but shadows of some higher truth, in which their apparent oppositions are merged in one harmonious whole. But when we attempt, from our limited point of view, to destroy the one, in order to establish the other more surely, we overlook the fact that our conception of General Law is to the full as human as that of Special Interposition; – that we are not really thereby acquiring a truer knowledge of the hidden things of God, but are measuring Him by a standard derived from the limited representations of man.

Subordinate to the Conception of Special Providence, and subject to the same laws of thought in its application, is that of *Miraculous Agency*. I am not now going to waste an additional argument in answer to that shallowest and crudest of all the assumptions of unbelief, which dictatorially pronounces that Miracles are impossible; – an assumption which is repudiated by the more philosophical among the leaders of Rationalism itself; and which implies, that he who maintains it has such a perfect and intimate acquaintance with the Divine Nature and Purposes, as to warrant him in asserting that God cannot or will not depart from the ordinary course of His Providence on any occasion whatever. If, as I have endeavoured to shew, the doctrine of Divine Interposition is not in itself more opposed to reason that that of General Law; and if the asserted immutability of the laws of nature is, at the utmost, tenable only on the supposition that material nature alone is spoken of, – we are not warranted, on any ground, whether of deduction from principles or of induction from experience, in denying the possible suspension of the Laws of Matter by the will of the Divine Mind. But the question on which it may still be desirable to say a few words, before concluding this portion of my argument, is one which is disputed, not necessarily between the believer and the unbeliever, but often between believers equally sincere and equally pious, differing only in their modes of representing to their own minds the facts and doctrines which both accept. Granting, that is to say, that variations from the established sequence of physical phenomena may take place, and have taken place, as Scripture bears witness; – are such variations to be represented as departures from or suspensions of natural law; or rather, as themselves the result of some higher law to us unknown, and as miraculous only from the point of view of our present ignorance?

Which of these representations, or whether either of them, is the true one, when such occurrences are considered in their relation to the Absolute Nature of God, our ignorance of that Nature forbids us to determine. Speculatively, to human understanding, it appears as little consistent with the nature of the Absolute and Infinite, to be subject to universal law, as it is to act at particular moments. But as a regulative truth, adapted to the religious wants of man's constitution, the more natural representation, that of a departure from the general law, seems to be also the more accurate. We are liable, in considering this question, to confound together two distinct notions under the equivocal name of *Law*. The first is a positive notion, derived from the observation of facts, and founded, with various modifications, upon the general idea of the *periodical recurrence of phenomena*. The other is a merely negative notion, deduced from a supposed apprehension of the Divine Nature, and professing to be based on the idea of the eternal Purposes of God. Of the former, the ideas of *succession* and *repetition* form an essential part. To the latter, the idea of Time, in any form, has no legitimate application; and it is thus placed beyond the sphere of human thought. Now when we speak of a Miracle as the possible result of some higher law, do we employ the term *law* in the former sense, or in the latter? do we mean, a law which actually exists in the knowledge of God; or one which, in the progress of science, may come to the knowledge of man? – one which might be discovered by a better acquaintance with the Divine Counsels; or one which might be inferred from a larger experience of natural phenomena? If we mean the former, we do not know that a more perfect acquaintance with the Divine Counsels, implying, as it does, the elevation of our faculties to a superhuman level, might not abolish the conception of Law altogether. If we mean the latter, we assume that which no experience warrants us in assuming; we endanger the religious significance and value of the miracle, only for the sake of removing God a few degrees further back from that chain of phenomena which is admitted ultimately to depend upon Him. A miracle, in one sense, need not be necessarily a violation of the laws of nature. God may make use of natural instruments, acting after their kind; as man himself, within his own sphere, does in the production of artificial combinations. The great question, however, still remains: Has God ever, for religious purposes, exhibited phenomena in certain relations, which the observed course of nature, and the artistic skill of man, are unable to bring about, or to account for?

I have thus far endeavoured to apply the principle of the Limits of Religious Thought to some of those representations which are usually objected to by the Rationalist, as in apparent opposition to the Speculative Reason of Man. In my next Lecture, I shall attempt to pursue the same argument, in relation to those doctrines which are sometimes regarded as repugnant to man's Moral Reason. The lesson to be derived from our present inquiry may be given in the pregnant sentence of a great philosopher, but recently taken from us: 'No difficulty emerges in Theology, which had not previously emerged in Philosophy'. The intellectual stumbling-blocks, which men find in the doctrines of Revelation, are not the consequence of any improbability or error peculiar to the things revealed; but are such as the thinker brings with him to the examination of the question; – such as meet him on every side, whether he thinks with or against the testimony of Scripture; being inherent in the constitution and laws of the Human Mind itself. But must we therefore acquiesce in the melancholy conclusion, that self-contradiction is the law of our intellectual being; – that the light of Reason, which is God's gift, no less than Revelation, is a delusive light, which we follow to our own deception? Far from it: the examination of the Limits of Thought leads to a conclusion the very opposite of this. Reason does not deceive us, if we will only read her witness aright; and Reason herself gives us warning, when we are in danger of reading it wrong. The light that is within us is not darkness; only it cannot illuminate that which is beyond the sphere of its rays. The self-contradictions, into which we inevitably fall, when we attempt certain courses of speculation, are the beacons placed by the hand of God in the mind of man, to warn us that we are deviating from the track that He designs us to pursue; that we are striving to pass the barriers which He has planted around us. The flaming sword turns every way against those who strive, in the strength of their own reason, to force their passage to the tree of life. Within her own province, and among her own objects, let Reason go forth, conquering and to conquer. The finite objects, which she can clearly and distinctly conceive, are her lawful empire and her true glory. The countless phenomena of the visible world; the unseen things which lie in the depths of the human soul; – these are given into her hand; and over them she may reign in unquestioned dominion. But when she strives to approach too near to the hidden mysteries of the Infinite; – when, not content with beholding afar off the partial and relative manifestations of God's presence, she would 'turn aside and see this great sight,' and know why God hath revealed Himself thus; – the voice of the Lord Himself is heard, as it were, speaking in warning from the midst: 'Draw not nigh hither: put off thy shoes from off thy feet; for the place whereon thou standest is holy ground.'[1]

[1] Exodus iii. 5.

8

From 'Essays and Reviews': 'Mosaic Cosmogony' by C. W. GOODWIN, and 'Bunsen's Biblical Researches' by ROWLAND WILLIAMS

Goodwin's Essay is not a work of great originality or power. But it provides perhaps the clearest contemporary account of the great dispute over Genesis, and it does so at the moment when it was most acute, in 1860, the year after the publication of Darwin's *Origin of Species*. Goodwin's personal position is very clearly summarized in his last paragraph, and he has a telling point when he says that those who profess to see in Genesis prophetic insight into future scientific investigation are really 'despoiling it of its consistency and grandeur'. It is interesting to note that, though Goodwin seems to have discarded the idea of Biblical Inspiration altogether, his essay was not made the subject of legal proceedings. This was no doubt because he was the only one of the seven contributors who was not a clergyman. He was a man of considerable versatility, and brother of the bishop of Carlisle. He was in turn barrister, Egyptologist and judge in the Far East.

In this essay we can see in its simplest and clearest form the 'liberal' or modernist account of the theological troubles of the nineteenth century. 'Theology', he complains, 'maintains but a shivering existence, shouldered and jostled by the sturdy growths of modern thought, and bemoaning itself for the hostility it encounters.' If theologians would look to history to find what God's procedure towards man has actually been, 'the so-called difficulties of theology would, for the most part, vanish of themselves.'

The main value of this essay does not lie, however, in the author's own argument, but in his fair and extensive summaries of the various views of the relation between geology and the Mosaic Cosmogony.

Williams's essay, together with another contribution to *Essays and Reviews* not printed here, was the subject of an unsuccessful prosecution for heresy. It is important in two ways. First, it heralds the long-delayed arrival of German Biblical scholarship into the Church of England itself. It had been familiar to a few people in England for a number of years, and George Eliot had finished her translation of Strauss's *LebenJesu* in 1846, fourteen years before the appearance of *Essays and Reviews*. But this essay made it for the first time a matter of public discussion. Williams was a Doctor of Divinity, and Vice-Principal of St David's College, Lampeter. Biblical Criticism had truly arrived when such a man could treat it sympathetically.

But the essay is perhaps even more important in another way which is less obvious. Its whole tendency is to attenuate or deny the concept of Revelation in religion, to soften all positive doctrines down into moral or psychological facts, and to treat sacraments and ordinances as mere symbols. The passage on Baptism is typical: 'The first Christians held that the heart was purified by faith; the accompanying symbol, water, became by degrees the instrument of purification.' And in another passage faith itself, the only positive theological word in the sentence just quoted, is fined down to mean little more than the peace of mind that comes from an untroubled conscience.

MOSAIC COSMOGONY

ON the revival of science in the 16th century, some of the earliest conclusions at which philosophers arrived were found to be at variance with popular and long-established belief. The Ptolemaic system of astronomy, which had then full possession of the minds of men, contemplated the whole visible universe from the earth as the immovable centre of things. Copernicus changed the point of view, and placing the beholder in the sun, at once reduced the earth to an inconspicuous globule, a merely subordinate member of a family of planets, which the terrestrials had until then fondly imagined to be but pendants and ornaments of their own habitation. The Church naturally took a lively interest in the disputes which arose between the philosophers of the new school and those who adhered to the old doctrines, inasmuch as the Hebrew records, the basis of religious faith, manifestly countenanced the opinion of the earth's immobility and certain other views of the universe very incompatible with those propounded by Copernicus. Hence arose the official proceedings against Galileo, in consequence of which he submitted to sign his celebrated recantation, acknowledging that 'the proposition that the sun is the centre of the world and immovable from its place is absurd, philosophically false, and formally heretical, because it is expressly contrary to the Scripture;' and that 'the proposition that the earth is not the centre of the world, nor immovable, but that it moves and also with a diurnal motion, is absurd, philosophically false, and at least erroneous in faith.'

The Romish Church, it is presumed, adheres to the old views to the present day. Protestant instincts, however, in the 17th century were strongly in sympathy with the augmentation of science, and consequently Reformed Churches more easily allowed themselves to be helped over the difficulty, which, according to the views of inspiration then held and which have survived to the present day, was in reality quite as formidable for them as for those of the old faith. The solution of the difficulty offered by Galileo and others was, that the object of a revelation or divine unveiling of mysteries, must be to teach man things which he is unable and must ever remain unable to find out for himself: but not physical truths, for the discovery of which he has faculties specially provided by his Creator. Hence it was not unreasonable, that in regard to matters of fact merely, the Sacred Writings should use the common language and assume the common belief of mankind, without purporting to correct errors upon points morally indifferent. So, in regard to such a text as 'The world is established, it cannot be moved,' though it might imply the sacred penman's ignorance of the fact that the earth does move, yet it does not put forth this opinion as an indispensable point of faith. And this remark is applicable to a number of texts which present a similar difficulty.

It might be thought to have been less easy to reconcile in men's minds the Copernican view of the universe with the very plain and direct averments contained in the opening chapter of Genesis. It can scarcely be said that this chapter is not intended in part to teach and convey at least some physical truth, and taking its words in their plain sense it manifestly gives a view of the universe adverse to that of modern science. It represents the sky as a watery vault in which the sun, moon, and stars are set. But the discordance of this description with facts does

C. W. GOODWIN

not appear to have been so palpable to the minds of the seventeenth century as it is to us. The mobility of the earth was a proposition startling not only to faith but to the senses. The difficulty involved in this belief having been successfully got over, other discrepancies dwindled in importance. The brilliant progress of astronomical science subdued the minds of men; the controversy between faith and knowledge gradually fell to slumber; the story of Galileo and the Inquisition became a school commonplace, the doctrine of the earth's mobility found its way into children's catechisms, and the limited views of the nature of the universe indicated in the Old Testament ceased to be felt as religious difficulties.

It would have been well if theologians had made up their minds to accept frankly the principle that those things for the discovery of which man has faculties specially provided are not fit objects of a divine revelation. Had this been unhesitatingly done, either the definition and idea of divine revelation must have been modified, and the possibility of an admixture of error have been allowed, or such parts of the Hebrew writings as were found to be repugnant to fact must have been pronounced to form no part of revelation. The first course is that which theologians have most generally adopted, but with such limitations, cautels, and equivocations as to be of little use in satisfying those who would know how and what God really has taught mankind, and whether anything beyond that which man is able and obviously intended to arrive at by the use of his natural faculties.

The difficulties and disputes which attended the first revival of science have recurred in the present century in consequence of the growth of geology. It is in truth only the old question over again – precisely the same point of theology which is involved, – although the difficulties which present themselves are fresh. The school-books of the present day, while they teach the child that the earth moves, yet assure him that it is a little less than six thousand years old, and that it was made in six days. On the other hand, geologists of all religious creeds are agreed that the earth has existed for an immense series of years, – to be counted by millions rather than by thousands; and that indubitably more than six days elapsed from its first creation to the appearance of man upon its surface. By this broad discrepancy between old and new doctrine is the modern mind startled, as were the men of the sixteenth century when told that the earth moved.

When this new cause of controversy first arose, some writers more hasty than discreet, attacked the conclusions of geologists, and

K 139

declared them scientifically false. This phase may now be considered past, and although school-books probably continue to teach much as they did, no well-instructed person now doubts the great antiquity of the earth any more than its motion. This being so modern theologians, forsaking the maxim of Galileo, or only using it vaguely as an occasional make-weight, have directed their attention to the possibility of reconciling the Mosaic narrative with those geological facts which are admitted to be beyond dispute. Several modes of doing this have been proposed which have been deemed more or less satisfactory. In a text-book of theological instruction widely used,[1] we find it stated in broad terms, 'Geological investigations, it is now known, all prove the perfect harmony between scripture and geology, in reference to the history of creation.'

In truth, however, if we refer to the plans of conciliation proposed, we find them at variance with each other and mutually destructive. The conciliators are not agreed among themselves, and each holds the views of the other to be untenable and unsafe. The ground is perpetually being shifted, as the advance of geological science may require. The plain meaning of the Hebrew record is unscrupulously tampered with, and in general the pith of the whole process lies in divesting the text of all meaning whatever. We are told that Scripture not being designed to teach us natural philosophy, it is in vain to attempt to make out a cosmogony from its statements. If the first chapter of Genesis conveys to us no information concerning the origin of the world, its statements cannot indeed be contradicted by modern discovery. But it is absurd to call this harmony. Statements such as that above quoted are, we conceive, little calculated to be serviceable to the interests of theology, still less to religion and morality. Believing, as we do, that if the value of the Bible as a book of religious instruction is to be maintained, it must be not by striving to prove it scientifically exact, at the expense of every sound principle of interpretation, and in defiance of common sense, but by the frank recognition of the erroneous views of nature which it contains, we have put pen to paper to analyse some of the popular conciliation theories. The inquiry cannot be deemed a superfluous one, nor one which in the interests of theology had better be let alone. Physical science goes on unconcernedly pursuing its own paths. Theology, the science whose object is the dealing of God with man as a moral being, maintains but a shivering existence, shouldered and jostled by the sturdy growths of modern thought, and bemoaning

1 Horne's *Introduction to the Holy Scriptures* (1856, tenth Edition).

itself for the hostility which it encounters. Why should this be, unless because theologians persist in clinging to theories of God's procedure towards man, which have long been seen to be untenable? If, relinquishing theories, they would be content to inquire from the history of man what this procedure has actually been, the so-called difficulties of theology would, for the most part, vanish of themselves.

The account which astronomy gives of the relations of our earth to the rest of the universe, and that which geology gives of its internal structure and the development of its surface, are sufficiently familiar to most readers. But it will be necessary for our purpose to go over the oft-trodden ground, which must be done with rapid steps. Nor let the reader object to be reminded of some of the most elementary facts of his knowledge. The human race has been ages in arriving at conclusions now familiar to every child.

This earth apparently so still and stedfast, lying in majestic repose beneath the ætherial vault, is a globular body of comparatively insignificant size, whirling fast through space round the sun as the centre of its orbit, and completing its revolution in the course of one year, while at the same time it revolves daily once about its own axis, thus producing the changes of day and night. The sun, which seems to leap up each morning from the east, and traversing the skyey bridge, slides down into the west, is relatively to our earth motionless. In size and weight it inconceivably surpasses it. The moon, which occupies a position in the visible heavens only second to the sun, and far beyond that of every other celestial body in conspicuousness, is but a subordinate globe, much smaller than our own, and revolving round the earth as its centre, while it accompanies it in yearly revolutions about the sun. Of itself it has no lustre, and is visible to us only by the reflected sunlight. Those beautiful stars which are perpetually changing their position in the heavens, and shine with a soft and moon-like light, are bodies, some much larger, some less, than our earth, and like it revolve round the sun, by the reflection of whose rays we see them. The telescope has revealed to us the fact that several of these are attended by moons of their own, and that besides those which the unassisted eye can see, there are others belonging to the same family coursing round the sun. As for the glittering dust which emblazons the nocturnal sky, there is reason to believe that each spark is a self-luminous body, perhaps of similar material to our sun, and that the very nearest of the whole tribe is at an incalculable distance from us, the very least of them of enormous size compared with our own humble globe. Thus has modern science reversed nearly all the *prima facie* views to which our senses lead us as to the constitution of the universe; but so thoroughly are the above statements wrought into the culture of the present day, that we are apt to forget that mankind once saw these things very differently, and that but a few centuries have elapsed since such views were startling novelties.

Our earth then is but one of the lesser pendants of a body which is itself only an inconsiderable unit in the vast creation. And now if we withdraw our thoughts from the immensities of space, and look into the construction of man's obscure home, the first question is whether it has ever been in any other condition than that in which we now see it, and if so, what are the stages through which it has passed, and what was its first traceable state. Here geology steps in and successfully carries back the history of the earth's crust to a very remote period, until it arrives at a region of uncertainty, where philosophy is reduced to mere guesses and possibilities, and pronounces nothing definite. To this region belong the speculations which have been ventured upon as to the original concretion of the earth and planets out of nebular matter of which the sun may have been the nucleus. But the first clear view which we obtain of the early condition of the earth, presents to us a ball of matter, fluid with intense heat, spinning on its own axis and revolving round the sun. How long it may have continued in this state is beyond calculation or surmise. It can only be believed that a prolonged period, beginning and ending we know not when, elapsed before the surface became cooled and hardened and capable of sustaining organized existences. The water which now enwraps a large portion of the face of the globe, must for ages have existed only in the shape of steam, floating above and enveloping the planet in one thick curtain of mist. When the cooling of the surface allowed it to condense and descend, then commenced the process by which the lowest stratified rocks were formed, and gradually spread out in vast layers. Rains and rivers now acted upon the scoriaceous integument, grinding it to sand and carrying it down to the depths and cavities. Whether organized beings co-existed with this state of things we know not, as the early rocks have been acted upon by interior heat to an extent which must have destroyed all traces of animal and vegetable life, if any such ever existed. This period has been named by geologists the Azoic, or that in which life was not. Its duration no one presumes to define.

It is in the system of beds which overlies these primitive formations that the first records of organisms present themselves. In the so-called

Silurian system we have a vast assemblage of strata of various kinds, together many thousands of feet thick, and abounding in remains of animal life. These strata were deposited at the bottom of the sea, and the remains are exclusively marine. The creatures whose exuviæ have been preserved belong to those classes which are placed by naturalists the lowest with respect to organization, the mollusca, articulata, and radiata. Analogous beings exist at the present day, but not their lineal descendants, unless time can effect transmutation of species, an hypothesis not generally accepted by naturalists. In the same strata with these inhabitants of the early seas are found remains of fucoid or seaweed-like plants, the lowest of the vegetable tribe, which may have been the first of this kind of existences introduced into the world. But, as little has yet been discovered to throw light upon the state of the dry land and its productions at this remote period, nothing can be asserted positively on the subject.[1]

In the upper strata of the Silurian system is found the commencement of the race of fishes, the lowest creatures of the vertebrate type, and in the succeeding beds they become abundant. These monsters clothed in mail who must have been the terror of the seas they inhabited, have left their indestructible coats behind them as evidence of their existence.

Next come the carboniferous strata, containing the remains of a gigantic and luxuriant vegetation, and here reptiles and insects begin to make their appearance. At this point geologists make a kind of artificial break, and for the sake of distinction, denominate the whole of the foregoing period of animated existences the Palæozoic, or that of antique life.

In the next great geological section, the so-called Secondary period, in which are comprised the oolitic and cretaceous systems, the predominant creatures are different from those which figured conspicuously in the preceding. The land was inhabited by gigantic animals, half-toad, half-lizard, who hopped about, leaving often their footprints like those of a clumsy human hand, upon the sandy shores of the seas they frequented. The waters now abounded with monsters, half-fish, half-crocodile, the well-known saurians, whose bones have been collected in abundance. Even the air had its tenantry from the same family type, for the pterodactyls were creatures, half-lizard, half-vampyre, provided with membranous appendages which must have enabled them to fly. In an early stage of this period traces of birds appear,

---

[1] It has been stated that a coal-bed, containing remains of land-plants, underlying strata of the lower Silurian class, has been found in Portugal.

and somewhat later those of mammals, but of the lowest class belonging to that division, namely, the marsupial or pouch-bearing animals, in which naturalists see affinities to the oviparous tribes. The vegetation of this period seems to have consisted principally of the lower classes of plants, according to the scale of organization accepted by botanists, but it was luxuriant and gigantic.

Lastly, comes the Tertiary period, in which mammalia of the highest forms enter upon the scene, while the composite growths of the Secondary period in great part disappear, and the types of creatures approach more nearly to those which now exist. During long ages this stage of things continued, while the earth was the abode principally of mastodons, elephants, rhinoceroses, and their thick-hided congeners, many of them of colossal proportions, and of species which have now passed away. The remains of these creatures have been found in the frozen rivers of the north, and they appear to have roamed over regions of the globe where their more delicate representatives of the present day would be unable to live. During this era the ox, horse, and deer, and perhaps other animals, destined to be serviceable to man, became inhabitants of the earth. Lastly, the advent of man may be considered as inaugurating a new and distinct epoch, that in which we now are, and during the whole of which the physical conditions of existence cannot have been very materially different from what they are now. Thus, the reduction of the earth into the state in which we now behold it has been the slowly continued work of ages. The races of organic beings which have populated its surface have from time to time passed away, and been supplanted by others, introduced we know not certainly by what means, but evidently according to a fixed method and order, and with a gradually increasing complexity and fineness of organization, until we come to man as the crowning point of all. Geologically speaking, the history of his first appearance is obscure, nor does archæology do much to clear this obscurity. Science has, however, made some efforts towards tracing man to his cradle, and by patient observation and collection of facts much more may perhaps be done in this direction. As for history and tradition, they afford little upon which anything can be built. The human race, like each individual man, has forgotten its own birth, and the void of its early years has been filled up by imagination, and not from genuine recollection. Thus much is clear, that man's existence on earth is brief, compared with the ages during which unreasoning creatures were the sole possessors of the globe.

We pass to the account of the creation contained in the Hebrew record. And it must be observed that in reality two distinct accounts are given us in the book of Genesis, one being comprised in the first chapter and the first three verses of the second, the other commencing at the fourth verse of the second chapter and continuing till the end. This is so philologically certain that it were useless to ignore it. But even those who may be inclined to contest the fact that we have here the productions of two different writers, will admit that the account beginning at the first verse of the first chapter, and ending at the third verse of the second, is a complete whole in itself. And to this narrative, in order not to complicate the subject unnecessarily, we intend to confine ourselves. It will be sufficient for our purpose to enquire, whether this account can be shown to be in accordance with our astronomical and geological knowledge. And for the right understanding of it the whole must be set out, so that the various parts may be taken in connexion with one another.

We are told that 'in the beginning God created the heaven and the earth.' It has been matter of discussion amongst theologians whether the word 'created' (Heb. *bara*) here means simply shaped or formed, or shaped or formed out of nothing. From the use of the verb *bara* in other passages, it appears that it does not necessarily mean to make out of nothing,[1] but it certainly might impliedly mean this in a case so peculiar as the present. The phrase 'the heaven and the earth,' is evidently used to signify the universe of things, inasmuch as the heaven in its proper signification has no existence until the second day. It is asserted then that God shaped the whole material universe, whether out of nothing, or out of pre-existing matter. But which sense the writer really intended is not material for our present purpose to enquire, since neither astronomical nor geological science affects to state anything concerning the first origin of matter.

In the second verse the earliest state of things is described; according to the received translation, 'the earth was without form and void.' The prophet Jeremiah uses[2] the same expression to describe the

---

[1] This appears at once from verse 21, where it is said that God created (*bara*) the great whales; and from verses 26 and 27, in the first of which we read, 'God said, Let us make (*hasah*) man in our image,' and in the latter, 'So God created (*bara*) man in his image.' In neither of these cases, can it be supposed to be implied that the whales, or man, were made out of nothing. In the second narrative, another word is used for the creation of man, *iatzer* – to mould; and his formation out of the dust is circumstantially described.

[2] Chap. iv 33.

desolation of the earth's surface occasioned by God's wrath, and perhaps the words 'empty and waste' would convey to us at present something more nearly approaching the meaning of *tohu va-bohu*, than those which the translators have used.

The earth itself is supposed to be submerged under the waters of the deep, over which the breath of God – the air or wind – flutters while all is involved in darkness. The first special creative command is that which bids the light appear, whereupon daylight breaks over the two primæval elements of earth and water – the one lying still enveloped by the other; and the space of time occupied by the original darkness and the light which succeeded, is described as the first day. Thus light and the measurement of time are represented as existing before the manifestation of the sun, and this idea, although repugnant to our modern knowledge, has not in former times appeared absurd. Thus we find Ambrose (*Hexaemeron*, lib. 4, cap. 3) remarking: 'We must recollect that the light of day is one thing, the light of the sun, moon, and stars another, – the sun by his rays appearing to add lustre to the daylight. For before sunrise the day dawns, but is not in full refulgence, for the mid-day sun adds still further to its splendour.' We quote this passage to show how a mind unsophisticated by astronomical knowledge understood the Mosaic statement; and we may boldly affirm that those for whom it was first penned could have taken it in no other sense than that light existed before and independently of the sun, nor do we misrepresent it when we affirm this to be its natural and primary meaning. How far we are entitled to give to the writer's words an enigmatical and secondary meaning, as contended by those who attempt to conciliate them with our present knowledge, must be considered further on.

The work of the second day of creation is to erect the vault of Heaven (Heb. *rakia*; Gr. στερέωμα; Lat. *firmamentum*) which is represented as supporting an ocean of water above it. The waters are said to be divided, so that some are below, some above the vault. That the Hebrews understood the sky, firmament, or heaven to be a permanent solid vault, as it appears to the ordinary observer, is evident enough from various expressions made use of concerning it. It is said to have pillars (Job xxvi. 11), foundations (2 Sam. xxii. 8), doors (Ps. lxxviii. 23), and windows (Gen. vii. 11). No quibbling about the derivation of the word *rakia*, which is literally something beaten out,[1] can affect

[1] The root is generally applied to express the hammering or beating out of metal plates; hence something beaten or spread out. It has been pretended that

the explicit description of the Mosaic writer, contained in the words 'the waters that are above the firmament', or avail to show that he was aware that the sky is but transparent space.

On the third day, at the command of God, the waters which have hitherto concealed the earth are gathered together in one place – the sea, – and the dry land emerges. Upon the same day the earth brings forth grass, herb yielding seed and fruit trees, the destined food of the animals and of man (v. 29). Nothing is said of herbs and trees which are not serviceable to this purpose, and perhaps it may be contended, since there is no vegetable production which may not possibly be useful to man, or which is not preyed upon by some animal, that in this description the whole terrestrial flora is implied. We wish, however, to call the attention of the reader to the fact, that trees and plants destined for food are those which are particularly singled out here as the earliest productions of the earth, as we shall have occasion to refer to this again presently.

On the fourth day, the two great lights, the sun and moon, are *made* (Heb. *hasah*) and *set* in the firmament of heaven to give light to the earth, but more particularly to serve as the means of measuring time, and of marking out years, days, and seasons. This is the most prominent office assigned to them (v. 14–18). The formation of the stars is mentioned in the most cursory manner. It is not said out of what materials all these bodies were made, and whether the writer regarded them as already existing, and only waiting to have a proper place assigned them, may be open to question. At any rate, their allotted receptacle – the firmament – was not made until the second day, nor were they set in it until the fourth; vegetation, be it observed, having already commenced on the third, and therefore independently of the warming influence of the sun.

On the fifth day the waters are called into productive activity, and bring forth fishes and marine animals, as also the birds of the air.[1] It is also said that God created or formed (*bara*) great whales and other creatures of the water and air. On the sixth day the earth brings forth living creatures, cattle, and reptiles, and also 'the beast of the field,' that is, the wild beasts. And here also it is added that God made (*hasah*) these creatures after their several kinds. The formation of man is

---

the word *rakia* may be translated *expanse*, so as merely to mean empty space. The context sufficiently rebuts this.

[1] In the second narrative of creation, in which no distinction of days is made, the birds are said to have been formed out of the ground. Gen. ii.

distinguished by a variation of the creative fiat. 'Let us make man in our image after our likeness.' Accordingly, man is made and formed (*bara*) in the image and likeness of God, a phrase which has been explained away to mean merely 'perfect, sinless,' although the Pentateuch abounds in passages showing that the Hebrews contemplated the Divine being in the visible form of a man.[1] Modern spiritualism has so entirely banished this idea, that probably many may not without an effort be able to accept the plain language of the Hebrew writer in its obvious sense in the 26th verse of the 1st chapter of Genesis, though they will have no difficulty in doing so in the 3rd verse of the 5th chapter, where the same words 'image' and 'likeness' are used. Man is said to have been created male and female, and the narrative contains nothing to show that a single pair only is intended.[2] He is commanded to increase and multiply, and to assume dominion over all the other tribes of beings. The whole of the works of creation being complete, God gives to man, beast, fowl, and creeping thing, the vegetable productions of the earth as their appointed food. And when we compare the verses Gen. i. 29, 30, with Gen. ix. 3, in which, after the Flood, animals are given to man for food in addition to the green herb, it is difficult not to come to the conclusion that in the earliest view taken of creation, men and animals were supposed to have been, in their original condition, not carnivorous. It is needless to say that this has been for the most part the construction put upon the words of the Mosaic writer, until a clear perception of the creative design which destined the tiger and lion for flesh-eaters, and latterly the geological proof of flesh-eating monsters having existed among the pre-adamite inhabitants of the globe, rendered it necessary to ignore this meaning.

The 1st, 2nd, and 3rd verses of the second chapter of Genesis, which have been most absurdly divided from their context, conclude the narrative.[3] On the seventh day God rests from His work, and blesses the day of rest, a fact which is referred to in the Commandment given from Sinai as the ground of the observance of Sabbatic rest imposed upon the Hebrews.

[1] See particularly the narrative in Genesis xviii.

[2] It is in the second narrative of creation that the formation of a single man, out of the dust of the earth, is described, and the omission to create a female at the same time, is stated to have been repaired by the subsequent formation of one from the side of the man.

[3] The common arrangement of the Bible in chapters is of comparatively modern origin, and is admitted, on all hands, to have no authority or philological worth whatever. In many cases, the division is most preposterous, and interferes greatly with an intelligent perusal of the text.

Remarkable as this narrative is for simple grandeur, it has nothing in it which can be properly called poetical. It bears on its face no trace of mystical or symbolical meaning. Things are called by their right names with a certain scientific exactness widely different from the imaginative cosmogonies of the Greeks, in which the powers and phenomena of nature are invested with personality, and the passions and qualities of men are represented as individual existences.

The circumstances related in the second narrative of creation are indeed such as to give at least some ground for the supposition that a mystical interpretation was intended to be given to it. But this is far from being the case with the first narrative, in which none but a professed mystifier of the school of Philo could see anything but a plain statement of facts. There can be little reasonable dispute then as to the sense in which the Mosaic narrative was taken by those who first heard it, nor is it indeed disputed that for centuries, putting apart the Philonic mysticism, which after all did not exclude a primary sense, its words have been received in their genuine nand atural meaning. That this meaning is *prima facie* one wholly adverse to the present astronomical and geological views of the universe is evident enough. There is not a mere difference through deficiency. It cannot be correctly said that the Mosaic writer simply leaves out details which modern science supplies, and that, therefore, the inconsistency is not a real but only an apparent one. It is manifest that the whole account is given from a different point of view from that which we now unavoidably take; that the order of things as we now know them to be, is to a great extent reversed, although here and there we may pick out some general analogies and points of resemblance. Can we say that the Ptolemaic system of astronomy is not at variance with modern science, because it represents with a certain degree of correctness some of the apparent motions of the heavenly bodies?

The task which sundry modern writers have imposed upon themselves is to prove that the Mosaic narrative, however apparently at variance with our knowledge, is essentially, and in fact true, although never understood properly until modern science supplied the necessary commentary and explanation.

Two modes of conciliation have been propounded which have enjoyed considerable popularity, and to these two we shall confine our attention.

The first is that originally brought into vogue by Chalmers and adopted by the late Dr Buckland in his Bridgewater Treatise, and which is probably still received by many as a sufficient solution of all difficulties. Dr Buckland's treatment of the case may be taken as a fair specimen of the line of argument adopted, and it shall be given in his own words.

The word *beginning* [he says], as applied by Moses in the first verse of the book of Genesis, expresses an undefined period of time which was antecedent to the last great change that affected the surface of the earth, and to the creation of its present animal and vegetable inhabitants, during which period a long series of operations may have been going on; which as they are wholly unconnected with the history of the human race, are passed over in silence by the sacred historian, whose only concern was barely to state, that the matter of the universe is not eternal and self-existent, but was originally created by the power of the Almighty. . . . The Mosaic narrative commences with a declaration that 'in the beginning God created the heaven and the earth.' These few first words of Genesis may be fairly appealed to by the geologist as containing a brief statement of the creation of the material elements, at a time distinctly preceding the operations of the first day; it is nowhere affirmed that God created the heaven and the earth in the *first day*, but in the *beginning*; this beginning may have been an epoch at an unmeasured distance, followed by periods of undefined duration during which all the physical operations disclosed by geology were going on.

The first verse of Genesis, therefore, seems explicitly to assert the creation of the universe; the heaven, including the sidereal systems; and the earth, more especially specifying our own planet, as the subsequent scene of the operations of the six days about to be described; no information is given as to events which may have occurred upon this earth, unconnected with the history of man, between the creation of its component matter recorded in the first verse, and the era at which its history is resumed in the second verse; nor is any limit fixed to the time during which these intermediate events may have been going on: millions of millions of years may have occupied the indefinite interval, between the beginning in which God created the heaven and the earth, and the evening or commencement of the first day of the Mosaic narrative.

The second verse may describe the condition of the earth on the opening of this first day (for in the Jewish mode of computation used by Moses each day is reckoned from the beginning of one evening to the beginning of another evening). This first evening may be considered as the termination of the indefinite time which followed the primeval creation announced in the first verse, and as the commencement of the first of the six succeeding days in which the earth was to be filled up, and peopled in a manner fit for the reception of mankind. We have in this second verse, a distinct mention of earth and waters, as already existing and involved in darkness; their condition also is described as a state of confusion and emptiness (*tohu bohu*), words which are usually interpreted by the vague and indefinite Greek term chaos, and which may be geologically considered as designating the wreck and ruins of a former world. At this intermediate point of time the preceding undefined geological periods had terminated, a new series of events commenced, and the work of the first morning of this new creation was the calling forth of light from a temporary darkness, which had overspread the ruins of the ancient earth.

With regard to the formation of the sun and moon, Dr Buckland observes, p. 27.

We are not told that the substance of the sun and moon was first called into existence on the fourth day; the text may equally imply that these bodies were then prepared and appointed to certain offices, of high importance to mankind, 'to give light upon the earth, and to rule over the day, and over the night, to be for signs, and for seasons, and for days, and for years.' The fact of their creation had been stated before in the first verse.

The question of the meaning of the word *bara*, create, has been previously touched upon; it has been acknowledged by good critics that it does not of itself necessarily imply 'to make out of nothing,' upon the simple ground that it is found used in cases where such a meaning would be inapplicable. But the difficulty of giving to it the interpretation contended for by Dr Buckland, and of uniting with this the assumption of a six days' creation, such as that described in Genesis, at a comparatively recent period, lies in this, that the heaven itself is distinctly said to have been formed by the division of the waters on the second day. Consequently during the indefinite ages which elapsed from the primal creation of matter until the first Mosaic day of creation, there was no sky, no local habitation for the sun, moon, and stars, even supposing those bodies to have been included in the original material. Dr Buckland does not touch this obvious difficulty, without which his argument that the sun and moon might have been contemplated as pre-existing, although they are not stated to have been set in the heaven until the fourth day, is of no value at all.

Dr Buckland appears to assume that when it is said that the heaven and the earth were created in the beginning, it is to be understood that they were created in their present form and state of completeness, the heaven raised above the earth as we see it, or seem to see it now. This is the fallacy of his argument. The circumstantial description of the framing of the heaven out of the waters, proves that the words 'heaven and earth,' in the first verse, must be taken either proleptically, as a general expression for the universe, the matter of the universe in its crude and unformed shape, or else the word *bara* must mean formed, not created, the writer intending to say 'God formed the heaven and earth in manner following,' in which case heaven is used in its distinct and proper sense. But these two senses cannot be united in the manner covertly assumed in Dr Buckland's argument.

Having, however, thus endeavoured to make out that the Mosaic account does not negative the idea that the sun, moon, and stars had 'been created at the indefinitely distant time designated by the word beginning,' he is reduced to describe the primæval darkness of the first day as 'a temporarary darkness, produced by an accumulation of dense vapours upon the face of the deep.'

An incipient dispersion of these vapours may have readmitted light to the earth, upon the first day, whilst the exciting cause of light was obscured, and the further purification of the atmosphere upon the fourth day, may have caused the sun and moon and stars to re-appear in the firmament of heaven, to assume their new relations to the newly modified earth and to the human race.

It is needless to discuss the scientific probability of this hypothesis, but the violence done to the grand and simple words of the Hebrew writer must strike every mind. 'And God said, Let there be light – and there was light – and God saw the light that it was good. And God divided the light from the darkness, and God called the light day, and the darkness called he night; and the evening and the morning were the first day.' Can any one sensible of the value of words suppose, that nothing more is here described, or intended to be described, than the partial clearing away of a fog? Can such a manifestation of light have been dignified by the appellation of day? Is not this reducing the noble description which has been the admiration of ages to a pitiful *caput mortuum* of empty verbiage?

What were the *new relations* which the heavenly bodies according to Dr Buckland's view, assumed to the newly modified earth and to the human race? They had, as we well know, marked out seasons, days and years, and had given light for ages before to the earth, and to the animals which preceded man as its inhabitants, as is shown, Dr Buckland admits, by the eyes of fossil animals, optical instruments of the same construction as those of the animals of our days, and also by the existence of vegetables in the early world, to the development of which light must have been as essential then as now.

The hypothesis adopted by Dr Buckland was first promulgated at a time when the gradual and regular formation of the earth's strata was not seen or admitted so clearly as it is now. Geologists were more disposed to believe in great catastrophes and sudden breaks. Buckland's theory supposes that previous to the appearance of the present races of animals and vegetables there was a great gap in the globe's history, – that the earth was completely depopulated, as well of marine as land animals; and that the creation of all existing plants and animals was coæval with that of man. This theory is by no means supported by geological phenomena, and is, we suppose, now rejected by all geologists whose authority is valuable. Thus writes Hugh Miller in 1857 –

> I certainly did once believe with Chalmers and with Buckland that the six days were simply natural days of twenty-four hours each – that they had comprised the entire work of the existing creation – and that the latest of the geologic ages was separated by a great chaotic gap from our own. My labours at the time as a practical geologist had been very much restricted to the palæozoic and secondary rocks, more especially to the old red and carboniferous systems of the one division, and the oolitic system of the other; and the long-extinct organisms which I found in them certainly did not conflict with the view of Chalmers. All I found necessary at the time to the work of reconciliation was some scheme that would permit me to assign to the earth a high antiquity, and to regard it as the scene of many succeeding creations. During the last nine years, however, I have spent a few weeks every autumn in exploring the late formations, and acquainting myself with their particular organisms. I have traced them upwards from the raised beaches and old coast lines of the human period, to the brick clays, Clyde beds, and drift and boulder deposits of the Pleistocene era; and again from them, with the help of museums and collections, up through the mammaliferous crag of England to its red and coral crags; and the conclusion at which I have been compelled to arrive is, that for many long ages ere man was ushered into being, not a few of his humbler contemporaries of the fields and woods enjoyed life in their present haunts, and that for thousands of years anterior to even *their* appearance, many of the existing molluscs lived in our seas. That *day* during which the present creation came into being, and in which God, when he had made 'the beast of the earth after his kind, and the cattle after their kind,' at length terminated the work by moulding a creature in His own image, to whom He gave dominion over them all, was not a brief period of a few hours' duration, but extended over, mayhap, millenniums of centuries. No blank chaotic gap of death and darkness separated the creation to which man belongs from that of the old extinct elephant, hippopotamus, and hyæna; for familiar animals, such as the red deer, the roe, the fox, the wild cat, and the badger, lived throughout the period which connected their time with our own; and so I have been compelled to hold that the days of creation were not natural but prophetic days, and stretched far back into the bygone eternity.[1]

Hugh Miller will be admitted by many as a competent witness to the untenability of the theory of Chalmers and Buckland on mere geological grounds. He had, indeed, a theory of his own to propose, which we shall presently consider; but we may take his word that it was not without the compulsion of what he considered irresistible evidence that he relinquished a view which would have saved him infinite time and labour, could he have adhered to it.

[1] *Testimony of the Rocks*, p. 10.

But whether contemplated from a geological point of view, or whether from a philological one, that is, with reference to the value of words, the use of language, and the ordinary rules which govern writers whose object it is to make themselves understood by those to whom their works are immediately addressed, the interpretation proposed by Buckland to be given to the Mosaic description will not bear a moment's serious discussion. It is plain, from the whole tenor of the narrative, that the writer contemplated no such representation as that suggested, nor could any such idea have entered into the minds of those to whom the account was first given. Dr Buckland endeavours to make out that we have here simply a case of leaving out facts which did not particularly concern the writer's purpose, so that he gave an account true so far as it went, though imperfect.

We may fairly ask [he argues] of those persons who consider physical science a fit subject for revelation, what point they can imagine short of a communication of Omniscience at which such a revelation might have stopped without imperfections of omission, less in degree, but similar in kind, to that which they impute to the existing narrative of Moses? A revelation of so much only of astronomy as was known to Copernicus would have seemed imperfect after the discoveries of Newton; and a revelation of the science of Newton would have appeared defective to La Place: a revelation of all the chemical knowledge of the eighteenth century would have been as deficient in comparison with the information of the present day, as what is now known in this science will probably appear before the termination of another age; in the whole circle of sciences there is not one to which this argument may not be extended, until we should require from revelation a full development of all the mysterious agencies that uphold the mechanism of the material world.

Buckland's question is quite inapplicable to the real difficulty, which is, not that circumstantial details are omitted – that might reasonably be expected, – but that what is told, is told so as to convey to ordinary apprehensions an impression at variance with facts. We are indeed told that certain writers of antiquity had already anticipated the hypothesis of the geologist, and two of the Christian fathers, Augustine and Theodoret, are referred to as having actually held that a wide interval elapsed between the first act of creation, mentioned in the Mosaic account, and the commencement of the six days' work.[1] If, however, they arrived at such a conclusion, it was simply because, like the modern geologist, they had theories of their own to support, which led them to make somewhat similar hypotheses.

'After all,' says Buckland, 'it should be recollected that the question is not respecting the correctness of the Mosaic narrative, but of our

[1] See Dr Pusey's note – Buckland's *Bridgewater Treatise*, pp. 24, 25.

interpretation of it,' a proposition which can hardly be sufficiently re-
probated. Such a doctrine, carried out unreservedly, strikes at the root
of critical morality. It may, indeed, be sometimes possible to give two
or three different interpretations to one and the same passage, even
in a modern and familiar tongue, in which case this may arise from the
unskilfulness of the writer or speaker who has failed clearly to express
his thought. In a dead or foreign language the difficulty may arise
from our own want of familiarity with its forms of speech, or in an
ancient book we may be puzzled by allusions and modes of thought
the key to which has been lost. But it is no part of the commentator's
or interpreter's business to introduce obscurity or find difficulties
where none exist, and it cannot be pretended that, taking it as a question
of the use of words to express thoughts, there are any peculiar difficulties
about understanding the first chapter of Genesis, whether in its original
Hebrew or in our common translation, which represents the original
with all necessary exactness. The difficulties arise for the first time,
when we seek to import a meaning into the language which it certainly
never could have conveyed to those to whom it was originally addressed. Unless we go the whole length of supposing the simple
account of the Hebrew cosmogonist to be a series of awkward equivocations, in which he attempted to give a representation widely different
from the facts, yet, without trespassing against literal truth, we can
find no difficulty in interpreting his words. Although language may be,
and often has been, used for the purpose, not of expressing, but con-
cealing thought, no such charge can fairly be laid against the Hebrew
writer.

'It should be borne in mind,' says Dr Buckland, 'that the object of
the account was, not to state *in what manner*, but *by whom* the world
was made.' Every one must see that this is an unfounded assertion
inasmuch as the greater part of the narrative consists in a minute and
orderly description of the manner in which things were made. We
can know nothing as to the *object* of the account, except from the
account itself. What the writer meant to state is just that which he has
stated, for all that we can know to the contrary. Or can we seriously
believe that if appealed to by one of his Hebrew hearers or readers as
to his intention, he would have replied, My only object in what I have
written is to inform you that God made the world; as to the manner of
His doing it, of which I have given so exact an account, I have no
intention that my words should be taken in their literal meaning.

We come then to this, that if we sift the Mosaic narrative of all definite meaning, and only allow it to be the expression of the most vague generalities, if we avow that it admits of no certain interpretation, of none that may not be shifted and altered as often as we see fit, and as the exigencies of geology may require, then may we reconcile it with what science teaches. This mode of dealing with the subject has been broadly advocated by a recent writer of mathematical eminence, who adopts the Bucklandian hypothesis, a passage from whose work we shall quote.[1]

The Mosaic account of the six days' work is thus harmonized by some. On the first day, while the earth was 'without form and void,' the result of a previous convulsion in nature, 'and darkness was upon the face of the deep,' God commanded light to shine upon the earth. This may have been effected by such a clearing of the thick and loaded atmosphere, as to allow the light of the sun to penetrate its mass with a suffused illumination, sufficient to dispel the total darkness which had prevailed, but proceeding from a source not yet apparent on the earth. On the second day a separation took place in the thick vapoury mass which lay upon the earth, dense clouds were gathered up aloft and separated by *an expanse* from the waters and vapours below. On the third day these lower vapours, or fogs and mists which hitherto concealed the earth, were condensed and gathered with the other waters of the earth into seas, and the dry land appeared. Then grass and herbs began to grow. On the fourth day the clouds and vapours so rolled into separate masses, or were so entirely absorbed into the air itself, that the sun shone forth in all its brilliancy, the visible source of light and heat to the renovated earth, while the moon and stars gave light by night, and God appointed them henceforth for signs, and for seasons, and for days, and for years, to his creatures whom he was about to call into existence, as he afterwards set or appointed his bow in the clouds, which had appeared ages before, to be a sign to Noah and his descendants. The fifth and sixth days' work needs no comment.

According to this explanation, the first chapter of Genesis does not pretend (as has been generally assumed) to be a cosmogony, or an account of the original creation of the material universe. The only cosmogony which it contains, in that sense at least, is confined to the sublime declaration of the first verse, 'In the beginning God created the heavens and the earth.' The inspired record thus stepping over an interval of indefinite ages with which man has no direct concern, proceeds at once to narrate the events preparatory to the introduction of man on the scene; employing phraseology strictly faithful to the *appearances* which would have met the eye of man, could he have been a spectator on the earth of what passed during those six days. All this has been commonly supposed to be a more detailed account of the general truth announced in the first verse, in short, a cosmogony; such was the idea of Josephus; such probably was the idea of our translators; for their version, without form and void, points to the primæval chaos, out of which all things

---

[1] *Scripture and Science not at Variance.* By J. H. Pratt, M.A., Archdeacon of Calcutta, 1859. Third edition, p. 24.

were then supposed to emerge; and these words standing *in limine*, have tended, perhaps more than anything else, to foster the idea of a cosmogony in the minds of general readers to this very day.

The foregoing explanation many have now adopted. It is sufficient for my purpose, if it be a possible explanation, and if it meet the difficulties of the case. That it is possible in itself, is plain from the fact above established, that the Scriptures wisely speak on natural things according to their *appearances* rather than their *physical realities*. It meets the difficulties of the case, because all the difficulties hitherto started against this chapter on scientific grounds proceeded on the principle that it is a cosmogony; which this explanation repudiates, and thus disposes of the difficulties. It is therefore an explanation satisfactory to my own mind. I may be tempted to regret that I can gain no certain scientific information from Genesis regarding the process of the original creation; but I resist the temptation, remembering the great object for which the Scripture was given – to tell man of his origin and fall, and to draw his mind to his Creator and Redeemer. Scripture was not designed to teach us natural philosophy, and it is vain to attempt to make a cosmogony out of its statements. The Almighty declares himself the originator of all things but he condescends not to describe the process or the laws by which he worked. All this he leaves for reason to decipher from the phenomena which his world displays.

This explanation, however, I do not wish to impose on Scripture; and am fully prepared to surrender it, should further scientific discovery suggest another better fitted to meet all the requirements of the case.

We venture to think that the world at large will continue to consider the account in the first chapter of Genesis to be a cosmogony. But as it is here admitted that it does not describe physical realities, but only outward appearances, that is, gives a description false in fact, and one which can teach us no scientific truth whatever, it seems to matter little what we call it. If its description of the events of the six days which it comprises be merely one of appearances and not of realities, it can teach us nothing regarding them.

Dissatisfied with the scheme of conciliation which has been discussed, other geologists have proposed to give an entirely mythical or enigmatical sense to the Mosaic narrative, and to consider the creative days described as vast periods of time. This plan was long ago suggested, but it has of late enjoyed a high degree of popularity, through the advocacy of the Scotch geologist Hugh Miller, an extract from whose work has been already quoted. Dr Buckland gives the following account of the first form in which this theory was propounded, and of the grounds upon which he rejected it in favour of that of Chalmers:[1]

A third opinion has been suggested both by learned theologians and by

---

[1] *Bridgewater Treatise*, p. 17.

geologists, and on grounds independent of one another – viz., that the days of the Mosaic creation need not be understood to imply the same length of time which is now occupied by a single revolution of the globe, but successive periods each of great extent; and it has been asserted that the order of succession of the organic remains of a former world accords with the order of creation recorded in Genesis. This assertion, though to a certain degree apparently correct, is not entirely supported by geological facts, since it appears that the most ancient marine animals occur in the same division of the lowest transition strata with the earliest remains of vegetables, so that the evidence of organic remains, as far as it goes, shows the origin of plants and animals to have been contemporaneous: if any creation of vegetables preceded that of animals, no evidence of such an event has yet been discovered by the researches of geology. Still there is, I believe, no sound critical or theological objection to the interpretation of the word 'day' as meaning a long period.

Archdeacon Pratt also summarily rejects this view as untenable:[1]

There is one other class of interpreters, however, with whom I find it impossible to agree – I mean those who take the six days to be six periods of unknown indefinite length. This is the principle of interpretation in a work on the *Creation and the Fall*, by the Rev. D. Macdonald; also in Mr Hugh Miller's posthumous work, the *Testimony of the Rocks*, and also in an admirable treatise on the *Præ-Adamite Earth* in Dr Lardner's *Museum of Science*. In this last it is the more surprising because the successive chapters are in fact an accumulation of evidence which points the other way, as a writer in the *Christian Observer*, Jan. 1858, has conclusively shown. The late M. D'Orbigny has demonstrated in his *Prodrome de Palæontologie*, after an elaborate examination of vast multitudes of fossils, that there have been at least twenty-nine distinct periods of animal and vegetable existence – that is, twenty-nine creations separated one from another by catastrophes which have swept away the species existing at the time, with a very few solitary exceptions, never exceeding one and a-half per cent. of the whole number discovered which have either survived the catastrophe, or have been erroneously designated. But not a single species of the preceding period survived the last of these catastrophes, and this closed the Tertiary period and ushered in the Human period. The evidence adduced by M. D'Orbigny shows that both plants and animals appeared in every one of those twenty-nine periods. The notion, therefore, that the 'days' of Genesis represent periods of creation from the beginning of things is at once refuted. The parallel is destroyed both in the number of the periods (thirty, including the Azoic, instead of six), and also in the character of the things created. No argument could be more complete; and yet the writer of the *Præ-Adamite Earth*, in the last two pages, sums up his lucid sketch of M. D'Orbigny's researches by referring the account in the first chapter of Genesis to the whole creation from the beginning of all things, a *selection* of epochs being made, as he imagines, for the six days or periods.

In this trenchant manner do theological geologists overthrow one another's theories. However, Hugh Miller was perfectly aware of the

[1] *Science and Scripture not at Variance*, p. 40, note.

difficulty involved in his view of the question, and we shall endeavour to show the reader the manner in which he deals with it.

He begins by pointing out that the families of vegetables and animals were introduced upon earth as nearly as possible according to the great classes in which naturalists have arranged the modern flora and fauna. According to the arrangement of Lindley, he observes –

Commencing at the bottom of the scale we find the thallogens, or flowerless plants, which lack proper stems and leaves – a class which includes all the algæ. Next succeed the acrogens, or flowerless plants that possess both stems and leaves – such as the ferns and their allies. Next, omitting an inconspicuous class, represented by but a few parasitical plants incapable of preservation as fossils, come the endogens – monocotyledonous flowering plants, that include the palms, the liliaceæ, and several other families, all characterized by the parallel venation of their leaves. Next, omitting another inconspicuous tribe, there follows a very important class, the gymnogens – polycotyledonous trees, represented by the coniferæ and cycadaceæ. And last of all come the dicotyledonous exogens – a class to which all our fruit and what are known as our forest trees belong, with a vastly preponderating majority of the herbs and flowers that impart fertility and beauty to our gardens and meadows.

The order in which fossils of these several classes appear in the strata, Hugh Miller states to be as follows: In the Lower Silurian we find only thallogens, in the Upper Silurian acrogens are added. The gymnogens appear rather prematurely, it might be thought, in the old red sandstone, the endogens (monocotyledonous) coming after them in the carboniferous group. Dicotyledonous exogens enter at the close of the oolitic period, and come to their greatest development in the tertiary. Again, the animal tribes have been introduced in an order closely agreeing with the geological divisions established by Cuvier, in the Silurian beds the invertebrate creatures, the radiata, articulata, and mollusca, appear simultaneously. At the close of the period, fishes, the lowest of the vertebrata, appear: before the old red sandstone period had passed away, reptiles had come into existence; birds, and the marsupial mammals, enter in the oolitic period; placental mammals in the tertiary; and man last of all.

Now, these facts do certainly tally to some extent with the Mosaic account, which represents fish and fowl as having been produced from the waters on the fifth day, reptiles and mammals from the earth on the sixth, and man as made last of all. The agreement, however, is far from exact, as according to geological evidence, reptiles would appear to have existed ages before birds and mammals, whereas here the creation of birds is attributed to the fifth day, that of reptiles to the sixth. There remains, moreover, the insuperable difficulty of the plants and trees being represented as made on the third day – that is, more than an age before fishes and birds; which is clearly not the case.

Although, therefore, there is a superficial resemblance in the Mosaic account to that of the geologists, it is evident that the bare theory that a 'day' means an age or immense geological period might be made to yield some rather strange results. What becomes of the evening and morning of which each day is said to have consisted? Was each geologic age divided into two long intervals, one all darkness, the other all light? and if so, what became of the plants and trees created in the third day or period, when the evening of the fourth day (the evenings, be it observed, precede the mornings) set in? They must have passed through half a seculum of total darkness, not even cheered by that dim light which the sun, not yet completely manifested, supplied on the morning of the third day. Such an ordeal would have completely destroyed the whole vegetable creation, and yet we find that it survived, and was appointed on the sixth day as the food of man and animals. In fact, we need only substitute the word 'period' for 'day' in the Mosaic narrative to make it very apparent that the writer at least had no such meaning, nor could he have conveyed any such meaning to those who first heard his account read.

'It has been held,' says Hugh Miller, 'by accomplished philologists, that the days of Mosaic creation may be regarded without doing violence to the Hebrew language, as successive periods of great extent.'[1] We do not believe that there is any ground for this doctrine. The word 'day' is certainly used occasionally in particular phrases, in an indefinite manner, not only in Hebrew, but other languages. As for instance, Gen. xxxix. 11 – 'About this time,' Heb. literally, 'about this day.' But every such phrase explains itself, and not only philology but common sense disclaims the notion, that when 'day' is spoken of in terms like those in the first chapter of Genesis, and described as consisting of an evening and a morning, it can be understood to mean a seculum.

Archdeacon Pratt, treating on the same subject, says (p. 41, note),

Were there no other ground of objection to this mode of interpretation, I think the wording of the fourth commandment is clearly opposed to it. Ex. xx. 8. 'Remember the Sabbath day to keep it holy. 9. Six days shalt thou labour and do all thy work. 10. But the seventh day is the Sabbath of the Lord thy God. In it, thou shalt not do any work, thou, nor thy son, nor thy daughter, thy manservant, nor thy maidservant, nor thy cattle, nor thy stranger

[1] *Testimony*, p. 133.

that is within thy gates. 11. For in six days the Lord made heaven and earth, the sea and all that in them is, and rested the seventh day; wherefore the Lord blessed the Sabbath day and hallowed it.

Is it not a harsh and forced interpretation to suppose that the six days in v. 9 do not mean the same as the six days in v. 11, but that in this last place they mean six periods? In reading through the eleventh verse, it is extremely difficult to believe that the seventh day is a long period, and the sabbath day an ordinary day, that is, that the same word day should be used in two such totally different senses in the same short sentence and without any explanation.

Hugh Miller saw the difficulty; but he endeavours to escape the consequences of a rigorous application of the periodic theory by modifying it in a peculiar, and certainly ingenious manner.

Waiving [he says] the question as a philological one, and simply holding with Cuvier, Parkinson, and Silliman, that each of the *six* days of the Mosaic account in the first chapter were what is assuredly meant by the *day*[1] referred to in the second, not natural days but lengthened periods, I find myself called on, as a geologist, to account for but three out of the six. Of the period during which light was created, of the period during which a firmament was made to separate the waters from the waters, or of the period during which the two great lights of the earth, with the other heavenly bodies, became visible from the earth's surface – we need expect to find no record in the rocks. Let me, however, pause for a moment, to remark the peculiar character of the language in which we are first introduced in the Mosaic narrative to the heavenly bodies – sun, moon, and stars. The moon, though absolutely one of the smallest lights of our system, is described as secondary and subordinate to only its greatest light, the sun. It is the apparent, then, not the actual, which we find in the passage – what *seemed* to be, not what *was*; and as it was merely what appeared to be greatest that was described as greatest, on what grounds are we to hold that it may not also have been what *appeared* at the time to be made that has been described as made? The sun, moon, and stars, may have been created long before, though it was not until this fourth day of creation that they became visible from the earth's surface.[2]

The theory founded upon this hint is that the Hebrew writer did not state facts, but merely certain appearances, and those not of things which really happened, as assumed in the explanation adopted by

[1] The expression, Gen. ii. 4, 'In the day that the Lord God created the earth and heaven,' to which Hugh Miller here refers, may possibly mean 'at the time when,' meaning a week, year, or other limited time. But there is not the smallest reason for understanding it to mean 'a *lengthened* period,' *i.e.*, an immense lapse of time. Such a construction would be inadmissible to the Hebrew, or any other language. It is difficult to acquit Hugh Miller of an equivocation here. In real truth, the second narrative is, as we have before observed, of distinct origin from the first, and we incline to the belief that, in this case also, 'day' is to be taken in its proper signification.

[2] *Testimony*, p. 134.

Archdeacon Pratt, but of certain occurrences which were presented to him in a vision, and that this vision greatly deceived him as to what he seemed to see; and thus, in effect, the real discrepancy of the narrative with facts is admitted. He had in all, seven visions, to each of which he attributed the duration of a day, although indeed each picture presented to him the earth during seven long and distinctly marked epochs. While on the one hand this supposition admits all desirable latitude for mistakes and misrepresentations, Hugh Miller, on the other hand, endeavours to show that a substantial agreement with the truth exists, and to give sufficient reason for the mistakes. We must let him speak for himself.

The geologist, in his attempts to collate the Divine with the geologic record, has, I repeat, only three of the six periods of creation to account for[1] – the period of plants, the period of great sea-monsters and creeping things, and the period of cattle and beasts of the earth. He is called on to question his systems and formations regarding the remains of these three great periods, and of them only. And the question once fairly stated, what, I ask, is the reply? All geologists agree in holding that the vast geological scale naturally divides into three great parts. There are many lesser divisions – divisions into systems, formations, deposits, beds, strata; but the master divisions, in each of which we find a type of life so unlike that of the others, that even the unpractised eye can detect the difference, are simply three: the palæozoic, or oldest fossiliferous division; the secondary, or middle fossiliferous division; and the tertiary, or latest fossiliferous division. In the first, or palæozoic division, we find corals, crustaceans, molluscs, fishes; and in its later formations, a few reptiles. But none of these classes give its leading character to the palæozoic; they do not constitute its prominent feature, or render it more remarkable as a scene of life than any of the divisions which followed. That which chiefly distinguished the palæozoic from the secondary and tertiary periods was its gorgeous flora. It was emphatically the period of plants – 'of herbs yielding seed after their kind.' In no other age did the world ever witness such a flora; the youth of the earth was peculiarly a green and umbrageous youth – a youth of dusk and tangled forests, of huge pines and stately araucarians, of the reed-like calamite, the tall tree-fern, the sculptured sigillaria, and the hirsute lepidodendrons. Wherever dry land, or shallow lakes, or running stream appeared, from where Melville Island now spreads out its icy coast under the star of the pole, to where the arid plains of Australia lie solitary beneath the bright cross of the south, a rank and luxuriant herbage cumbered every foot-breadth of the dank and steaming soil; and even to distant planets our earth must have shone through the developing cloud

---

[1] A very inadmissible assertion. Any one, be he geologist, astronomer, theologian, or philologist, who attempts to explain the Hebrew narrative, is bound to take it with all that really belongs to it. And in truth, if the fourth day really represented an epoch of creative activity, geology would be able to give some account of it. There is no reason to suppose that any intermission has taken place.

with a green and delicate ray. . . . The geologic evidence is so complete as to be patent to all, that the first great period of organized being was, as described in the Mosaic record, peculiarly a period of herbs and trees 'yielding seed after their kind.'

The middle great period of the geologist – that of the secondary division – possessed, like the earlier one, its herbs and plants, but they were of a greatly less luxuriant and conspicuous character than their predecessors, and no longer formed the prominent trait or feature of the creation to which they belonged. The period had also its corals, its crustaceans, its molluscs, its fishes, and in some one or two exceptional instances, its dwarf mammals. But the grand existences of the age – the existences in which it excelled every other creation, earlier or later – were its huge creeping things – its enormous monsters of the deep, and, as shown by the impressions of their footprints stamped upon the rocks, its gigantic birds. It was peculiarly the age of egg-bearing animals, winged and wingless. Its wonderful *whales*, not however, as now, of the mammalian, but of the reptilian class, – ichthyosaurs, plesiosaurs, and cetosaurs, must have tempested the deep; its creeping lizards and crocodiles, such as the teliosaurus, megalosaurus, and iguanodon – creatures, some of which more than rivalled the existing elephant in height, and greatly more than rivalled him in bulk – must have crowded the plains, or haunted by myriads the rivers of the period; and we know that the foot-prints of at least one of its many birds are of fully twice the size of those made by the horse or camel. We are thus prepared to demonstrate, that the second period of the geologist was peculiarly and characteristically a period of whale-like reptiles of the sea, of enormous creeping reptiles of the land, and of numerous birds, some of them of gigantic size; and in meet accordance with the fact, we find that the second Mosaic period with which the geologist is called on to deal, was a period in which God created the fowl that flieth above the earth, with moving (or creeping) creatures, both in the waters and on land, and what our translation renders great whales, but that I find rendered in the margin great sea-monsters. The tertiary period had also its prominent class of existences. Its flora seems to have been no more conspicuous than that of the present time; its reptiles occupy a very subordinate place; but its beasts of the field were by far the most wonderfully developed, both in size and numbers, that ever appeared on earth. Its mammoths and its mastodons, its rhinoceri and its hippopotami, its enormous dinotherium, and colossal megatherium, greatly more than equalled in bulk the hugest mammals of the present time, and vastly exceeded them in number.* * * 'Grand, indeed,' says an English naturalist, 'was the fauna of the British Islands in these early days. Tigers as large again as the biggest Asiatic species lurked in the ancient thickets; elephants of nearly twice the bulk of the largest individuals that now exist in Africa or Ceylon roamed in herds; at least two species of rhinoceros forced their way through the primæval forest; and the lakes and rivers were tenanted by hippopotami as bulky and with as great tusks as those of Africa.' The massive cave-bear and large cave-hyæna belonged to the same formidable group, with at least two species of great oxen (*Bos longifrons* and *Bos primigenius*), with a horse of smaller size, and an elk (*Megaceros Hibernicus*) that stood ten feet four inches in height. Truly, this Tertiary age – this third and last of the great geologic periods –

was peculiarly the age of great 'beasts of the earth after their kind, and cattle after their kind.'

Thus by dropping the invertebrata, and the early fishes and reptiles of the Palæozoic period as inconspicuous and of little account, and bringing prominently forward the carboniferous era which succeeded them as the most characteristic feature of the first great division, by classing the great land reptiles of the secondary period with the moving creatures of the waters (for in the Mosaic account it does not appear that any inhabitants of the land were created on the fifth day), and evading the fact that terrestrial reptiles seem to have preceded birds in their order of appearance upon earth, the geologic divisions are tolerably well assimilated to the third, fifth, and sixth Mosaic days. These things were represented, we are told, to Moses in visionary pictures, and resulted in the short and summary account which he has given.

There is something in this hypothesis very near to the obvious truth, while at the same time something very remote from that truth is meant to be inferred. If it be said the Mosaic account is simply the speculation of some early Copernicus or Newton who devised a scheme of the earth's formation, as nearly as he might in accordance with his own observations of nature, and with such views of things as it was possible for an unassisted thinker in those days to take, we may admire the approximate correctness of the picture drawn, while we see that the writer, as might be expected, took everything from a different point of view from ourselves, and consequently represented much quite differently from the fact. But nothing of this sort is really intended. We are asked to believe that a vision of creation was presented to him by Divine power, for the purpose of enabling him to inform the world of what he had seen, which vision inevitably led him to give a description which has misled the world for centuries, and in which the truth can now only with difficulty be recognised. The Hebrew writer informs us that on the third day 'the earth brought forth grass, the herb yielding seed after his kind, and the tree yielding fruit, whose seed was in itself, after his kind:' and in the 29th verse, that God on the sixth day said, 'Behold, I have given you every herb bearing seed, which is upon the face of all the earth, and every tree in the which is the fruit of a tree yielding seed, to you it shall be for meat. And to every beast of the earth, and to every fowl of the air, and to everything that creepeth upon the earth, wherein there is life, I have given every green herb for meat.' Can it be disputed that the writer here conceives that grass, corn, and fruit, were created on the third day, and with a view to the future nourishment of man and beast? Yet, according to the vision hypothesis, he must have been greatly deceived; for that luxuriant vegetation which he saw on the third day, consisted not of plants destined for the food of man, but for his fuel. It was the flora of the carboniferous period which he beheld, concerning which Hugh Miller makes the following remark, p. 24:

The existing plants whence we derive our analogies in dealing with the vegetation of this early period, contribute but little, if at all, to the support of animal life. The ferns and their allies remain untouched by the grazing animals. Our native club-mosses, though once used in medicine, are positively deleterious; the horsetails, though harmless, so abound in silex, which wraps them round with a cuticle of stone, that they are rarely cropped by cattle; while the thickets of fern which cover our hill-sides, and seem so temptingly rich and green in their season, scarce support the existence of a single creature, and remain untouched in stem and leaf from their first appearance in spring, until they droop and wither under the frosts of early winter. Even the insects that infest the herbaria of the botanist almost never injure his ferns. Nor are our resin-producing conifers, though they nourish a few beetles, favourites with the herbivorous tribes in a much greater degree. Judging from all we yet know, the earliest terrestrial flora may have covered the dry land with its mantle of cheerful green, and served its general purposes, chemical and others, in the well-balanced economy of nature; but the herb-eating animals would have fared but ill, even where it throve most luxuriantly; and it seems to harmonize with the fact of its unedible character that up to the present time we know not that a single herbivorous animal lived amongst its shades.

The Mosaic writer is, however, according to the theory, misled by the mere appearance of luxuriant vegetation, to describe fruit trees and edible seed-bearing vegetables as products of the third day.

Hugh Miller's treatment of the description of the first dawn of light is not more satisfactory than that of Dr Buckland. He supposes the prophet in his dream to have heard the command 'Let there be light' enunciated, whereupon

straightway a grey diffused light springs up in the east, and casting its *sickly gleam* over a cloud-limited expanse of steaming vaporous sea, journeys through the heavens towards the west. One heavy, sunless day is made the representative of myriads; the faint light waxes fainter, – it sinks beneath the dim, undefined horizon.

We are then asked to imagine that a second and a third day, each representing the characteristic features of a great distinctly-marked epoch, and the latter of them marked by the appearance of a rich and luxuriant vegetation, are presented to the seer's eye; but without sun, moon, or stars as yet entering into his dream. These appear first in his fourth vision, and then for the first time we have 'a brilliant day,' and the seer, struck with the novelty, describes the heavenly bodies as being the most conspicuous objects in the picture. In reality we know that he represents them (v. 16) as having been *made* and *set* in the heavens on that day, though Hugh Miller avoids reminding us of this.

In one respect the theory of Hugh Miller agrees with that advocated by Dr Buckland and Archdeacon Pratt. Both these theories divest the Mosaic narrative of real accordance with fact; both assume that appearances only, not facts, are described, and that in riddles, which would never have been suspected to be such, had we not arrived at the truth from other sources. It would be difficult for controversialists to cede more completely the point in dispute, or to admit more explicitly that the Mosaic narrative does not represent correctly the history of the universe up to the time of man. At the same time, the upholders of each theory see insuperable objections in details to that of their allies, and do not pretend to any firm faith in their own. How can it be otherwise when the task proposed is to evade the plain meaning of language, and to introduce obscurity into one of the simplest stories ever told, for the sake of making it accord with the complex system of the universe which modern science has unfolded? The spectacle of able and, we doubt not, conscientious writers engaged in attempting the impossible is painful and humiliating. They evidently do not breathe freely over their work, but shuffle and stumble over their difficulties in a piteous manner; nor are they themselves again until they return to the pure and open fields of science.

It is refreshing to return to the often-echoed remark, that it could not have been the object of a Divine revelation to instruct mankind in physical science, man having had faculties bestowed upon him to enable him to acquire this knowledge by himself. This is in fact pretty generally admitted; but in the application of the doctrine, writers play at fast and loose with it according to circumstances. Thus an inspired writer may be permitted to allude to the phenomena of nature according to the vulgar view of such things, without impeachment of his better knowledge; but if he speaks of the same phenomena assertively, we are bound to suppose that things are as he represents them, however much our knowledge of nature may be disposed to recalcitrate. But if we find a difficulty in admitting that such misrepresentations can find a place in revelation, the difficulty lies in our having previously assumed what a Divine revelation ought to be. If God made use of imperfectly informed men to lay the foundations of that higher knowledge for which the human race was destined, is it wonderful that they should have committed themselves to assertions not in accordance with facts, although they may have believed them to be true? On what grounds has the popular notion of Divine revelation been built up? Is it not plain that the plan of Providence for the education of man is a progressive one, and as imperfect men have been used as the agents for teaching mankind, is it not to be expected that their teachings should be partial and, to some extent, erroneous? Admitted, as it is, that physical science is not what the Hebrew writers, for the most part, profess to convey, at any rate, that it is not on account of the communication of such knowledge that we attach any value to their writings, why should we hesitate to recognise their fallibility on this head?

Admitting, as is historically and in fact the case, that it was the mission of the Hebrew race to lay the foundation of religion upon the earth, and that Providence used this people specially for this purpose, is it not our business and our duty to look and see how this has really been done? not forming for ourselves theories of what a revelation ought to be, or how we, if entrusted with the task, would have made one, but enquiring how it has pleased God to do it. In all his theories of the world, man has at first deviated widely from the truth, and has only gradually come to see how far otherwise God has ordered things than the first daring speculator had supposed. It has been popularly assumed that the Bible, bearing the stamp of Divine authority, must be complete, perfect, and unimpeachable in all its parts, and a thousand difficulties and incoherent doctrines have sprung out of this theory. Men have proceeded in the matter of theology, as they did with physical science before inductive philosophy sent them to the feet of nature, and bid them learn in patience and obedience the lessons which she had to teach. Dogma and groundless assumption occupy the place of modest enquiry after truth, while at the same time the upholders of these theories claim credit for humility and submissiveness. This is exactly inverting the fact; the humble scholar of truth is not he who, taking his stand upon the traditions of rabbins, Christian fathers, or school-men, insists upon bending facts to his unyielding standard, but he who is willing to accept such teaching as it has pleased Divine Providence to afford, without murmuring that it has not been furnished more copiously or clearly.

The Hebrew race, their works, and their books, are great facts in the history of man; the influence of the mind of this people upon the rest of mankind has been immense and peculiar, and there can be no difficulty in recognising therein the hand of a directing Providence. But we may not make ourselves wiser than God, nor attribute to Him methods of procedure which are not His. If, then, it is plain that He has not thought it needful to communicate to the writer of the Cosmogony that knowledge which modern researches have revealed, why do we not acknowledge this, except that it conflicts with a human theory which presumes to point out how God ought to have instructed man? The treatment to which the Mosaic narrative is subjected by the theological geologists is anything but respectful. The writers of this school, as we have seen, agree in representing it as a series of elaborate equivocations – a story which 'palters with us in a double sense.' But if we regard it as the speculation of some Hebrew Descartes or Newton, promulgated in all good faith as the best and most probable account that could be then given of God's universe, it resumes the dignity and value of which the writers in question have done their utmost to deprive it. It has been sometimes felt as a difficulty to taking this view of the case, that the writer asserts so solemnly and unhesitatingly that for which he must have known that he had no authority. But this arises only from our modern habits of thought, and from the modesty of assertion which the spirit of true science has taught us. Mankind has learnt caution through repeated slips in the process of tracing out the truth.

The early speculator was harassed by no such scruples, and asserted as facts what he knew in reality only as probabilities. But we are not on that account to doubt his perfect good faith, nor need we attribute to him wilful misrepresentation, or consciousness of asserting that which he knew not to be true. He had seized one great truth, in which, indeed, he anticipated the highest revelation of modern enquiry – namely, the unity of the design of the world, and its subordination to one sole Maker and Lawgiver. With regard to details, observation failed him. He knew little of the earth's surface, or of its shape and place in the universe; the infinite varieties of organized existences which people it, the distinct floras and faunas of its different continents, were unknown to him. But he saw that all which lay within his observation had been formed for the benefit and service of man, and the goodness of the Creator to his creatures was the thought predominant in his mind. Man's closer relation to his Maker is indicated by the representation that he was formed last of all creatures, and in the visible likeness of God. For ages, this simple view of creation satisfied the wants of man, and formed a sufficient basis of theological teaching, and if modern research now shows it to be physically untenable, our respect for the narrative which has played so important a part in the culture of our race need be in nowise diminished. No one contends that it can be used as a basis of astronomical or geological teaching, and those who profess to see in it an accordance with facts, only do this *sub modo*, and by processes which despoil it of its consistency and grandeur, both which may be preserved if we recognise in it, not an authentic utterance of Divine knowledge, but a human utterance, which it has pleased Providence to use in a special way for the education of mankind.

BUNSEN'S BIBLICAL RESEARCHES

WHEN geologists began to ask whether changes in the earth's structure might be explained by causes still in operation, they did not disprove the possibility of great convulsions, but they lessened the necessity for imagining them. So, if a theologian has his eyes opened to the Divine energy as continuous and omnipresent, he lessens the sharp contrast of epochs in Revelation, but need not assume that the stream has never varied in its flow. Devotion raises time present into the sacredness of the past; while Criticism reduces the strangeness of the past into harmony with the present. Faith and Prayer (and great marvels answering to them) do not pass away: but, in prolonging their range as a whole, we make their parts less exceptional. We hardly discern the truth, for which they are anxious, until we distinguish it from associations accidental to their domain. The truth itself may have been apprehended in various degrees by servants of God, of old, as now. Instead of, with Tertullian, *what was first is truest,* we may say, what comes of God is true, and He is not only afar, but nigh at hand; though His mind is not changed.

Questions of miraculous interference do not turn merely upon our conceptions of physical law, as unbroken, or of the Divine Will, as all-pervading: but they include inquiries into evidence, and must abide by verdicts on the age of records. Nor should the distinction between poetry and prose, and the possibility of imagination's allying itself with affection, be overlooked. We cannot encourage a remorseless criticism of Gentile histories and escape its contagion when we approach Hebrew annals; nor acknowledge a Providence in Jewry without owning that it may have comprehended sanctities elsewhere. But the moment we examine fairly the religions of India and of Arabia, or even those of primæval Hellas and Latium, we find they appealed to the better side of our nature, and their essential strength lay in the elements of good which they contained, rather than in any satanic corruption.

Thus considerations, religious and moral, no less than scientific and critical, have, where discussion was free, widened the idea of Revelation for the old world, and deepened it for ourselves; not removing the footsteps of the Eternal from Palestine, but tracing them on other shores; and not making the saints of old orphans, but ourselves partakers of their sonship. Conscience would not lose by exchanging that repressive idea of revelation, which is put over against it as an adversary, for one to which the echo of its best instincts should be the witness. The moral constituents of our nature, so often contrasted with Revelation, should rather be considered parts of its instrumentality. Those cases in which we accept the miracle for the sake of the moral lesson prove the ethical element to be the more fundamental. We see this more clearly if we imagine a miracle of cruelty wrought (as by Antichrist) for immoral ends; for then only the technically miraculous has its value isolated; whereas by appealing to *good* 'WORKS' (however wonderful) for his witness, Christ has taught us to have faith mainly in goodness. This is too much overlooked by some apologists. But there is hardly any greater question than whether history shows Almighty God to have trained mankind by a faith which has reason and conscience for its kindred, or by one to whose miraculous tests their pride must bow; that is, whether His Holy Spirit has acted through the channels which His Providence ordained, or whether it has departed from these so signally that comparative mistrust of them ever afterwards becomes a duty. The first alternative, though invidiously termed philosophical, so that to which free nations and Evangelical thinkers tend; the second has a greater show of religion, but allies itself naturally with priestcraft or formalism; and not rarely with corruptness of administration or of life.

In this issue converge many questions anciently stirred, but recurring in our daylight with almost uniform[1] accession of strength to the

---

[1] It is very remarkable that, amidst all our Biblical illustration from recent travellers, Layard, Rawlinson, Robinson, Stanley, &c., no single point has been discovered to tell in favour of an irrational supernaturalism; whereas numerous discoveries have confirmed the more liberal (not to say, rationalizing) criticism which traces Revelation historically within the sphere of nature and humanity. Such is the moral, both of the Assyrian discoveries, and of all travels in the East, as well as the verdict of philologers at home. Mr G. Rawlinson's proof of this is stronger, because undesigned.

liberal side. Such questions turn chiefly on the law of growth, traceable throughout the Bible, as in the world; and partly on science, or historical inquiry: but no less on the deeper revelations of the New Testament, as compared to those of the Old. If we are to retain the old Anglican foundations of research and fair statement, we must revise some of the decisions provisionally given upon imperfect evidence; or, if we shrink from doing so, we must abdicate our ancient claim to build upon the truth; and our retreat will be either to Rome, as some of our lost ones have consistently seen, or to some form, equally evil, of darkness voluntary. The attitude of too many English scholars before the last Monster out of the Deep is that of the degenerate senators before Tiberius. They stand, balancing terror against mutual shame. Even with those in our universities who no longer repeat fully the required Shibboleths, the explicitness of truth is rare. He who assents most, committing himself least to baseness, is reckoned wisest.

Bunsen's enduring glory is neither to have paltered with his conscience nor shrunk from the difficulties of the problem; but to have brought a vast erudition, in the light of a Christian conscience, to unroll tangled records, tracing frankly the Spirit of God elsewhere, but honouring chiefly the traditions of His Hebrew sanctuary. No living author's works could furnish so pregnant a text for a discourse on Biblical criticism. Passing over some specialities of Lutheranism, we may meet in the field of research which is common to scholars; while even here, the sympathy, which justifies respectful exposition, need not imply entire agreement.

In the great work upon Egypt,[1] the later volumes of which are now appearing in English, we do not find that picture of home life which meets us in the pages of our countryman, Sir G. Wilkinson. The interest for robust scholars is not less, in the fruitful comparison of the oldest traditions of our race, and in the giant shapes of ancient empires, which flit like dim shadows, evoked by a master's hand. But for those who seek chiefly results, there is something wearisome in the elaborate discussion of authorities; and, it must be confessed, the German refinement of method has all the effect of confusion. To give details here is impossible (though the more any one scrutinizes them, the more substantial he will find them), and this sketch must combine suggestions, which the author has scattered strangely apart, and sometimes repeated

---

[1] *Egypt's Place in Universal History,* by Christian C. J. Bunsen, &c. London. 1848, vol. i. 1854, vol. ii.

without perfect consistency. He dwells largely upon Herodotus, Eratosthenes, and their successors, from Champollion and Young to Lepsius. Especially the dynastic records of the Ptolemaic priest, Manetho,[1] are compared with the accounts of the stone monuments. The result, if we can receive it, is to vindicate for the civilized kingdom of Egypt, from Menes downward, an antiquity of nearly four thousand years before Christ. There is no point in which archæologists of all shades were so nearly unanimous as in the belief that our Biblical chronology was too narrow in its limits; and the enlargement of our views, deduced from Egyptian records, is extended by our author's reasonings on the development of commerce and government, and still more of languages, and physical features of race. He could not have vindicated the unity of mankind if he had not asked for a vast extension of time, whether his petition of twenty thousand years be granted or not. The mention of such a term may appear monstrous to those who regard six thousand years as a part of Revelation. Yet it is easier to throw doubt on some of the arguments than to show that the conclusion in favour of a vast length is improbable. If pottery in a river's mud proves little, its tendency may agree with that of the discovery of very ancient pre-historic remains in many parts of the world. Again, how many years are needed to develope modern French out of Latin, and Latin itself out of its original crude forms? How unlike is English to Welsh, and Greek to Sanskrit – yet all indubitably of one family of languages! What years were required to create the existing divergence of members of this family! How many more for other families, separated by a wide gulf from this, yet retaining traces of a primæval aboriginal affinity, to have developed themselves, either in priority or collaterally! The same consonantal roots, appearing either as verbs inflected with great variety of grammatical form, or as nouns with case-endings in some languages, and with none in others, plead as convincingly as the succession of strata in geology, for enormous lapses of time. When, again, we have traced our Gaelic and our Sanskrit to their inferential pre-Hellenic stem, and when reason has convinced

---

[1] See an account of him, and his tables, in the Byzantine Syncellus, pp. 72–145, vol. i, ed. Dind., in the *Corpus Historiæ Byzantinæ*, Bonn. 1829. But with this is to be compared the Armenian version of Eusebius's Chronology, discovered by Cardinal Mai. The text, the interpretation, and the historical fidelity, are all controverted. Baron Bunsen's treatment of them deserves the provisional acceptance due to elaborate research, with no slight concurrence of probabilities; and if it should not ultimately win a favourable verdict from Egyptologers, no one who summarily rejects it as arbitrary or impossible can have a right to be on the iury.

us that the Semitic languages which had as distinct an individuality four thousand years ago as they have now, require a cradle of larger dimensions than Archbishop Ussher's chronology, what farther effort is not forced upon our imagination, if we would guess the measure of the dim background in which the Mongolian and Egyptian languages, older probably than the Hebrew, became fixed, growing early into the type which they retain? Do we see an historical area of nations and languages extending itself over nearly ten thousand years: and can we imagine less than another ten thousand, during which the possibilities of these things took body and form? Questions of this kind require from most of us a special training for each: but Baron Bunsen revels in them, and his theories are at least suggestive. He shows what Egypt had in common with that primæval Asiatic stock, represented by Ham, out of which, as raw material, he conceives the divergent families, termed Indo-European[1] and Semitic (or the kindreds of Europe and of Palestine), to have been later developed. Nimrod is considered as the Biblical representative of the earlier stock, whose ruder language is continued, by affiliation or by analogy, in the Mongolian races of Asia and in the negroes of Africa.

The traditions of Babylon, Sidon, Assyria, and Iran, are brought by our author to illustrate and confirm, though to modify our interpretation of, Genesis. It is strange how nearly those ancient cosmogonies[2] approach what may be termed the philosophy of Moses, while they fall short in what Longinus called his 'worthy conception of the divinity.' Our deluge takes its place among geological phenomena, no longer a disturbance of law from which science shrinks, but a prolonged play of the forces of fire and water, rendering the primæval regions of North Asia uninhabitable, and urging the nations to new abodes. We learn approximately its antiquity, and infer limitation in its range, from finding it recorded in the traditions of Iran and Palestine (or of Japhet and Shem), but unknown to the Egyptians and Mongolians, who left earlier the cradle of mankind. In the half ideal half traditional notices[3] of the beginnings of our race, compiled in Genesis, we

---

[1] The common term was Indo-Germanic. Dr Prichard, on bringing the Gael and Cymry into the same family, required the wider term Indo-European. Historical reasons, chiefly in connexion with Sanskrit, are bringing the term Aryan (or Aryas) into fashion. We may adopt whichever is intelligible, without excluding, perhaps, a Turanian or African element surviving in South Wales. Turanian means nearly Mongolian.

[2] *Aegypten's Stelle in der Weltgeschichte*, pp. 186–400; B. v. 1–3. Gotha. 1856.

[3] *Aegypten's Stelle*, &c., B. v. 4–5, pp. 50–142. Gotha. 1857.

are bid notice the combination of documents, and the recurrence of barely consistent genealogies. As the man Adam begets Cain, the man Enos begets Cainan. Jared and Irad, Methuselah and Methusael, are similarly compared. Seth, like El, is an old deity's appellation, and MAN was the son of Seth in one record, as Adam was the son of God in the other. One could wish the puzzling circumstance, that the etymology of some of the earlier names seems strained to suit the present form of the narrative, had been explained. That our author would not shrink from noticing this, is shown by the firmness with which he relegates the long lives of the first patriarchs to the domain of legend, or of symbolical cycle. He reasonably conceives that the historical portion begins with Abraham, where the lives become natural, and information was nearer. A sceptical criticism might, indeed, ask, by what right he assumes that the moral dimensions of our spiritual heroes can not have been idealized by tradition, as he admits to have been the case with physical events and with chronology rounded into epical shape. But the first principles of his philosophy, which fixes on personality (or what we might call force of character) as the great organ of Divine manifestation in the world, and his entire method of handling the Bible, lead him to insist on the genuineness, and to magnify the force, of spiritual ideas, and of the men who exemplified them. Hence, on the side of religion, he does not intentionally violate that reverence with which Evangelical thinkers view the fathers of our faith. To Abraham and Moses, Elijah and Jeremiah, he renders grateful honour. Even in archæology his scepticism does not outrun the suspicions often betrayed in our popular mind; and he limits, while he confirms these, by showing how far they have ground. But as he says, with quaint strength, 'there is no chronological element in Revelation.' Without borrowing the fifteen centuries which the Greek Church and the Septuagint would lend us, we see, from comparing the Bible with the Egyptian records and with itself, that our common dates are wrong, though it is not so easy to say how they should be rectified. The idea of bringing Abraham into Egypt as early as 2876 B.C. is one of our author's most doubtful points, and may seem hardly tenable. But he wanted time for the growth of Jacob's family into a people of two millions, and he felt bound to place Joseph under a native Pharaoh, therefore, before the Shepherd Kings. He also contends that Abraham's horizon in Asia is antecedent to the first Median conquest of Babylon in 2234. A famine, conveniently mentioned under the twelfth dynasty of Egypt, completes his proof. Sesortosis, therefore, is the Pharaoh to whom Joseph was minister; the stay of the Israelites in Egypt is extended to fourteen centuries; and the date 215 represents the time of oppression. Some of these details are sufficiently doubtful to afford ground of attack to writers whose real quarrel is with our author's Biblical research, and its more certain, but not therefore more welcome, conclusions. It is easier to follow him implicitly when he leads us, in virtue of an over-whelming concurrence of Egyptian records and of all the probabilities of the case, to place the Exodus as late as 1320 or 1314. The event is more natural in Egypt's decline under Menephthah, the exiled son of the great Ramses, than amidst the splendour of the eighteenth dynasty. It cannot well have been earlier, or the Book of Judges must have mentioned the conquest of Canaan by Ramses; nor later, for then Joshua would come in collision with the new empire of Ninus and Semiramis. But Manetho places, under Menephthah, what seems the Egyptian version of the event, and the year 1314, one of our alternatives, is the date assigned it by Jewish tradition. Not only is the historical reality of the Exodus thus vindicated against the dreams of the Drum-monds and the Volneys, but a new interest is given it by its connexion with the rise and fall of great empires. We can understand how the ruin on which Ninus rose made room in Canaan for the Israelites, and how they fell again under the satraps of the New Empire, who appear in the Book of Judges as kings of the provinces. Only, if we accept the confirmation, we must take all its parts. Manetho makes the con-querors before whom Menephthah retreats into Ethiopia Syrian shepherds, and gives the human side of an invasion, or war of libera-tion;[1] Baron Bunsen notices the 'high hand' with which Jehovah led forth his people, the spoiling of the Egyptians, and the lingering in the peninsula, as signs, even in the Bible, of a struggle conducted by human means. Thus, as the pestilence of the Book of Kings becomes in Chronicles the more visible angel, so the avenger who slew the first-born may have been the Bedouin host, akin nearly to Jethro, and more remotely to Israel.

So in the passage of the Red Sea, the description may be interpreted with the latitude of poetry: though, as it is not affirmed that Pharaoh was drowned, it is no serious objection that Egyptian authorities con-tinue the reign of Menephthah later. A greater difficulty is that we find

---

[1] νόμον ἔθετο μήτε προσκυνεῖν Θεοὺς ... συνάπτεσθαι δὲ μηδενὶ πλὴν τῶν συνωμοσμένων· αὐτὸς δὲ ... ἔπεμψε πρέσβεις πρὸς τοὺς ὑπὸ Τεθμώσεως ἀπελαθέντας ποιμένας ... καὶ ἠξίου συνε πιστρατεύειν κ.τ.λ. Manetho, apud Jos. c. Apion. The whole passage has the stamp of genuine history.

but three centuries thus left us from the Exodus to Solomon's Temple. Yet less stress will be laid on this by whoever notices how the numbers in the Book of Judges proceed by the eastern round number of forty, what traces the whole book bears of embodying history in its most popular form, and how naturally St Paul or St Stephen would speak after received accounts.

It is not the importance severally, but the continual recurrence of such difficulties, which bears with ever-growing induction upon the question, whether the Pentateuch is of one age and hand, and whether subsequent books are contemporary with the events, or whether the whole literature grew like a tree rooted in the varying thoughts of successive generations, and whether traces of editorship, if not of composition, between the ages of Solomon and Hezekiah, are manifest to whoever will recognise them. Baron Bunsen finds himself compelled to adopt the alternative of gradual growth. He makes the Pentateuch Mosaic, as indicating the mind and embodying the developed system of Moses, rather than as written by the great lawgiver's hand. Numerous fragments of genealogy, of chronicle, and of spiritual song go up to a high antiquity, but are imbedded in a crust of later narrative, the allusions of which betray at least a time when kings were established in Israel. Hence the idea of composition out of older materials must be admitted; and it may in some cases be conceived that the compiler's point of view differed from that of the older pieces, which yet he faithfully preserved. If the more any one scrutinizes the sacred text, the more he finds himself impelled to these or like conclusions respecting it, the accident of such having been alleged by men more critical than devout should not make Christians shrink from them. We need not fear that what God has permitted to be true in history can be at war with the faith in Himself taught us by His Son.

As in his *Egypt* our author sifts the historical date of the Bible, so in his *Gott in der Geschichte*,[1] he expounds its directly religious element. Lamenting, like Pascal, the wretchedness of our feverish being, when estranged from its eternal stay, he traces, as a countryman of Hegel, the Divine thought bringing order out of confusion. Unlike the despairing school, who forbid us trust in God or in conscience, unless we kill our souls with literalism, he finds salvation for men and States only in becoming acquainted with the Author of our life, by whose reason the world stands fast, whose stamp we bear in our forethought, and

---

[1] *Gott in der Geschichte* (i.e. the Divine Government in History). Books i and ii. Leipzig. 1857.

whose voice our conscience echoes. In the Bible, as an expression of devout reason, and therefore to be read with reason in freedom, he finds record of the spiritual giants whose experience generated the religious atmosphere we breathe. For, as in law and literature, so in religion we are debtors to our ancestors; but their life must find in us a kindred apprehension, else it would not quicken; and we must give back what we have received, or perish by unfaithfulness to our trust. Abraham the friend of God, Moses the inspired patriot, Elijah the preacher of the still small voice, and Jeremiah the foreseer of a law written on the conscience, are not ancestors of Pharisees who inherit their flesh and name, so much as of kindred spirits who put trust in a righteous God above offerings of blood, who build up free nations by wisdom, who speak truth in simplicity though four hundred priests cry out for falsehood, and who make self-examination before the Searcher of hearts more sacred than the confessional. When the fierce ritual of Syria, with the awe of a Divine voice, bade Abraham slay his son, he did not reflect that he had no perfect theory of the absolute to justify him in departing from traditional revelation, but trusted that the FATHER, whose voice from heaven he heard at heart, was better pleased with mercy than with sacrifice; and this trust was his righteousness. Its seed was sown from heaven, but it grew in the soil of an honest and good heart. So in each case we trace principles of reason and right, to which our heart perpetually responds, and our response to which is a truer sign of faith than such deference to a supposed external authority as would quench these principles themselves.

It may be thought that Baron Bunsen ignores too peremptorily the sacerdotal element in the Bible, forgetting how it moulded the form of the history. He certainly separates the Mosaic institutions from Egyptian affinity more than our Spencer and Warburton would permit; more, it seems, than Hengstenberg considers necessary. But the distinctively Mosaic is with him, not the ritual, but the spiritual, which generated the other, but was overlaid by it. Moses, he thinks, would gladly have founded a free religious society, in which the primitive tables written by the Divine finger on man's heart should have been law; but the rudeness or hardness of his people's heart compelled him to a sacerdotal system and formal tablets of stone. In favour of this view, it may be remarked, that the tone of some passages in Exodus appears less sacerdotal than that of later books in the Pentateuch. But, be this as it may, the truly Mosaic (according to our author) is not the Judaic, but the essentially human; and it is not the Semitic form, often divergent from our modes of conception, but the eternal truths of a righteous God, and of the spiritaul sacrifices with which He is pleased, that we ought to recognise as most characteristic of the Bible; and these truths the same Spirit which spoke of old speaks, through all variety of phrase, in ourselves.

That there was a Bible before our Bible, and that some of our present books, as certainly Genesis and Joshua, and perhaps Job, Jonah, Daniel, are expanded from simpler elements, is indicated in the book before us rather than proved as it might be. Fuller details may be expected in the course of the revised *Bible for the People*,[1] that grand enterprise of which three parts have now appeared. So far as it has gone, some amended renderings have interest, but are less important than the survey of the whole subject in the Introduction. The word JEHOVAH has its deep significance brought out by being rendered THE ETERNAL. The famous Shiloh (Gen. xlix. 10) is taken in its local sense, as the sanctuary where the young Samuel was trained; which, if doctrinal perversions did not interfere, hardly any one would doubt to be the true sense. The three opening verses of Genesis are treated as *side*-clauses (*when* God created, &c.), so that the first direct utterance of the Bible is in the fourth verse, '*God said*, LET THERE BE LIGHT.' Striking as this is, the Hebrew permits, rather than requires it. Less admissible is the division after verse 4 of the 2nd chapter, as if 'This is the history' was a summary of what precedes, instead of an announcement of what follows. But the first three verses of the 2nd chapter belong properly to the preceding. Sometimes the translator seems right in substance but wrong in detail. He rightly rejects the perversions which make the cursing Psalms evangelically inspired; but he forgets that the bitterest curses of Psalm 109 (from verse 6 to 19) are not the Psalmist's own, but a speech in the mouth of his adversary, as the change of number shows. These are trifles, when compared with the mass of information, and the manner of wielding it, in the prefaces to the work. There is a grasp of materials and a breadth of view from which the most practised theologian may learn something, and persons least versed in Biblical studies acquire a comprehensive idea of them. Nothing can be more dishonest than the affectation of contempt with which some English critics endeavoured to receive this instalment of a glorious work. To sneer at demonstrated criticisms as 'old,' and to brand fresh discoveries as 'new,' is worthy of men who neither understand the Old Testament nor love the New. They to whom the Bible is dear for the truth's sake will

1 *Bibel-werk für die Gemeinde*. I and II. Leipzig. 1858.

wish its illustrious translator life to accomplish a task as worthy of a Christian statesman's retirement as the Tusculans of Cicero were of the representative of Rome's lost freedom.

Already in the volume before-mentioned Baron Bunsen has exhibited the Hebrew Prophets as witnesses to the Divine Government. To estimate aright his services in this province would require from most Englishmen years of study. Accustomed to be told that modern history is expressed by the Prophets in a riddle, which requires only a key to it, they are disappointed to hear of moral lessons, however important. Such notions are the inheritance of days when Justin could argue, in good faith, that by the riches of Damascus and the spoil of Samaria were intended the Magi and their gifts, and that the King of Assyria signified King Herod (!);[1] or when Jerome could say, '*No one doubts that by Chaldeans are meant Demons*,'[2] and the Shunammite Abishag could be no other than heavenly wisdom, for the honour of David's old age[3] – not to mention such things as Lot's daughters symbolizing the Jewish and Gentile Churches.[4] It was truly felt by the early fathers that Hebrew prophecy tended to a system more spiritual than that of Levi; and they argued unanswerably that circumcision and the Sabbath[5] were symbols for a time, or means to ends. But when, instead of using the letter as an instrument of the spirit, they began to accept the letter in all its parts as their law, and twisted it into harmony with the details of Gospel history, they fell into inextricable contradictions; the most rational interpreter among them is Jerome, and the perusal of his

[1] Isaiah viii. 4. Trypho § 77, 8, 9. Well might Trypho answer, that such interpretations are strained, if not blasphemous.

[2] On Isaiah xliii. 14–15, and again, on ch. xlviii. 12–16. He also shows on xlviii. 22, that the Jews of that day had not lost the historical sense of their prophecies; though mystical renderings had already shown themselves. But the later mysticists charitably prayed for HILLEL, because his expositions had been historical. (See Pearson's Notes on Art. iii.) When will *our* mysticists show as Christian a temper as the Jewish ones? *Condonet Dominus hoc R. Hillel!*

[3] To Nepotian. Letter 52.

[4] Presbyteri apud Irenuæm.

[5] Trypho § 41–43. This tract of Justin's shows strikingly a transition from the utmost evangelical freedom, with simplicity of thought, to a more learned, but confused speculation and literalism. He still thinks reason a revelation, Socrates a Christian, prophecy a necessary and perpetual gift of God's people, circumcision temporary, *because not natural*; and lustral washings, which he contrasts with mental baptism, superstitious. His view of the Sabbath is quite St Paul's. His making a millennial resurrection the Christian doctrine, as opposed to the heathen immortality of the soul, is embarrassing, but perhaps primitive. But his Scriptural interpretations are dreams, and his charge against the Jews of corrupting the Prophets as suicidal as it is groundless.

criticisms is their ample confutation.[1] Nor could the strong intellect of Augustine compensate for his defect of little Greek, which he shared with half, and of less Hebrew, which he shared with most of the Fathers. But with the revival of learning began a reluctant and wavering, yet inevitable, retreat from the details of patristic exposition, accompanied with some attempts to preserve its spirit. Even Erasmus looked that way; Luther's and Calvin's strong sense impelled them some strides in the same direction; but Grotius, who outweighs as a critic any ten opposites, went boldly on the road. In our own country each successive defence of the prophecies, in proportion as its author was able, detracted something from the extent of literal prognostication; and either laid stress on the moral element, or urged a second, as the spiritual sense. Even Butler foresaw the possibility, that every prophecy in the Old Testament might have its elucidation in contemporaneous history; but literature was not his strong point, and he turned aside, endeavouring to limit it, from an unwelcome idea. Bishop Chandler is said to have thought twelve passages in the Old Testament directly Messianic; others restricted this character to five. Paley ventures to quote only one. Bishop Kidder[2] conceded freely an historical sense in Old Testament texts remote from adaptations in the New. The apostolic Middleton pronounced firmly for the same principle; Archbishop Newcome[3] and others proved in detail its necessity. Coleridge, in a suggestive letter, preserved in the memoirs of Cary, the translator of Dante, threw secular prognostication altogether out of the idea of prophecy.[4] Dr Arnold, and his truest followers, bear, not always consistently, on the same side. On the other hand, the declamatory assertions, so easy in pulpits or on platforms, and aided some-

[1] Thus he makes Isaac's hundredfold increase, Gen. xxvi. 12, mean 'multiplication of virtues,' because no grain is specified! *Quæst. Hebraie. in Gen.* ch. xxvi. When Jerome Origenises, he is worse than Origen, because he does not, like that great genius, distinguish the historical from the mystical sense.

[2] Collected in the *Boyle Lectures.*

[3] *A Literal Translation of the Prophets, from Isaiah to Malachi,* with Notes, by Lowth, Blaney, Newcome, Wintle, Horsley, &c. London. 1836. A book unequal, but useful for want of a better, and of which a revision, if not an entire recast, with the aid of recent expositors, might employ our Biblical scholars.

[4] 'Of prophecies in the sense of *prognostication* I utterly deny that there is any instance delivered by one of the illustrious Diadoche, whom the Jewish church comprised in the name *Prophets* – and I shall regard *Cyrus* as an exception, when I believe the 137th Psalm to have been composed by David. . . .

' Nay, I will go farther, and assert that the contrary belief, the hypothesis of prognostication, is in irreconcileable oppugnancy to our Lord's declaration, that the *times* hath the Father reserved to Himself.' – *Memoir of Cary,* vol. ii. p. 180.

times by powers, which produce silence rather than conviction, have
not only kept alive but magnified with uncritical exaggeration, whatever the Fathers had dreamt or modern rhetoric could add, tending to
make prophecy miraculous. Keith's edition of Newton need not be
here discussed. Davison, of Oriel, with admirable skill, threw his
argument into a series as it were of hypothetical syllogisms, with only
the defect (which some readers overlook) that his minor premise can
hardly in a single instance be proved. Yet the stress which he lays on
the moral element of prophecy atones for his sophistry as regards the
predictive. On the whole, even in England, there is a wide gulf between the arguments of our genuine critics, with the convictions of
our most learned clergy, on the one side, and the assumptions of popular
declamation on the other. This may be seen on a comparison of Kidder
with Keith.[1] But in Germany there has been a pathway streaming
with light, from Eichhorn to Ewald, aided by the poetical penetration

[1] Amongst recent authors, Dr Palfrey, an American scholar, has expounded in
five learned volumes the difficulties in current traditions about prophecy; but
instead of remedying these by restricting the idea of revelation to Moses and the
Gospels, he would have done better to seek a definition of revelation which
should apply to the Psalms, and Prophets, and Epistles.

Mr Francis Newman, in his *Hebrew Monarchy*, is historically consistent in his
expositions, which have not been controverted by any serious argument; but his
mind seems to fail in the *Ideal* element; else he would see, that the typical ideas
(of patience or of glory) in the Old Testament, find their culminating fulfilment
in the New.

Mr Mansel's *Bampton Lectures* must make even those who value his argument,
regret that to his acknowledged dialectical ability he has not added the rudiments
of Biblical criticism. In all his volume not one text of Scripture is elucidated, nor
a single difficulty in the evidences of Christianity removed. Recognised mis-
translations, and misreadings, are alleged as arguments, and passages from the
Old Testament are employed without reference to the illustration, or inversion,
which they have received in the New. Hence, as the eristic arts of logic without
knowledge of the subject-matter become powerless, the author is a mere gladiator
hitting in the dark, and his blows fall heaviest on what it was his duty to defend.
As to his main argument (surely a strange parody of Butler), the sentence from
Sir W. Hamilton prefixed to his volume, seems to me its gem, and its confutation.
Of the *reasoning*, which would bias our interpretation of Isaiah, by telling us
Feuerbach was an atheist, I need not say a word.

We are promised from Oxford farther elucidations of the Minor Prophets by
the Regius Professor of Hebrew, whose book seems launched sufficiently to catch
the gales of friendship, without yet tempting out of harbour the blasts of criticism.
Let us hope when the work appears, its interpretations may differ from those of
a *Catena Aurea*, published under high auspices in the same university, in which
the narrative of Uriah is improved by making David represent Christ, and Uriah
the devil; so that the crime which 'displeased the Lord', becomes a prophecy of
Him who was harmless and undefiled! This comes from Anselm on St Matthew,
ch. i.

of Herder and the philological researches of Gesenius, throughout which the value of the moral element in prophecy has been progressively raised, and that of the directly predictive, whether secular or Messianic, has been lowered. Even the conservatism of Jahn amongst Romanists, and of Hengstenberg amongst Protestants, is free and rational, compared to what is often in this country required with denunciation, but seldom defended by argument.

To this inheritance of opinion Baron Bunsen succeeds. Knowing these things, and writing for men who know them, he has neither the advantage in argument of unique knowledge, nor of unique ignorance. He dare not say, though it was formerly said, that David foretold the exile, because it is mentioned in the Psalms. He cannot quote Nahum denouncing ruin against Nineveh, or Jeremiah against Tyre, without remembering that already the Babylonian power threw its shadow across Asia, and Nebuchadnezzar was mustering his armies. If he would quote the book of Isaiah, he cannot conceal, after Gesenius, Ewald, and Maurer have written, that the book is composed of elements of different eras. Finding Perso-Babylonian, or new-coined words, such as *sagans* for officers, and Chaldaic forms of the Hebrew verb, such as *Aphel* for *Hiphil*, in certain portions, and observing that the political horizon of these portions is that of the sixth century, while that of the elder or more purely Hebraic portions belonged to the eighth, he must accept a theory of authorship and of prediction, modified accordingly. So, if under the head of Zechariah he finds three distinct styles and aspects of affairs, he must acknowledge so much, whether he is right or wrong in conjecturing the elder Zechariah of the age of Isaiah to have written the second portion, and Uriah in Jeremiah's age the third. If he would quote Micah, as designating Bethlehem for the birthplace of the Messiah, he cannot shut his eyes to the fact that the Deliverer to come from thence was to be a contemporary shield against the Assyrian. If he would follow our version in rendering the second Psalm, *Kiss the son*; he knows that Hebrew idiom convinced even Jerome[1] the true meaning was, *worship purely*. He may read in Psalm xxxiv. that, 'not a bone of the righteous shall be broken,' but he must feel a difficulty in detaching this from the context, so as to make it a prophecy of the crucifixion. If he accepts mere versions of Psalm, xxii. 17, he may wonder how 'piercing the hands and the feet' can fit into the whole passage; but if he prefers the most ancient Hebrew reading, he finds,

[1] Cavillatur ... quod posuerim, ... *Adorate purè* ... ne violentus viderer interpres, et Jud. locum darem. – *Hieron. c. Ruffin.* § 19.

instead of 'piercing,' the comparison 'like a lion,' and this corresponds sufficiently with the 'dogs' of the first clause; though a morally certain emendation would make the parallel more perfect by reading the word 'lions' in both clauses.[1] In either case, the staring monsters are intended, by whom Israel is surrounded and torn. Again he finds in Hosea that the Lord loved Israel when he was young, and called him out of Egypt to be his son; but he must feel, with Bishop Kidder, that such a citation is rather accommodated to the flight of Joseph into Egypt, than a prediction to be a ground of argument. Fresh from the services of Christmas, he may sincerely exclaim, *Unto us a child is born*; but he knows that the Hebrew translated *Mighty God*, is at least disputable, that perhaps it means only Strong and Mighty One, Father of an Age; and he can never listen to any one who pretends that the Maiden's Child of Isaiah vii. 16, was not to be born in the reign of Ahaz, as a sign against the Kings Pekah and Rezin. In the case of Daniel, he may doubt whether all parts of the book are of one age, or what is the starting point of the seventy weeks; but two results are clear beyond fair doubt, that the period of weeks ended in the reign of Antiochus Epiphanes, and that those portions of the book, supposed to be specially predictive, are a history of past occurrences up to that reign. When so vast an induction on the destructive side has been gone through, it avails little that some passages may be doubtful, one perhaps in Zechariah, and one in Isaiah, capable of being made directly Messianic, and a chapter possibly in Deuteronomy foreshadowing the final fall of Jerusalem. Even these few cases, the remnant of so much confident rhetoric, tend to melt, if they are not already melted, in the crucible of searching inquiry. If our German had ignored all that the masters of philology have proved on these subjects, his countrymen would have raised a storm of ridicule, at which he must have drowned himself in the Neckar.

Great then is Baron Bunsen's merit, in accepting frankly the belief of scholars, and yet not despairing of Hebrew Prophecy as a witness to the kingdom of God. The way of doing so left open to him, was to show, pervading the Prophets, those deep truths which lie at the heart of Christianity, and to trace the growth of such ideas, the belief in a righteous God, and the nearness of man to God, the power of prayer, and the victory of self-sacrificing patience, ever expanding in men's hearts, until the fulness of time came, and the ideal of the Divine

---

[1] By reading בלביאים for כלבים. The Septuagint version may have arisen from חקיבוני, taken as from נקף.

thought was fulfilled in the Son of Man. Such accordingly is the course our author pursues, not with the critical finish of Ewald, but with large moral grasp. Why he should add to his moral and meta-physical basis of prophecy, a notion of foresight by vision of particulars, or a kind of *clairvoyance*, though he admits it to be[1] a natural gift, consistent with fallibility, is not so easy to explain. One would wish he might have intended only the power of seeing the ideal in the actual, or of tracing the Divine Government in the movements of men. He seems to mean more than presentiment or sagacity; and this element in his system requires proof.

The most brilliant portion of the prophetical essays is the treatment of the later Isaiah. With the insertion of four chapters concerning Hezekiah from the histories of the kings, the words and deeds of the elder Isaiah apparently close. It does not follow that all the prophecies arranged earlier in the book are from his lips; probably they are not; but it is clear to demonstration,[2] that the later chapters (xl, &c.) are upon the stooping of Nebo, and the bowing down of Babylon, when the Lord took out of the hand of Jerusalem the cup of trembling; for the glad tidings of the decree of return were heard upon the mountains; and the people went forth, not with haste, or flight, for their God went before them, and was their rereward (ch. lii). So they went forth with joy, and were led forth with peace (ch. liv). So the arm of the Lord was laid bare, and his servant who had foretold it was now counted wise though none had believed his report. We cannot take a portion out of this continuous song, and by dividing it as a chapter, separate its primary meaning from what precedes and follows. The servant in chapters lii and liii must have relation to the servant in chapters xlii and xlix. Who was this servant, that had foretold the exile and the return, and had been a man of grief, rejected of his people, imprisoned and treated as a malefactor? The oldest Jewish tradition, preserved in Origen,[3] and to be inferred from Justin,[4] said

---

[1] 'Die Kraft des Schauens, die im Menschen verborgen liegt, und, von der Naturnothwendigkeit befreit, im hebräischen Prophetenthum sich zur wahren Weltanschauung erhoben hat . . . ist der Schlüssel,' &c. *Gott in der Geschichte*, p. 149.
'Jene Herrlichkeit besteht nicht in dem Vorhersagen . . . Dieses haben sie gemein mit manchen Aussprüchen der Pythia, . . . und mit vielen Weissagungen der Hellseherinnen dieses Jahrhunderts . . . *id.* p. 151.

[2] To prove this, let any one read Jerome's arguments against it; if the sacred text itself be not sufficient proof. '*Go ye forth of Babylon*,' &c., ch. xlviii. 20.

[3] *C. Celsum*, i. 55. (Quoted by Pearson.)

[4] For, in making the Gentiles mean *Proselytes*, they must have made the servant

the chosen people – in opposition to heathen oppressors – an opinion which suits ch. xlix. ver. 3. Nor is the[1] later exposition of the Targum altogether at variance; for though Jonathan speaks of the Messiah, it is in the character of a Judaic deliverer: and his expressions about '*the holy people's being multiplied*,' and seeing their sanctuary rebuilt, especially when he calls the holy people a *remnant*,[2] may be fragments of a tradition older than his time. It is idle, with Pearson,[3] to quote Jonathan as a witness to the Christian interpretation, unless his conception of the Messiah were ours. But the idea of the Anointed One, which in some of the Psalms belongs to Israel, shifted from time to time, being applied now to people, and now to king or prophet, until at length it assumed a sterner form, as the Jewish spirit was hardened by persecutions into a more vindicative hope. The first Jewish expositor who loosened, without breaking Rabbinical fetters, R. Saadiah,[4] in the 9th century, named Jeremiah as the man of grief, and emphatically the prophet of the return, rejected of his people. Grotius, with his usual sagacity, divined the same clue; though Michaelis says upon it, *pessimè Grotius*. Baron Bunsen puts together, with masterly analysis, the illustrative passages of Jeremiah; and it is difficult to resist the conclusion to which they tend. Jeremiah compares his whole people to sheep going astray,[5] and himself to 'a lamb or an ox, brought to the slaughter.'[6] He was taken from prison;[7] and his generation, or posterity, none took account of;[8] he interceded for his people in prayer:[9] but was not the less despised, and a man of grief, so that no sorrow was like his;[10] men assigned his grave with the wicked,[11] and his tomb with

---

Israel. ἀλλὰ τί; οὐ πρὸς τὸν νόμον λέγει, καὶ τοὺς φωτιζομένους ὑπ' αὐτοῦ, κ.τ.λ. — *Trypho*, § 122.

[1] Later, because it implies the fall of Jerusalem. It is thought to have been compiled in the fourth century of our era. It is very doubtful, whether the Jewish schools of the middle ages had (except in fragments) any Hermeneutic tradition so old as what we gather from the Church fathers, however unfairly this may be reported. My own belief is clear, that they had not.

[2] יסנון חולרח קורשא, and רעמידן יח שארא. – *Targum on Isaiah* liii.

[3] In Pearson's hands, even the Rabbins become more Rabbinical. His citations from Jonathan and from Jarchi are most unfair; and in general he makes their prose more prosaic.

[4] Titulary styled Gaon, as president of the Sora school.

[5] Jer. xxiii. 1–2; l. 6–17; xii. 3.   [6] Jer. xi. 19.

[7] Jer. xxxviii. 4–6, 13; xxxvii. 16.

[8] Jer. xi. 19–23; xx. 10; xxxvi. 19; xlv. 2–3.

[9] Jer. xviii. 20; xiv. 11; xv. i.

[10] Jer. xviii. 18; xx. 9–17; Lam. iii. 1–13.

[11] Lam. iii. 52, 53, 54; Jer. xxvi. 11–15, 23; xliv. 15, 16; i, 18, 19.

the oppressors; all who followed him seemed cut off out of the land of the living,[1] yet his seed prolonged their days;[2] his prophecy was fulfilled,[3] and the arm of the Eternal laid bare; he was counted wise on the return; his place in the book of Sirach[4] shows how eminently he was enshrined in men's thoughts as the servant of God; and in the book of Maccabees[5] he is the gray prophet, who is seen in vision, fulfilling his task of interceding for the people.

This is an imperfect sketch, but may lead readers to consider the arguments for applying Isaiah lii. and liii. to Jeremiah. Their weight (in the master's hand) is so great, that if any single person should be selected, they prove Jeremiah should be the one. Nor are they a slight illustration of the historical sense of that famous chapter, which in the original is a history.[6] Still the general analogy of the Old Testament which makes collective Israel, or the prophetic remnant, especially the servant of Jehovah, and the comparison of c. xlii, xlix may permit us to think the oldest interpretation the truest; with only this admission, that the figure of Jeremiah stood forth amongst the Prophets, and tinged the delineation of the true Israel, that is, *the faithful remnant* who had been disbelieved – just as the figure of Laud or Hammond might represent the Caroline Church in the eyes of her poet.

If this seems but a compromise, it may be justified by Ewald's phrase, '*Die wenigen Treuen im Exile, Jeremjah und andre,*'[7] though he makes the servant idealized Israel.

If any sincere Christian now asks, is not then our Saviour spoken of in Isaiah; let him open his New Testament, and ask therewith John the Baptist, whether he was Elias? If he finds the Baptist answering *I am not,* yet our Lord testifies that in spirit and power this was Elias; a little reflexion will show how the historical representation in Isaiah liii. is of some suffering prophet or remnant, yet the truth and patience, the grief and triumph, have their highest fulfilment in Him who said, 'Father, not my will, but thine.' But we must not distort the prophets,

[1] Jer. xlv. 1–3; xi. 19; xli. 2–3: with xli. 9–10.; xlii. 1–2, 10.
[2] Psalms cxx. cxxii. cxxvi. cxxix. &c.; Isaiah xliii. 1–5, 10–14.
[3] Lam. i. 17; Jer. xvi. 15, xxx. 1, 2, 3, 10, 18; xxx. 6–12; Isaiah xliv. 7–8; xlvi. 1–9, 10; l. 5–6; lii. 10–13.
[4] Eccles. xlix. 6–7, and Jer. i.
[5] 2 Macc. xv. 13, 14.
[6] The tenses from verse 2 onward are rather historical than predictive; and in ver. 8, for *he was stricken,* the Hebrew is, נגע למו, the *stroke was upon them;* i.e., on the generation of the faithful, which was cut off; when the blood of the Prophets was shed on every side of Jerusalem.
[7] *Die Propheten, d, A. B.* 2ter Baund. pp. 438–453.

to prove the Divine WORD incarnate, and then from the incarnation reason back to the sense of prophecy.

Loudly as justice and humanity exclaim against such traditional distortion of prophecy as makes their own sacred writings a ground of cruel prejudice against the Hebrew people, and the fidelity of this remarkable race to the oracles of their fathers a handle for social obloquy, the cause of Christianity itself would be the greatest gainer, if we laid aside weapons, the use of which brings shame. Israel would be acknowledged, as in some sense still a Messiah, having borne centuries of reproach through the sin of the nations; but the Saviour who fulfilled in his own person the highest aspiration of Hebrew seers and of mankind, thereby lifting the ancient words, so to speak, into a new and higher power, would be recognised as having eminently the function of a prophet whose words die not, of a priest in a temple not made with hands, and of a king in the realm of thought, delivering his people from a bondage of moral evil, worse than Egypt or Babylon. If already the vast majority of the prophecies are acknowledged by our best authorities to require some such rendering, in order to Christianize them, and if this acknowledgment has become uniformly stronger in proportion as learning was unfettered, the force of analogy leads us to anticipate that our Isaiah too must require a similar interpretation. No new principle is thrust upon the Christian world, by our historical understanding of this famous chapter; but a case which had been thought exceptional, is shown to harmonize with a general principle.

Whether the great prophet, whose triumphant thanksgiving on the return from Babylon forms the later chapters of our Isaiah, is to remain without a name, or whether Baron Bunsen has succeeded in identifying him with BARUCH, the disciple, scribe, and perhaps biographer or editor of Jeremiah, is a question of probability. Most readers of the argument for the identity will feel inclined to assent; but a doubt may occur, whether many an unnamed disciple of the prophetic school may not have burnt with kindred zeal, and used diction not peculiar to any one; while such a doubt may be strengthened by the confidence with which our critic ascribes a recasting of Job, and of parts of other books, to the same favourite Baruch. Yet, if kept within the region of critical conjecture, his reasons are something more than ingenious. It may weigh with some Anglicans, that a letter ascribed to St Athanasius mentions Baruch among the canonical prophets.[1]

---

[1] Ἱερεμίας, καὶ σὺν αὐτῷ Βαρούχ, Θρῆνοι, Ἐπιστολὴ καὶ μετ᾽ αὐτὸν Ἰεζεκιήλ, κ.τ.λ. – Ep. Fest.

In distinguishing the man Daniel from our book of Daniel, and in bringing the latter as low as the reign of Epiphanes, our author only follows the admitted necessities of the case.[1] Not only Macedonian words, such as *symphonia*[2] and *psanterion*, but the texture of the Chaldaic, with such late forms as לְכוֹן ,דָּן and אֶלֵּן the pronominal ם and ה having passed into ן, and not only minute description of Antiochus's reign, but the stoppage of such description at the precise date 169 B.C., remove all philological and critical doubt as to the age of the book. But what seems peculiar to Baron Bunsen, is the interpretation of the four empires' symbols with reference to the original Daniel's abode in Nineveh; so that the winged lion traditionally meant the Assyrian empire; the bear was the Babylonian symbol; the leopard that of the Medes and Persians; while the fourth beast represented, as is not uncommonly held, the sway of Alexander. A like reference is traced in the mention of Hiddekel, or the Tigris, in ch. x; for, if the scene had been Babylon under Darius, the river must have been the Euphrates. The truth seems, that starting like many a patriot bard of our own, from a name traditionally sacred, the writer used it with no deceptive intention, as a dramatic form which dignified his encouragement of his countrymen in their great struggle against Antiochus. The original place of the book,[3] amongst the later Hagiographa of the Jewish canon, and the absence of any mention of it by the son of Sirach, strikingly confirm this view of its origin; and, if some obscurity rests upon details, the general conclusion, that the book contains no predictions, except by analogy and type, can hardly be gainsaid. But it may not the less, with some of the latest Psalms, have nerved the men of Israel, when they turned to flight the armies of the aliens; and it suggests, in the godless invader, no slight forecast of Caligula again invading the Temple with like abomination, as well as of whatever exalts itself against faith and conscience, to the end of the world. It is time for divines to recognise these things, since, with their opportunities of study, the current error is as discreditable to them, as for the well-meaning crowd, who are taught to identify it with their creed, it is a matter of grave compassion.

It provokes a smile on serious topics to observe the zeal with which

[1] Auberlen indeed defends, but says, 'Die Unächtheit Daniels ist in der modernen Theologie zum Axiom geworden.' – *Der Prophet Daniel*. Basel. 1854.

[2] Compare 'Philosophy of Universal History' (part of the *Hippolytus*), vol. i. pp. 217–219, with *Gott in der Deschichte*, istr Theil. pp. 514–540.

[3] The saying that later Jews changed the place of the book in the canon, seems to rest on no evidence.

our critic vindicates the personality of Jonah, and the originality of his hymn (the latter being generally thought doubtful), while he proceeds to explain that the narrative of our book, in which the hymn is imbedded, contains a late legend,[1] founded on misconception. One can imagine the cheers which the opening of such an essay might evoke in some of our own circles, changing into indignation as the distinguished foreigner developed his views. After this he might speak more gently of mythical theories.

But, if such a notion alarms those who think that, apart from omniscience belonging to the Jews, the proper conclusion of reason is atheism; it is not inconsistent with the idea that Almighty God has been pleased to educate men and nations, employing imagination no less than conscience, and suffering His lessons to play freely within the limits of humanity and its shortcomings. Nor will any fair reader rise from the prophetical disquisitions without feeling that he has been under the guidance of a master's hand. The great result is to vindicate the work of the Eternal Spirit; that abiding influence, which as our church teaches us in the Ordination Service, underlies all others, and in which converge all images of old time and means of grace now; temple, Scripture, finger, and hand of God; and again, preaching, sacraments, waters which comfort, and flame which burns. If such a Spirit did not dwell in the Church the Bible would not be inspired, for the Bible is, before all things, the written voice of the congregation. Bold as such a theory of inspiration may sound, it was the earliest creed of the Church, and it is the only one to which the facts of Scripture answer. The Sacred Writers acknowledge themselves men of like passions with ourselves, and we are promised illumination from the Spirit which dwelt in them. Hence when we find our Prayer-book constructed on the idea of the Church being an inspired society, instead of objecting that every one of us is fallible, we should define inspiration consistently with the facts of Scripture, and of human nature. These would neither exclude the idea of fallibility among Israelites of old, nor teach us to quench the Spirit in true hearts for ever. But if any one prefers thinking the Sacred Writers passionless machines, and calling Luther and Milton 'uninspired,' let him co-operate in researches by which his theory, if true, will be triumphantly confirmed. Let him join in considering it a religious duty to print the most genuine text of those words which he calls Divine; let him yield no grudging

[1] The present writer feels excused from repeating here the explanation given in the appendix to his *Sermon on Christian Freedom*. London, 1858.

assent to the removal of demonstrated interpolations in our text or errors in our translation; let him give English equivalents for its Latinisms, once natural, but now become deceptive; let him next trace fairly the growth of our complex doctrines out of scriptural germs, whether of simple thought or of Hebrew idiom; then, if he be not prepared to trust our Church with a larger freedom in incorporating into her language the results of such inquiry and adapting one-sided forms to wider experience, he will at least have acquired such a knowledge of this field of thought as may induce him to treat labourers in it with respect. A recurrence to first principles, even of Revelation, may, to minds prudent or timid, seem a process of more danger than advantage; and it is possible to defend our traditional theology, if stated reasonably, and with allowance for the accidents of its growth. But what is not possible, with honesty, is to uphold a fabric of mingled faith and speculation, and in the same breath to violate the instinct which believed, and blindfold the mind which reasoned. It would be strange if God's work were preserved, by disparaging the instruments which His wisdom chose for it.

9

From A. P. STANLEY: *Judgement on 'Essays and Reviews', 'Edinburgh Review', July 1864*

Stanley's Essays on Church and State, which first appeared in various journals such as Fraser's and the *Edinburgh Review*, are among the most intelligent and fascinating of all comments on Victorian religion, and should be read complete by anyone really interested in the period.

The passage selected for inclusion here shows Stanley as usual judiciously keeping his head in time of crisis, and as usual defending the party attacked. His chief aim was not to defend the essayist but to keep the Church of England as inclusive as possible. In the same spirit he had defended a person of utterly different views, W. G. Ward, when the University tried to degrade him. The particular importance of this passage is that it shows how Erastianism can, in the mind of a man like Stanley, be a truly religious principle. Most Erastians, undoubtedly, are so because they care little about religion; but Stanley was one because he believed that the State was the only religious authority that could ensure spiritual liberty in the Church. Stanley writes here and always with beautiful clearness; and though not Newman's equal in range and complexity of thought, he is perhaps his only equal in the period for persuasiveness and controversial force.

O N this case, so argued, Dr Lushington, on the 25th of June, 1862, delivered his memorable judgment. There are many points in that judgment which are open to criticism, and which have been clearly pointed out in an able pamphlet by Professor Grote of Cambridge. But, taking it as a whole, and considering the subtlety of the questions on the one hand, and on the other the great age and multifarious avocations of the Judge, it is a document deserving of warm admiration and serious attention. Guiding himself by the principles laid down in the Gorham

Judgment – the Magna Charta, as it has been truly called, of the liberties of the English Church – he at once discarded all questions of Biblical interpretation and criticism as entirely beyond and beside the range of the Articles or Prayer Book. All charges of heresy founded on questions of authorship or date, of parabolical or historical construction, of prediction or of prophecy – all charges founded on general impressions of the scope and design of the book – he set aside with an impartial courage the more remarkable, because it was evident that he himself to some degree shared the popular alarm which the book had awakened. On the only passage in the Formularies (the answer of the Deacon in the Ordination Service) that might have seemed to bear on the extent of belief to be required in the various parts of the Canonical Scriptures, he had placed a construction which admits the widest latitude that the extremest Essayist ever claimed.[1]

When he left the judgment-seat, out of thirty-two charges, five alone remained; and for those five transgressions of the law, as he deemed them, he pronounced no heavier penalty than that of a year's suspension. It might have seemed that, with a victory so nearly complete, and a punishment so slight, the accused parties, thus acquitted of by far the greater number of charges which had roused the most inveterate prejudice against them, would have found it the safest course to have rested on the judgment of the Court of Arches, without incurring the risk of further appeal. It was determined otherwise; and the five remaining charges were brought before the Judicial Committee of the Privy Council. The Law Lords[2] in this great appeal were the Lord Chancellor Westbury, Lord Cranworth, Lord Chelmsford, and Lord Kingsdown, with the two Primates, and the Bishop of London,[3] sitting, not as in the case of Mr Gorham, as assessors, but as judges.[4] The appellants took what many thought the hazardous course of pleading their own case. Their danger was increased by the circumstance that two of the judges – the Archbishop of Canterbury in his Charge and on other public occasions, and the Archbishop of York by having edited a volume ex-

1 For the Judgments both of the Dean of Arches and of the Privy Council, see Broderick and Fremantle's *Judgments of the Privy Council*, pp. 253–280, pp. 281–290.

2 It appears that these Members of the Judicial Committee were summoned by Her Majesty's command, because they are the four acting Members of the Committee highest in rank; each of them has held or might have held the Great Seal; two are Equity and two may be considered Common lawyers; two are Whigs and two are Tories.

3 [Archbishops Longley, Thomson, and Tait.]

4 Under the terms of 3 & 4 Vict. c. 86.

pressly intended to attack their views – had already pledged themselves
to an adverse opinion on the main questions stirred by the inculpated
Essays; and the Bishop of London had also joined in the general censure
pronounced by the Episcopal Manifesto of 1861.

The pleadings were concluded in July, 1863. The defence of Mr
Wilson remains on record, he having taken the precaution of confining
himself to a written statement. Whatever may be thought of the truth
or falsehood of his theological tenets, there was, we believe, but one
opinion amongst friends and foes as to the force of the masterly, yet
dignified and pathetic argument with which he pleaded for his own
and for the freedom of the English Church against the new yoke which,
as he contended, was for the first time attempted to be imposed. In the
course of those pleadings two of the five charges were dismissed or
withdrawn, and there remained but three; these, however, as we shall
see, each involving issues of the largest consequence. After six months'
delay, the Judgment, to which the Church, not of England only, but of
foreign nations also, had been looking forward with intense expectation, was at last pronounced. No one who was present can forget the
interest with which the audience in that crowded Council Chamber
listened to sentence after sentence as they rolled along from the smooth
and silvery tongue of the Lord Chancellor, enunciating with a lucidity
which made it seem impossible that any other statement of the case was
conceivable, and with a studied moderation of language which, at times,
seemed to border on irony – first the principles on which the judgment was to proceed, and then the examination, part by part, and word
by word, of each of the three charges that remained, till, at the close,
not one was left, and the appellants remained in possession of the field.

As in the acquittal by Dr Lushington, so in the acquittal by the final
Court of Appeal, fresh force was added to the Judgment by the constant disclaimers of sympathy with the appellants; and also by the fact
that the Bishop of London completely adhered to the Judgment, and
that there was a partial adhesion, much to their credit, even of the two
Primates whose bias against the Essayists had been so openly and
strongly avowed.

We have thought it necessary to recapitulate the course of these proceedings, in order to put on record in these pages the most important
event which has taken place in the settlement of the English Church
since the Gorham controversy. As the Gorham Judgment established
beyond question the legal position of the Puritan or so-called Evangelical party in the Church of England; as the Denison Judgment would,

had it turned on the merits of the case instead of a technical flaw, have established the legal position of the High Church or Sacramental party; so the Judgment in the case of Mr Wilson and Dr Williams established the legal position of those who have always claimed the right of free enquiry and latitude of opinion equally for themselves and for both the other sections of the Church; and it therefore becomes necessary to state at this point precisely the questions on which this liberty of opinion has been won.

We have seen that by Dr Lushington's Judgment ample freedom was left to all detailed criticism of the Sacred Text, so long as it did not go to the length of denying the canonicity of any one of the Canonical Books. The questions, whether there be one Isaiah or two – two Zechariahs or three – who wrote the Epistle to the Hebrews, and who wrote the Pentateuch – whether Job and Jonah be historical or parabolical – whether the 53rd chapter of Isaiah and the 2nd Psalm be directly or indirectly prophetic – what are the precise limits of the natural and preternatural – what is the relative weight of internal and external evidence – whether the Apocalypse refers to the Emperor Nero or the Pope of Rome, – are determined to be all alike open to all clergymen of the English Church. In the course of the pleadings before the Privy Council, two charges were abandoned by the prosecutors themselves – one, that which insisted on the necessity of a distinction between the covenanted and uncovenanted mercies of God; the other, turning on a phase of the controversy of Justification.

But three important questions were still left; and, although, as the Judicial Committee frequently and justly observed, all the charges on which they were called to pronounce were contained in a few meagre and disjointed sentences, those few meagre sentences did, in fact, involve the settlement of doctrines containing the pith and marrow of the recent controversy.

The first question raised was as to the doctrine of the Church of England on the Divine authority and inspiration of the Bible. The general fact of their Divine authority and inspiration was admitted by both parties.[1] But the doctrine maintained by the prosecutors, and alleged to have been contradicted by the Essayists, amounted to this (we quote the perspicuous language in which it is drawn out by the

[1] This is fully acknowledged by one of the opponents of the Essayists in his answer to them in the *Aids to Faith* (p. 404): 'We are agreed on both sides that there *is* such a thing as Inspiration in reference to the Scriptures, and we are further agreed that the Scriptures themselves are the best sources of information on the subject.'

Judicial Committee): 'Every part of the canonical Books of the Old and New Testaments, upon any subject whatever, however unconnected with religious faith and moral duty, was written under the inspiration of the Holy Spirit.' The doctrine maintained by the Essayists (again we sum up their position in the same lucid language) is this: 'The Bible was inspired by the Holy Spirit that has ever dwelt and still dwells in the Church, which dwelt also in the Sacred Writers of Holy Scripture, and which will aid and illuminate the minds of those who read Holy Scripture, trusting to receive the guidance and assistance of that Spirit.' And again, that, 'inasmuch as Holy Scripture containeth all things necessary for salvation from the revelations of the Holy Spirit, the Bible may well be denominated "Holy," and said to be "the Word of God," "God's Word written," or "Holy Writ" ' – yet that 'those terms cannot be affirmed to be clearly predicated of every statement and representation contained in every part of the Old and New Testament.'

It was maintained by the Court that the doctrine alleged by the prosecutors to be the doctrine of the Church was not found either in its Articles or in any of its formularies, and that the doctrine maintained by the appellants was not contradicted by or plainly inconsistent with the Articles or formularies which the accusers alleged against them.

The framers of the Articles have not used the word 'Inspiration' as applied to the Holy Scriptures; nor have they laid down anything as to the fitness, extent, or limits of that operation of the Holy Spirit. The caution of the framers of our Articles prohibits our treating their language as implying more than is expressed; nor are we warranted in ascribing to them corollaries expressed in new forms of words, involving minute and subtle matters of controversy.

The two remaining charges differed from that which we have just noticed, in that they relate not to the main question stirred by the appearance of the volume of 'Essays and Reviews,' but to questions which were hardly thought of in connexion with this peculiar controversy, and were only brought into this trial from the extreme anxiety of the prosecutors to leave no sentence or phrase unturned which could by any possibility bring the Essayists within reach of the law.

But they are not the less important on this account. One of them turned on a hope expressed that, at the Day of Judgment, those men who are not admitted to happiness may be so dealt with as that 'the perverted may be restored,' and 'all, both small and great, may ultimately find a refuge in the bosom of the Universal Parent.' The Judges came to their conclusion after a few weighty arguments, founded on the well-known ambiguity of the original words translated by the English word 'everlasting,' on the liberty of opinion which has always existed without restraint among eminent English divines on this subject, and on the fact that the Thirty-nine Articles, as now established, omitted that which in the original Articles of 1552 had stood as the Forty-second, and condemned the doctrine, that 'all men will be saved at the length.' Their conclusion was that 'they do not find in the formularies any such distinct declaration of our Church upon the subject as to require them to condemn as penal the expression of hope by a clergyman, that even the ultimate pardon of the wicked, who are condemned in the Day of Judgment, may be consistent with the will of Almighty God.'

The last charge to be noticed was that extracted from an ambiguous hint, that 'Justification by Faith might mean the peace of mind or sense of Divine approval which comes of trust in a righteous God, rather than a fiction of merit by transfer.' The Judges are in doubt as to what was actually meant, but they declare that the important Eleventh Article – the only one which treats directly of Justification by Faith, 'is wholly silent as to the merits of Jesus Christ being transferred to us; that, therefore, they cannot declare it to be penal for a clergyman to speak of merit by transfer as a fiction, however unseemingly that word may be when used in connexion with such a subject.'

Such was this famous Judgment. The Judges, indeed, still maintained a prudent reticence on the design and general tendency of the book called 'Essays and Reviews,' and on the effect or aim of the whole Essay of Dr Williams, or of the whole Essay of Mr Wilson. They even in one passage leave the impression that they concur in the alarm excited by the appearance of the volume, as a whole. They express no opinion on the theological merits of the case. But every particular charge of contravening the Formularies of the Church, was by the Court of Arches or by the Judicial Committee declared to be untenable. Everything had been staked by the prosecuting party on the issue of this trial, and everything, as it seemed, was lost.

We cannot wonder that the result of this Judgment, after its first stunning effect, should have been a widespread panic. Those who remember the Gorham Judgment will call to mind all the same features of alarm and of agitation. There was one important difference – that whereas in the Gorham Judgment only one great party in the Church was aggrieved at being obliged to tolerate its adversary, in this case two parties were combined against a third. By the skilful guidance of the mysterious oracle, which spoke through the lips of the 'Quarterly Review,' the suggestion of a close alliance founded on a common antipathy to persons whom both alike dreaded or disliked had marvellously succeeded. And this bond of union, which had been formed in a moment of triumph, was tightened by the sense of the common misery of unexpected defeat, such as proverbially unites the strangest bedfellows.

But what the opposition to the recent Judgment thus gained in numerical strength, above the opposition to the Gorham Judgment, it lost in force and consistency. It is impossible not to be struck by the sincerity and conviction with which the opponents of the Gorham Judgment drew up the Resolutions respecting the doctrine[1] of Baptismal Regeneration, on the maintenance of which, as they supposed, the salvation of the English Church depended. The interest of those Resolutions has now passed by. But they remain as a monument of what could be said and done by a party which knew its own mind, and could act freely, without regard to ulterior consequences.

Far other was the conduct of the allied forces on the present occasion. The anger of the leaders, the alarm of the followers, as we have said, was indeed extreme, and, we doubt not, conscientious. The ecclesiastical world was first startled by the unwonted apparition of a letter of Dr Pusey to the editor of the 'Record' newspaper, calling for united action against the 'recent miserable, soul-destroying Judgment.' Such an adhesion to a journal which not only denounces in the strongest terms the doctrines which he and his party have habitually represented as essential to Christianity, but has been conspicuous even amongst its own partisans for its incessant attacks on all who do not adopt its own peculiar creed, was, no doubt, a significant fact. It was followed almost immediately by a meeting hastily called in the Music Hall at Oxford (on occasion of a Convocation convened to determine a matter of Academical Examinations), in which, amidst much confusion and disorder, a committee was appointed consisting of seven clergymen, selected from the extreme sections of the two aggrieved parties of the Church, to draw up a protest in accordance with Dr Pusey's letter.

Before the results of their labours were distinctly made known to the world, another event occurred, which served to show the passions which agitated the theological mind. The too celebrated vote by which the non-residents of Oxford threw out a statute for the endowment

[1] They are given in Dr Manning's Letter on *The Crown in Council*, p. 4.

of its most eminent Professor and its most useful Chair, against the feelings of the vast majority of residents, and, we may add, of the whole intelligence of the country, including even Dr Pusey himself – was ascribed, and justly no doubt, to the determination of the leading agitators, and of the clergy who acted under the terror of the moment, to mark their displeasure at the recent Judgment by condemning a Professor whose opinions could only be assailed by such an oblique blow. We note this curious act as a proof of the vehemence of party feeling roused, and as forming one episode of the irregular warfare which a large portion of the clergy has been led to wage against the Judgment which they had themselves invoked. Of the vote itself we need say no more than to refer to the strong expression of public opinion on the subject in the House of Lords, during the discussions on the endowment of the Greek Professorship by a Canonry, which the Lord Chancellor had for this object generously proposed to surrender, with the view of rectifying this acknowledged wrong. In the face of the severest censures, hardly a voice was raised in defence of the vote of the University – not a Bishop or Archbishop rose to vindicate an act which, if right at all, required the most positive expression of sympathy from the Episcopal Bench.

Close upon this act of 'wild justice,' or 'injustice,' followed the publication of the Declaration, drawn up by the Oxford Committee, and sent to every clergyman of the Established Church of England and Ireland, with an adjuration, 'for the love of God,' to sign it.[1]

We are unwilling to weaken, by any words of our own, the weighty judgment pronounced by two of the most eminent members of the Episcopal Order, on 'this melancholy Declaration,' to which signatures have been obtained 'by a kind of moral torture,' and 'in a way quite unworthy of the character of those who put it forth, and deserving of the gravest reprobation.'[2]

We do not call in question the sincerity or the ability of those who drew up this Declaration. The sinister appearance which it bears was the

[1] See Essay II, p. 55. 'We, the undersigned Presbyters and Deacons in Holy Orders of the Church of England and Ireland, hold it to be our bounden duty to the Church and to the souls of men to declare our firm belief that the Church of England and Ireland, in common with the whole Catholic Church, maintains without reserve or qualification the Inspiration and Divine Authority of the whole Canonical Scriptures, as not only containing but being the Word of God, and further teaches, in the words of Our Blessed Lord, that the "punishment" of the "cursed," equally with "the life" of "the righteous," is "everlasting."'

[2] The speeches of Bishop Tait and of Bishop Thirlwall in the Upper House of Convocation, as reported in the *Guardian* of April 27, 1864.

almost inevitable result of their embarking on an impossible enterprise. They wished to controvert and contradict what Dr Pusey had called 'the miserable and soul-destroying Judgment' of the Privy Council, and yet they were unwilling – justly unwilling – to state openly their opposition to the declared law of the Church. Hence followed the palpable absurdity of signatures being attached to the protest against the Judgment by clergymen who confessed that nothing could induce them to sign if the Declaration were meant to contravene the Judgment, or who insisted as a special condition of signing that they must be understood not to impugn its legal correctness. They wished to re-affirm as the doctrine of the Church the opinion of verbal inspiration and of the hopeless torments of future punishment, which the Judgment had declared not to be the doctrine of the Church, and yet they did not venture to state distinctly what that opinion was. Hence came forth a document, of which the intention indeed was manifest from the language of its framers and the occasion of its publication, but of which the language was so signally ambiguous, that, but for its obvious intention, it might have been signed by those against whom it was intended to protest, and it was in fact signed by persons who, agreeing substantially with the doctrines which the Judgment had asserted, yet were able, under the cover of this ambiguity, to give their names to a protest really aimed against themselves. The pointed expression, that 'the Church maintains without reserve or qualification the inspiration of the whole Canonical Scriptures,' was explained under the pressure of enquiry to mean that signatures might be given by those who did make large 'reserves and qualifications' in the inspiration of Scripture, provided only that they would assert their belief that the doctrine of inspiration, however qualified and reserved, was maintained by the Church *bonâ fide*, and without evasion. The Declaration was intended to be a precise test against heterodox opinions; yet being composed by two contending parties, each of whom had a few years ago believed each other to be fundamentally heterodox, it had to be so framed as to conceal the differences which smouldered under this apparent agreement. The High Church framers were obliged to keep out of view their belief in the Divine authority of tradition, and of the Inspiration of the Apocrypha. The Low Church framers were obliged to surrender altogether their doctrine of imputed righteousness and transfer of merit. The only point on which they were really at one with each other was that of endless future punishment, and even on this the High Church party were obliged to suppress their own solution of the matter, as furnished in the Purgatorial views sanctioned by Tract XC and its adherents.

No wonder that amidst such a complication of difficulties, the ambiguity of this new Fortieth Article far exceeded the ambiguity even of the celebrated Thirty-nine, to which it was to be an adjunct. No wonder that, 'though unmistakable in its intention,' it should have been considered, even by its own admirers, as 'awkward in form, construction, and language.'[1] No wonder that it should exhibit in its vacillation and feebleness of statement a strong contrast to the decisive and vigorous, if not altogether lucid, enunciation of the High Church dogma of Baptismal Regeneration, to which we just now referred, before the leaders of that party had condescended, for the sake of crushing a common antagonist, to dilute their strength by union with their own mortal foes. 'I have,' writes an able and learned ecclesiastic, 'another sufficient reason for refusing to sign the Declaration. I do not understand it. Or rather, since it may be answered that this is my misfortune, I must venture to say that I understand it sufficiently to be satisfied that it is unintelligible.'[2]

What amount of authority would hang on even the most distinguished names, attached to such a nullity as this document, may be seen from the fact that the Bishop of St David's, than whom no one has spoken of it with stronger condemnation, declares that he himself could have subscribed it, if taken with the qualification which even the actual subscribers had forced upon the framers. What amount of authority hangs on the names which are in fact attached to it, we will presently show. The longer the catalogue is, the more it calls to mind the memorable image so felicitously applied by the eminent Prelate whom we have just cited: 'I cannot[3] consider them in the light of so many ciphers which add to the value of the figures which they follow; but I consider them in the light of a row of figures preceded by a decimal point, so that however far the series may be prolonged, it can never rise to the value of a single unit.' The famous slaughter of St Ursula and her 11,000 companions at Cologne has been by modern critics resolved into the misfortune of a single princess, accompanied by a single handmaid named Undecemilla; and it is much to be apprehended that the procession of the 11,000 clergy would in like manner, as far as mere authority is concerned, resolve themselves into the seven names which

[1] *Quart. Rev.*, April 1864, p. 539.
[2] An able pamphlet on *The Oxford Declaration*, by Robert Anchor Thompson, M.A.   [3] *Guardian* newspaper, April 27, 1864.

headed the movement. Indeed, considering the extreme ambiguity of the document, and the powerful inducements, temporal, social, and spiritual, brought to bear specially on the younger country clergy, the number is less than we should have expected. A moment's reflection will elucidate the real value even of the signatures thus obtained. Every one will acknowledge that on matters requiring so much thought, study, and experience of life, the opinion of the Academical and Metropolitan clergy would far outweigh that of the rural districts. The opinion of those who preside over our seats of education and of the most learned dignitaries, both in the cathedrals and the universities, would outweigh them all. What is the actual case? We believe, in point of fact, that of the London clergy, the signatures amount only to one-third; out of the Professors at Oxford, nine, of those at Cambridge, one only, have signed; out of the thirty English deans, eight only; out of all the head-masters of our public schools, two only; out of the fifty clerical contributors to the Biblical Dictionary only six names appear attached to a document so sternly requiring an exact knowledge of the Sacred Volume; and, in spite of the system of terrorism set on foot in the provinces, there are still more than half the clergy who have stood aloof altogether, and when the document was presented at Lambeth, only four out of the twenty-eight Bishops lent their countenance to its formal reception.

The next attempt of the defeated party was to attack their opponents by a condemnation in the Convocation of Canterbury – a measure of doubtful legality, which goes far to justify the apprehensions excited by the remembrance of the history of that body in the years preceding its long suspension. That branch of Convocation consists of two Houses, – the Upper containing the Archbishop and Bishops of the Southern Province, the Lower containing the representatives of its different dioceses and chapters, as well as its Deans and Archdeacons. In both Houses, the question of this condemnation was debated with an animation and vigour unequalled since the revival of the body in 1852. In the Upper House the discussion called forth those remarkable speeches of the Bishops of London and St David's which we have already quoted. In spite of their energetic remonstrances, backed by the moderate and judicious support of the Bishops of Lichfield, Lincoln, and Ely,[1] it was determined by the casting vote of the President, that a Committee should be appointed to survive the dying embers of the controversy, and the result was a general censure of the book, in which the Lower

1 [Bishops Lonsdale, Jackson, and Browne.]

House was invited to express its concurrence. It was evidently expected that this censure would be carried by a stroke of hand without discussion. A vote of thanks and approval was proposed, even before the Report had been read, on which the act of condemnation was founded, and was pressed on the Lower House with all the impassioned eagerness natural to those who thought that the welfare of the Church depended on the repudiation, by whatever means, of the obnoxious opinions which the Supreme Court of Appeal had acquitted. But instead of submission, there came the most determined resistance which the Lower House has in these latter days offered to their episcopal brethren of the Upper House. At every turn the Synodical Condemnation was opposed by Deans, Archdeacons, Canons, – on every conceivable ground, of justice, decorum, precedent, law, reason, and charity, – by arguments which were, in great part, conceded by their opponents, who, it is only fair to say, listened to these unpalatable truths with a praiseworthy forbearance and courtesy. But to minds already pledged to condemn before they heard, and despite of whatever they could hear, argument was addressed in vain. 'For the sake of repudiating these opinions,' it had been said, 'we must sacrifice all minor considerations.' 'All minor considerations,' replied one of the speakers in language worthy alike of his sacred profession[1] and of his own high character, 'I would sacrifice for such an object. But not "the minor considerations" of justice, mercy, and truth.' It was urged still more emphatically, 'All that has been said against the censure is true. It is ambiguous, indiscriminate, unfair. But the men have been acquitted by the highest legal Court; and hanged they must be – and if they cannot be hanged by Law, they shall be hanged by Lynch Law.' This outspoken sentiment of one of the most respected and straightforward of the supporters of the censure, expressed, in fact, the sentiments of nearly all: and in the uncompromising determination, which it implied, to secure victims at any cost, we are reminded of the passage in Holy Writ which Archbishop Whately used to give as the best example of the dogged pertinacity of mistaken zeal: 'We will have no silver nor gold of Saul, nor of his house. . . . Let seven men of his sons be delivered unto us, and we will hang them up unto the Lord in Gibeah of Saul.'

With the close of these proceedings in Convocation, in all probability this long controversy will have reached its conclusion – and the thrice slain and thrice revived book, which has cost such oceans of gall, will be allowed to sleep in quiet – and the Protests and Declarations and

1 [Lord Arthur Hervey, now Bishop of Bath and Wells.]

Synodical Judgments will pass with it into the same grave as that to which during the last two hundred years have descended so many other Protests against imaginary dangers which have themselves passed away in like manner.

But what happily will not pass away, will be the permanent blessings bestowed on the Church and country by the timely decision of the highest Court of Appeal. And first, let us clearly ascertain its legal effect. The Judicial Committee, on this occasion as always, has distinctly laid down that

> This Court has no jurisdiction or authority to settle matters of faith, or to determine what ought in any particular to be the doctrine of the Church of England. Its duty extends only to the consideration of that which is by law established to be the doctrine of the Church of England, upon the true and legal construction of her Articles and Formularies.

This in fact is the highest point to which any authority in any existing Church, at least any existing Protestant Church, can attain. Individual bishops, individual theologians, may declare their own belief as to the truth or the theological importance of any particular doctrine. But not any bishop, nor all the bishops together, even if they had legal power, can authoritatively do more than declare as binding that which is already incorporated in the Formularies, unless they make or procure to be made a new law to increase or to diminish the stock of the existing legal doctrines. Even in the Roman Catholic Church, the Pope himself has not, unless in exceptional instances, pretended to any larger power than to enforce dogmas already received by the Church, or to give a new legal sanction (as in the case of the Immaculate Conception) to an opinion floating in the minds of men, but hitherto unauthorised by any such formal sanction. The Judicial Committee, acting in the name of the Sovereign and under the authority of the Legislature, has had this charge entrusted to it; and for this purpose its decision, until repealed, becomes at once the law of the Church.

It is not surprising that Western ecclesiastics, with that impatience of the civil power which they have inherited from the Roman clergy, should be unwilling to acknowledge this exercise of the Royal Supremacy. We regret to see that even the two Primates who concurred in the larger part of the Judgment, allowed themselves to be carried away for the moment by the current of clerical agitation. One of them is reported to have stated in a public speech[1] that, whilst the Judgment of

[1] Speech at the Church Missionary Society, on May 2nd, 1864. (*Guardian* newspaper, May 11, 1864.)

the Judicial Committee had 'some shadow of colour from authority' – 'the real authority of the Church of England is the voice of the clergy of the Church of "England." '

Such declarations, however well meant, are, if not absolutely ground-less, exceedingly misleading. There are solemn declarations of the Church of England to the effect that, not the voice of its clergy, but the Crown (that is the Law) is supreme over all cases, ecclesiastical as well as civil. The first Act for the Uniformity of Common Prayer and Worship in the Church, the foundation of all ecclesiastical legislation in England, is one of the few Acts, if it be not the only one, that bears on its face the mark of having passed through Parliament without the con-currence of the spiritual peers.[1] In a yet more important Act of the same momentous period – the only Act which declares what heresy is – the sole authority in this realm to which it assigns the adjudication of this question, is the High Court of Parliament (not by the judgment, but) with the assent of the clergy in Convocation.[2] Even in the Church of Rome, as we have just observed, so dangerous a doctrine has never been openly avowed, as that the opinion, even though unanimous, of the clergy on any given question is the real authority of the Church. The opinion of the Immaculate Conception was held, as the Bishop of St David's has well pointed out, with at least as much unanimity amongst the Roman Catholic clergy as the opinion of verbal inspiration is by the English clergy at this moment – yet it was never received as a dogma till it had received the legal sanction of the highest Court of Appeal in that Church, on December 8, 1854.

It is of some importance to remove these misapprehensions, because this is the only mode in which, in such matters, the Queen's supremacy over the Church can be exercised.[3] When by the Act of the first year of Elizabeth the preeminence and jurisdiction spiritual and ecclesiastical was reannexed to the Crown, it was provided that the kings or queens of this realm should have authority to name commissioners to exercise this ecclesiastical jurisdiction. The appeals formerly addressed to Rome

[1] Stat. 1 Eliz. c. 2. ss. 3, 15. All the bishops present dissented.
[2] Stat. 1 Eliz. c. 1. s. 36.
[3] 1 Eliz. cap. 1, sect. 17. 'All such jurisdictions, privileges, superiorities and preeminences spiritual and ecclesiastical, *as by any spiritual or ecclesiastical person or authority hath heretofore been*, or may lawfully be exercised or used, for the visitation of the ecclesiastical state and persons, and for reformation, order, and correction of the same, and of all manner of errors, heresies, schisms, abuses, offences, contempts, and enormities, shall for ever by authority of this present Parliament *be united and annexed to the Imperial Crown of this Realm*.' [See Preface to Broderick and Fremantle's *Judgments of the Privy Council*, pp. x–lxxv.]

lay to the King in Chancery, that is to the Court of Delegates; and it deserves notice, that if this jurisdiction had not been transferred in 1832 to the King in Council, the Delegates alone would have decided the very causes now under discussion. But it is a far more decorous and constitutional arrangement to vest in the judicial portion of the Privy Council the duty of advising and guiding the Crown in the exercise of this branch of its ecclesiastical authority. By a subsequent Act, the prelates, being Privy Councillors, were added to the Court, and are bound in this capacity to tender their advice to their Sovereign. Unless it be contended that an irreconcilable difference is to prevail between the theological opinions of the episcopate and the propositions of theology legally established by the Articles and Formularies of the Church of England – so that the Sovereign is to be assailed by the terrors of heresy on the one hand, and bound by strict legal obligations on the other – it is not easy to devise any safer mode of dealing with these disputes.

Any attempt to remove the Bishops from the Judicial Committee would be a direct slight on the Episcopal order, as though they were incapable of taking a calm and judicial view of what under any circumstances must be a legal and not a theological question. And it would also directly tend to encourage that mischievous separation of the civil and ecclesiastical powers, which it has been the object of all wise statesmanship to conciliate, and which the whole constitution of the Church of England, as expressed in its formal acts, and defended by its greatest writers, has hitherto tended to bind together in indissoluble union. We have not cited the proceedings of Convocation for the sake of pointing any inference against the permission tacitly conceded by the Crown for the exercise of speech in the English Convocations. In a certain point of view these proceedings even serve a useful purpose as a safety-valve for the free expression and collision of opinion amongst the clergy. But they show conclusively what amount of justice and moderation might be expected if 'the voice of the clergy is really the voice of the Church of England,' – if, as was claimed by one of the disputants in Convocation, 'the House of Convocation was really the highest Court of Appeal' in the Church. We have learned from these proceedings to know that 'the minor considerations' – of justice and equity – would go at once to the wall; that accused parties would be condemned without being heard; that condemnations for opinions expressed with impunity by others would be passed against them, without any definite statement of that wherein their offence consisted.

In the presence of such dangers, we cannot but observe with regret and surprise that some distinguished laymen, as well as clergymen, have signed an address to the two Primates, expressing their deep gratitude for the Pastorals on which we have felt it our duty to animadvert. But our regret, if not our surprise, is greatly diminished by the reflection that, unless it means to express a concurrence in the opinions of these Pastorals (which one of the most respectable subscribers has openly repudiated), this pompous address means absolutely nothing. It asserts merely that the subscribers believe in the Christian Faith, and it asserts this in terms so general, that not only all members whosoever of the English Church, but all persons professing the Christian Faith at all – Roman Catholics, Quakers, and Unitarians – might equally have adopted the language used. It is strange that persons of such exalted station should wish to receive, or should consent to sign, a document which either exposes itself to the grave charge of saying one thing and meaning another, or else is entirely futile. We trust that in the freedom of these remarks we have said nothing inconsistent with our respect for the high public position and the private worth of the persons concerned. And we are thankful to know, that if the distinguished occupants of the two metropolitical sees have for the time been led into an apparent opposition to the law, and an apparent acquiescence in these questionable compliments, the sounder feeling of the English Church has found its expression in the Bishop of London. He may rest satisfied with the assurance that his just and courageous conduct on this occasion has won the esteem and admiration of thousands whose voice will never reach him; and we trust that in the blessings which will descend on his labours for the good of his great diocese, he will receive his best reward and compensation.

Such being the legal character of the Judgment, there remains still the important question, what are the advantages which will accrue to the Church of England, and to the Christian faith itself, from the whole situation in which it leaves the doctrines at issue?

When the Spartan general Brasidas, within the besieged city of Amphipolis, looked out on the approaching enemy, his keen eye caught through the gates the sight of the uncertain desultory movement of the troops without. 'The day is ours,' he exclaimed –'I see the shaking of the spears.' We, too, have seen 'the shaking of the spears.' The resistance to the Judgment, formidable as it may appear at first sight, is really an acquiescence in it. The unsteady vacillating motion which has marked the advance of the phalanx, shows that the alarm and the animosity engendered has no deep seat in the convictions of the

Church and the nation, but will pass away when the real merits of the case are more fully appreciated.

We have been compelled to state clearly the nature of the Judgment and the close of the legal process, which has wound up the long personal controversy of the last three years; but God forbid that we should regard it as the triumph of a party. In the civil wars of ancient Rome there were no triumphs; and in this case, so far as it is a triumph at all, it is a triumph, not of a party but of the whole Church, in which we are convinced that, sooner of later, the whole Church will thankfully acquiesce.

Cast a rapid glance over the three questions on which the Privy Council was called to decide. It is now declared to be no doctrine of the Church of England that 'every part of the Bible is inspired, or is the Word of God.' Surely this is the actual doctrine of every intelligent and devout Christian, who has not committed himself irretrievably to the narrow trammels of a school. 'Inspired' in the general sense in which our Liturgy uses the word, in the only passages where it uses the word at all – 'inspired' with a peculiar fulness by the Divine Spirit, by whose inspiration every good thought comes into the heart of man – in this sense, the Bible,[1] taken as a whole, is 'inspired' from Genesis to Revelation. 'The Word of God' it is, in the same general sense, as containing the Divine revelation; as we speak of a church as 'the House of God,' or a prophet as 'the Man of God.' In this wide and obvious sense it is used occasionally for the Bible in our Formularies. But in order to give to this general sense of inspiration, and this general application of the phrase 'the Word of God' a meaning which shall contravene the position declared by the Judgment to be admissible within the Church of England, the two phrases have been extended to mean the exact and literal truth of every verse of the Bible, indeed we fear that we must add, every verse of the Received Text of the Authorised Version. For, unless it means this, the dreaded alternative which is put forth by the opponents of the Judgment meets us at every turn – namely, that 'there is no touchstone which shall test for us whether a given passage is part of the Word of God or of the word of man therewith entangled.'

[1] It is satisfactory to observe that in one passage of his letter to the *Record* this general sense of inspiration, as given in the Judgment, is adopted by Dr Pusey as 'expressing our common faith.' *O si sic omnia!* It is as if for a moment the free generous spirit which breathed through his earlier work on German Theology had again taken possession of a mind too widely and deeply learned, to submit, without a struggle, to the trammels of the modern schools of thought, with which he has allowed himself of late to be shackled.

These are the express words in which this alternative has been put forward. But in actual fact it is accepted by hardly any educated man. Even the Pastoral of the Archbishop of Canterbury allows an unquestioned right of rejecting spurious passages. The 'touchstone' which rejects the verse of the Three Witnesses is neither more nor less than 'the verifying faculty' of Biblical criticism; and unless each single word of the Authorised Text is protected by the law from criticism, each student of the sacred text must apply, and does apply, that touchstone for himself. The able writer in the 'Quarterly,'[1] who appears to speak with all but episcopal authority, and who has adopted a far more reasonable ground since the commencement of his first attack, has no scruple in applying the touchstone further still. 'Christianity,' he says, 'no more looks to the Bible for scientific teaching than it searches for the Articles of Faith in Algebra.' 'Nothing is less to be encouraged than the nervous shrinking from the discovery of the truth which marks some feeble religionists, unless, indeed, it be the fussy anxiety with which others rush eagerly about to invent schemes for the hasty reconciliation of every seeming contradiction,' &c. He condemns 'passionate assertions of the absolute verbal inspiration of the sacred text, which, in fact, exclude altogether the human element, and hazard the truth of Revelation on the correctness of Biblical statements as to science and history.' He agrees with the Judgment that 'there may be parts of the Canonical Books . . . not written under the inspiration of the Holy Spirit.' In like manner, many even of the subscribers to the Oxford Declaration claim the right of believing that there must be a reserve and qualification in the inspiration of Scripture. There are, we will venture to say, not above fifty clergymen in England who fully and from their heart believe the precepts of Leviticus or the pedigrees in the Book of Chronicles, the description of the hare as a ruminant animal, or the imprecations of Nehemiah on his enemies, to be immediately and absolutely the Word of God, in the same sense, or anything like the same sense as they believe this of the Sermon on the Mount or the farewell Discourses in St John's Gospel. What the Privy Council has done is to legalise the latent – our enemies would say 'heterodoxy,' but we boldly say – the latent 'orthodoxy,' of the great mass of English opinion on this subject. Had it determined otherwise, it would, for the sake of courting a momentary popularity, have closed the doors of the Church of England against the belief held, we freely admit inconsistently and imperfectly, but still held by all those who have not a theory to defend or a party to accuse. 'The

[1] April 1864, pp. 530, 551, 552.

Word of God,' as the Bishop of St David's well observes in that powerful Charge which must both by friends and foes be acknowledged to be
fully worthy of his ancient fame – 'cannot in any passage[1] of the New
Testament, be substituted for the Bible without manifest absurdity.'
And what Scripture nowhere enjoins, and hardly allows, a church or an
individual must be very bold to assert without reserve or qualification.
'The Word of God' is the Divine Effluence which visited the patriarchs,
which inspired the prophets, which spake by the Evangelists and
Apostles, which is uttered and expressed in all the forms of Revelation
and of Reason, which in its highest and most perfect sense is applied by
St John to the Eternal Son. The Articles speak quite correctly of 'God's
Word written,' that is, 'God's word as far as it is expressed in writing.'
But this is but one form – and a very limited form – of the Word of
God – a sense in which it is never, as we have seen, used in Scripture,
very rarely, we believe, by the Fathers of the Church. And nothing is
more debasing to the true conception of that exalted term, which may
be traced through all the religious annals of the world, than to apply it
to the Bible so as to identify the Bible with it, as if it were that and
nothing else.

Still less can any argument for the absolute correctness of every part
of the sacred books be drawn from the expression 'Canonical Scriptures.' True it is that the Scriptures, as a whole, contain the rule of faith
and practice, yet this is not the meaning of the word *Canonical*, nor can
any inference be drawn from it as to the character of the books so designated. The highest, because the most learned, authority on this subject
in England – we allude to Mr Westcott[2] – has proved beyond all question that the words as applied to the Scriptures, mean not the books
which rule, or contain the rule, but the books which are ruled, or placed
in the rule, by the Church. It describes simply an historical fact that
certain books have been so received by Christendom. What those books
are has been ruled differently by different portions of the Christian
world. The Church of the first centuries often included the Book of
Baruch, and excluded the Book of Esther, or included the Epistles of
Clement and Barnabas, and excluded the Apocalypse. The Church of
Rome excludes the Epistles of Clement and Barnabas, and includes the
Apocrypha. The Church of Armenia includes the History of Joseph and
Asenath, and the Third Epistle of St Paul to the Corinthians. The
Church of England, before the Reformation, included for several

[1] Charge of the Bishop of St David's, p. 102.
[2] See article 'Canon' in the *Dictionary of the Bible*.

centuries the Epistle to the Laodiceans, and since the Reformation has excluded the Apocryphal books in its Articles, though describing two of them in its Homilies as of Divine authority. But nothing has been determined either in Articles, Prayer-book, or Homilies, as to the precise nature of this authority, save only that the books named in the Sixth Article contain all things necessary to salvation; in other words contain, but are not coextensive with, the Word of God, in that exalted and exact sense in which alone it can be recognised in theological definitions or legal obligations. We might multiply quotations from English divines past and present, but we will confine ourselves to one from a useful but unpretending little work by a well-known clergyman of the so-called Evangelical School, which incorporates some of the most decisive from former times.[1]

I do earnestly plead in behalf of Holy Scripture, that instead of demands for it which end in outrages upon it, we abide by the doctrine of the Sixth Article, and the Homilies of our Church. Of the Sixth Article, when, it declares 'Holy Scripture containeth all things necessary to Salvation.' Of the Homilies, when they say, 'Unto a Christian man there can be nothing either more necessary or profitable than the knowledge of Holy Scripture; forasmuch as *in it is contained God's true Word*, setting forth His glory, and also man's duty.' 'For in Holy Scripture is fully *contained* what we ought to do and what to eschew, what to believe, what to love, and what to look for at God's hands.' (Homily I.) 'For the Holy Scriptures are *God's treasure-house*, wherein are found all things needful for us to see, to hear, to learn, and to believe, necessary for the attaining of eternal life.'

And this principle is re-echoed by Hooker: 'The *principal intent* of Scripture is to deliver the laws of *duties supernatural*.' (I. 14.) And again, 'Scripture teaches us that *saving truth* which God hath discovered unto the world by revelation'. (iii. 8.) And still more emphatically, 'The *main drift* of the whole New Testament is that which St John setteth down as the purpose of his own history, "These things are written that ye might believe that Jesus Christ is the Son of God, and that believing *ye might have life* through His name." The drift of the Old, that which the Apostle mentioneth to Timothy, "The Holy Scriptures are able to make thee *wise unto salvation*." So that the general end both of Old and New is one.' With which accord the deeply suggestive words of Bacon, 'Some have pretended to find the truth of all natural philosophy in the Scriptures. . . . But neither do they give honour to the Scriptures, *as they suppose*, but much embase them. For to seek heaven and earth in the Word of God, is *to seek temporary things amongst eternal*: to seek philosophy in divinity is to seek the dead among the living; neither are the pots or lavers, whose place was in the outward part of the temple, to be sought in the holiest place of all, where the ark of the testimony was seated. The scope or purpose of the Spirit of God is not to express *matters of nature* in the Scriptures otherwise than *in passage*,

---

[1] *A Plea for Holy Scripture.* By Thomas Griffin, A.M., Prebendary of St Paul's.

and for application to man's capacity and to *matters moral or divine*. For it is a true rule, "Auctoris *aliud agentis* parva auctoritas." '

The sufficiency of Scripture is not asserted as to anything else but this. It has not to do with settling matters of Science, or Philosophy, or History, or Ethnology; it has to do only with the Revelation of the one True God in His relation to man.

There are indeed other things in Scripture, of infinite truth and beauty, but they are all subordinate to this. There are its historical elements, its poetical, its legal, its political, its prophetical, its philosophical, its moral, its mystical. It has something to tell us about everything that has interested or can interest the human mind. But the one thing which makes it to us emphatically 'God's Treasure-house' is its Disclosure, amidst all these accessory matters, of the otherwise unknown and unknowable God – His character, His works, His ways.

Still more conducive to the interests of religion has been the refusal of the Supreme Court of Appeal to pledge itself and the Church to any popular theory of the future punishment of the wicked or of the mode of justification. These questions were not, properly speaking, part of the original controversy which has precipitated this decision. But they are not less momentous in their bearings on Christian Theology; and of these, no less than of the question of Inspiration, it is obvious that the opinion of the clergy is not sufficiently matured to require any definition, beyond that which has been given. The doctrine of the endlessness of future punishment might, indeed, at first seem to have a stronger hold, and in a more precise form, than that of verbal inspiration. But here, again, the moment we press the prevalent belief, we feel that it is either altogether fluctuating, or else expresses itself in forms wholly untenable. The 'tacit repugnance'[1] with which, from the days of Origen downwards, some of the leading spirits of the Christian Church have rejected the sterner dogma, has constantly kept alive a protest which no traditional weight has been able entirely to smother. Perhaps of all the secondary arguments that Mr Wilson used in his defence, none was more effective than that in which he cited the well-known sermon of Archbishop Tillotson, and then asked whether, after elaborately preaching such a doctrine, one man should have been raised to the Primacy of this great Church, whilst for merely expressing a hope that there may be conditions of restoration and recovery for God's erring creatures, another should be suspended from his functions –

Ille crucem sceleris pretium tulit, hic diadema.

But it is more to our present point to observe that the doctrine of

[1] Dean Milman's *History of Latin Christianity*, vi. 253.

endless torments, if held, is not practically taught by the vast majority of the English clergy. How rarely in these modern days have our pulpits resounded with the detailed descriptions of future punishments, which abound in the writings of the seventeenth century! How rarely does any one even of the strictest sect venture to apply such descriptions to any one that he has personally known! And when we read the actual grounds on which the belief is rested by those who now put it forth as one of the essential articles of the faith, we find that it reposes almost entirely on the doubtful interpretation, in a single passage, of a single word, which in far the larger proportion of passages where it occurs in the Bible, cannot possibly bear the meaning commonly put upon it in this particular text. We must, we are told, believe in the endless punishment of the wicked, because in one verse in St Matthew's Gospel, 'the punishment of the cursed equally with the life of the righteous is called everlasting.' We do not now dwell on the real meaning of the Greek and Hebrew words translated 'everlasting' in this or in any other passages. We do admit as the obvious fact that the true meaning of Our Lord's parable where this solemn warning occurs is not to determine the nature of the future state, but to recognise the just deserts of those who, however unconsciously, have served Him by serving His brethren, and of those who, amidst whatever professions, have neglected the practical duties of life. However this may be, it is certain that the true Christian belief in the blessedness of the good rests not on the sense of any single word, or of any single text, but on the conviction pressed upon us alike by conscience and by the whole tenour of Scripture, that God's essential attributes are unchangeable – that of all His attributes none is more essential or more unchangeable than His love for those who love Him, and His desire to recover those who have gone astray from Him. It is the love of God and the fear of God, the love of goodness and the hatred of sin, not the hope of heaven or the fear of hell, that in the Bible are made the foundations of human action – the way to eternal life. The excellent men who put forward the Oxford Declaration could hardly have weighed the whole force of their expression when they entreated their younger brethren, 'for the love of God,' and 'in common with the whole Catholic Church,' to sign a statement which, if taken literally, was (as they were reminded in a remarkable letter from a High Churchman of no wavering faith), 'making private and heretical opinions the measure of the Church's faith – defining where neither the Catholic Church nor the Scriptures have defined.' 'You assert,' he proceeds, 'that eternity –

must be understood in precisely the same sense of the creature as of the Creator, of evil as of good, of union to Satan as of union to God. Surely a very little thought might have taught you better. The words 'eternal' and 'everlasting,' or phrases answering to these, are constantly used in a relative sense in the Old Testament Scriptures with reference to Jewish ordinances designed to pass away, and they signify 'indefinite and continuous,' until superseded by a higher law or principle, never tending to come to an end of themselves. Is it necessary to teach learned men like you that whatever begins in time may also know an end in time; that there is this essential and infinite difference between the eternity of good and of evil – that the one has never begun, but was from all eternity; that the other has begun, and may therefore end; that it is nothing less than blasphemous to draw comparisons between the eternity of the everlasting Son of God and the relative eternity of his sinful creatures; that evil having nothing Divine in it is essentially finite, not infinite; that it consists in rebellion to the will of God, and has no inherent endless vitality; that the happiness of the blessed rests not on a word, or a syllable, but on their perfect union with God, who is infinite life and joy; that we have no 'data' whatever on which to ground the assertion that the eternity of sin, of pain, and of evil, is equally unlimited, absolute, and infinite; that these are 'the deep things of God' which really wise men will not seek to fathom or define too closely; that Catholics content themselves with using the language of Scripture and the creeds without attempting to do what the whole Catholic Church never has done, sound the limits and take the accurate measure of that love of Christ concerning which an inspired Apostle prays for his brethren that they might be able to comprehend 'what is the breadth, and length, and depth, and height, and know that love of Christ which passeth knowledge?'

All honour to the wise laymen, therefore, who, in our highest court of appeal, with the assistance of the three highest ecclesiastical assessors in the land, have delivered on these grave questions a sound and Catholic judgment, against which you are now urging an heretical, a disloyal, and a most unhappy movement; disturbing the hearts and minds of Christ's people, exciting the weak, practically to the desertion of our communion, and driving all young, generous and noble spirits into scepticism and open infidelity.[1]

It was no sceptical philosopher no rationalist theologian, but the most devout and saintly of the most Christian kings,' to whom, as it was believed by his contemporaries, was vouchsafed the vision, in which his envoys met, by the shores of Palestine, a woman of stately form approaching them, with a brazier of burning coals in one hand, and a vase of water in the other. They asked her who she was, and what she bore in her hand. 'I am,' she answered, 'the Christian Religion – and I come with these burning coals to dry up the rivers of Paradise, and with these streams of water to quench the fires of hell that henceforth mankind may serve me for myself alone – may hate sin and cleave to good, for the love of God and for the love of goodness.' A bold, perhaps too

[1] Letter of the Rev. Archer Gurney to the Editor of the *Daily News*.

bold, conception, but representing a truth on which all Christian teachers would do well to meditate. It is not in the interests of philosophy, but in the interests of Religion herself, that we are bound to avoid exaggerated statements of the details of that future state, which transcends all human thought. It is from relying not on the dictates of a presumptuous reason, but on the revelations of the nature of God made in the Bible itself, that we shrink from closing for ever that door of hope which He in His infinite mercy, not in one passage only, but in many of the sacred Scriptures, has appeared to some of the holiest and purest Christians to leave open. The Bible is either silent, or speaks with a voice which conveys to some the brighter, as to others the darker, conclusion. The Church in its formal documents is silent altogether. The Forty-second Article, affirming the harsher doctrine, has been long ago struck out of the Articles of the English Church. The clergy waver in their own teaching respecting it. Those (if any there be) who really hold it, and really teach it, can hold and teach it now more effectively, from the fact that they will be known to do so, not from any imaginary compulsion of the law, but from their own unbiassed convictions. Now that the liberty to teach and to think freely on this mysterious subject is openly allowed and avowed, we doubt not that the true Biblical doctrine, whatever it is, will, through the manifold fluctuations of human belief respecting it, be at last clearly and consistently set forth.

There remains the question, perhaps in itself the most thorny of all – and that which appeared most directly to infringe on the language of the Articles – the doctrine of 'transfer by merit;' or as it is sometimes called, of 'substitution,' or of 'imputed righteousness.' Unlike the questions of Inspiration, and of Future Punishment – on which subjects no one has pretended that any Article has expressly spoken, and on which all the allegations in the recent controversies were drawn only by way of remote inference – here was a doctrine, to which one Article at least distinctly and exclusively refers. There is no Article on Inspiration. There is no Article on Hell Fire. But there is an Article on the doctrine of Justification by Faith only. In this great Article, however, the Judgment has ruled that we must not, or we need not, interpret its language beyond the exact letter of what it lays down. It asserts, so say all the Judges, that we are justified 'for the merits,' it does not assert that we are justified 'by the transfer of the merits of Christ.' We might have thought that no part of the Judgment would have provoked a more determined resistance from the whole Puritanical party in the Church, than this announcement that no theory of transferred or imputed righteousness is involved in the 'Article of a falling or standing Church.' But here came in the advantage of the union between the two contending parties. To High Churchmen as to Roman Catholics, imputed righteousness is a heresy. Their cooperation could be secured by their ancient enemies only at the cost of not raising once more this ancient feud. Not entirely without a struggle, but with a struggle so faint as to have left no traces behind, every protest on this point was abandoned. This part, perhaps the most important part of the whole Judgment, has been received without a murmur; and the voice, or the silence, of the whole English clergy has acquiesced in the clearance of these entangling and vexatious theories from the great doctrine of the Redemption of man. We will not dwell on the lasting benefits of this particular result of the Judgment; but we are satisfied that they will, in a few years, be acknowledged even by that party, or, more properly speaking, that class of mind, which has hitherto most eagerly caught at such theories, as though they were the very bulwarks of the Faith. Firmly compacted as the popular theology seemed to be on this special point, on none, we are convinced, is it more entirely (to use the sacred phrase) 'ready to wax old and vanish away;' and we are, therefore, proportionably thankful that nothing has occurred in the recent Judgment to stand in the way of this peaceful and gradual disappearance of scholastic forms, which only commended themselves to the truly devout mind because of the Eternal Truth which those forms represented, and which will shine out more clearly than ever, now that it is disencumbered, in law as well as in fact, from the theories which disfigured and concealed it.

That on each of these three questions, the conclusions of the clergy, at present so fluctuating and unsettled, should thus be left free to form themselves, is in itself an immense boon. As our great historian describes the unconscious benefits of the Peace of Ryswick,[1] so we doubt not that when the immediate pressure and panic of the moment have passed away, every English clergyman, even in the most secluded parish or amidst the most arduous pastoral work, will find his course easier, and be made aware, without knowing the cause, that the atmosphere has become lighter and the heavens brighter. He will find weapons of attack against his neighbours not so ready at hand as they used to be; he will find the means of agreement and mutual cooperation increased tenfold. Controversy perhaps will still roll on, but it will not be embittered by the taunts of dishonesty and unfaithfulness to a Church

1 Macaulay's *Hist. of England*, vol. iv. p. 810.

which has now proclaimed itself able and willing to bear the shock of free enquiry. It will be recognised that the Articles which would have admitted the doubts of Calvin, and the difficulties of Luther, on the Sacred Books, and the Prayer-book, which was read with a safe conscience by Archbishop Tillotson, have not closed the doors against their spiritual descendants. We shall have lost the expensive luxury of prosecutions, but we shall have gained the blessings of truth and peace. 'And the land had rest forty years.'

IO

J. W. COLENSO: *Preface to 'The Pentateuch and Book of Joshua Critically Examined'*

F. D. Maurice said of Colenso, with just about the degree of unfairness that may be permitted in an epigram, that his idea of history was that it is a branch of arithmetic. The whole essay on the Pentateuch is an immensely detailed and somewhat repetitive demonstration that the numerical element in the Pentateuch is often erroneous. Why did Colenso feel that this proof was of such great moment to himself and the Church?

Colenso was a Cornishman of humble birth, with a gift for mathematics, who became a Fellow of St John's College, Cambridge. The Church of England has never been very strong in Cornwall, any more than it has in Wales. Colenso grew up believing that there was no fundamental difference between the Church of England and the sects. For both, the unshakeable basis of faith was the Bible and nothing but the Bible; and Colenso, like those around him, interpreted the idea of Biblical Inspiration with the greatest possible rigour and literalness. This view he always retained, as can be seen here in the way he treats the story of the Flood. 'Of course, I am well aware that some have attempted to show that Noah's Deluge was only a *partial* one. But such attempts have ever seemed to me to be made in the very teeth of the Scripture statements, which are plain and explicit as words can possibly be.' No one with any literary sense could have written that, one is tempted to say, for the same method of interpreting Gray's Elegy would lead to the conclusion that the poet was claiming, in the first stanza, to be the only person left alive on earth. But such a comment would not be quite fair, because Biblical interpretation was then so literalistic that even people possessed of literary sense, tended to make no use of it, when reading the Bible.

Colenso's type of religion, undogmatic, high-minded ethical Protestantism, leant very heavily for its effectiveness on the agreed decencies of English life. It was the Zulus, as the Preface clearly shows, who upset Colenso, quite as much as his own restless mathematical mind. If he had stayed in England he would have been a happier man, but he would now be quite forgotten. For although, in theory, the Bible was supreme and unquestionable for the theological school to which Colenso belonged, it was not asked in practice to bear so much weight by those who remained in England. English ethical traditions kept men of Colenso's type on the rails, and needed little help in the task from doctrinal theology. But when Colenso had become a missionary, he was plunged into a world of alien traditions, and the one support, the belief in Biblical Inspiration, had to bear a weight which it was not equipped to carry.

What is particularly touching about this preface, though, apart from its deeply felt sincerity, is the way Colenso, even as he sorrowfully rejected the Bible, retained all the Hebrew moral fervour, which he and generations of Englishmen had derived from it. 'My heart Answered in the words of the Prophet, "Shall a man speak lies in the Name of the Lord?" Zech. xiii. 3.' We fully believe him when he says, 'The question has been to me a matter of life and death.'

Only one other point seems to need comment here – his puzzled references to *Essays and Reviews*. The authors of this book might well have been grouped in the public mind with Colenso. But, in reality, they were far apart. The essayists were pleading for a free hand with Scripture, the right to reject what was improbable or repulsive in their eyes. Colenso held firm to an extreme form of literalism, and then, as a result of his rigid mathematical outlook, found it break in his hand. The essayists were liberals; Colenso was a kind of radical of the right. It is not surprising that Colenso was puzzled to find himself bundled by force of circumstances on to the same side in public controversy.

THE circumstances under which this book has been written, will be best indicated by the following extracts from a letter, which I addressed some time ago, (though I did not forward it,) to a Professor of Divinity in one of our English Universities.

'My remembrance of the friendly intercourse, which I have enjoyed with you in former days, would be enough to assure me that you will excuse my troubling you on the present occasion, were I not also certain that, on far higher grounds, you will gladly lend what aid you can to a brother in distress, and in very great need of advice and assistance, such as few are better able to give than yourself. You will easily understand that, in this distant colony, I am far removed from the possibility of converse with those, who would be capable of appreciating my difficulties, and helping me with friendly sympathy and counsel. I have many friends in England; but there are few, to whom I would look more readily than to yourself, for the help which I need, from regard both to your public position and private character; and you have given evidence, moreover, in your published works, of that extensive reading and sound judgment the aid of which I specially require under my present circumstances.

'You will, of course, expect that, since I have had the charge of this Diocese, I have been closely occupied in the study of the Zulu tongue, and in translating the Scriptures into it. Through the blessing of God, I have now translated the New Testament completely, and several parts of the Old, among the rest the books of Genesis and Exodus. In this work I have been aided by intelligent natives; and, having also published a Zulu Grammar and Dictionary, I have acquired sufficient knowledge of the language, to be able to have intimate communion with the native mind, while thus engaged with them, so as not only to avail myself freely of their criticisms, but to appreciate fully their objections and difficulties. Thus, however, it has happened that I have been brought again face to face with questions, which caused me some uneasiness in former days, but with respect to which I was then enabled to satisfy my mind sufficiently for practical purposes, and I had fondly hoped to have laid the ghosts of them at last for ever. Engrossed with parochial and other work in England, I did what, probably, many other clergymen have done under similar circumstances, – I contented myself with silencing, by means of the specious explanations, which are given in most commentaries, the ordinary objections against the historical character of the early portions of the Old Testament, and settled down into a willing acquiescence in the general truth of the narrative, whatever difficulties might still hang about particular parts of it. In short, the doctrinal and devotional portions of the Bible were what were needed most in parochial duty. And, if a passage of the Old Testament formed at any time the subject of a sermon, it was easy to draw from it practical lessons of daily life, without examining closely into the historical truth of the narrative. It is true, there were one or two stories, which presented great difficulties, too prominent not to be noticed, and which were brought every now and then before us in the Lessons of the Church, such e.g. as the account of the Creation and the Deluge. But, on the whole, I found so much of Divine Light and Life in these and other parts of the Sacred Book, so much wherewith to feed my own soul and the souls of others, that I was content to take all this for granted, as being true in the main, however wonderful, and as being at least capable, in an extreme case, of *some* sufficient explanation.

'Here, however, as I have said, amidst my work in this land, I have been brought face to face with the very questions which I then put by. While translating the story of the Flood, I have had a simple-minded, but intelligent, native, – one with the docility of a child, but the reasoning powers of mature age, – look up, and ask, "Is all that true? Do you really believe that all this happened thus, – that all the beasts, and birds, and creeping things, upon the earth, large and small, from hot countries and cold, came thus by pairs, and entered into the ark with Noah? And did Noah gather food for them *all*, for the beasts and birds of prey, as well as the rest?" My heart answered in the words of the Prophet, "Shall a man speak lies in the Name of the LORD?" Zech. xiii. 3. I dared not do so. My own knowledge of some branches of science, of Geology in particular, had been much increased since I left England; and I now knew for certain, on geological grounds, a fact, of which I had only had misgivings before, viz. that a *Universal* Deluge, such as the Bible manifestly speaks of, could not possibly have taken place in the way described in the Book of Genesis, not to mention other difficulties which the story contains. I refer especially to the circumstance, well known to all geologists, (see Lyell's *Elementary Geology*, p. 197, 198,) that volcanic hills exist of immense extent in Auvergne and Languedoc, which must have been formed ages before the Noachian Deluge, and which are covered with light and loose substances, pumice-stone, &c., that must have been swept away by a Flood, but do not exhibit the slightest sign of having ever been so disturbed. Of course, I am well aware that some have attempted to show that Noah's Deluge was only a *partial* one. But such attempts have ever seemed to me to be made in the very teeth of the Scripture statements, which are as plain and explicit as words can possibly be. Nor is anything really gained by supposing the Deluge to have been partial. For, as waters must find their own level on the Earth's surface, without a special miracle, of which the Bible says nothing, a Flood, which should begin by covering the top of Ararat, (if that were conceivable,) or a much lower mountain, must necessarily become universal, and in due time sweep over the hills of Auvergne. Knowing this, I felt that I dared not, as a servant of the God of Truth, urge my brother man to believe that, which I did not myself believe, which I knew to be untrue, as a matter-of-fact, historical, narrative. I gave him, however, such a reply as satisfied him for the time, without throwing any discredit upon the general veracity of the Bible history.

'But I was thus driven, – against my will at first, I may truly say, – to search more deeply into these questions; and I have since done so, to the best of my power, with the means at my disposal in this colony. And now I tremble at the result of my enquiries, rather, I should do so, were it not that I believe firmly in a God of Righteousness and Truth and Love, who both "IS, and is a rewarder of them that diligently seek him." Should all else give way beneath me, I feel that His Everlasting Arms are still under me. I am sure that the solid ground is there, on which my feet can rest, in the knowledge of Him, "in whom I live, and move, and have my being," who is my "faithful Creator," my "Almighty and most Merciful Father." *That* Truth I see with my spirit's eyes, once opened to the light of it, as plainly as I see the Sun in the heavens. And that Truth, I know, more or less distinctly apprehended, has been the food of living men, the strength of brave souls that "yearn for light," and battle for the right and the true, the support of struggling and sorrow-stricken hearts, in all ages of the world, in all climes, under all religions.'

[The letter then proceeded to state some of the principal difficulties in the account of the Exodus, which are set forth at full length in this volume, and concluded as follows.]

'Will you oblige me by telling me if you know of any books, which to your own mind deal with these questions satisfactorily, or, rather, will you kindly direct Messrs —— to send to me the book or books you may recommend, with others which I have ordered from them? Among the rest, I have sent for Hengstenberg's book on the Pentateuch, which I see commended in a remarkable article in the Quarterly on "Essays and Reviews." That article, however, appears to me to shrink from touching the real question at issue, and, instead of meeting the essayists with argument, to be chiefly occupied with pitying or censuring them. Certainly, there are not a few points on which I differ strongly from those writers. But I cannot think it to be a fair way of proceeding to point out, as the *apparent consequence* of the course they are pursuing, that it will necessarily lead to infidelity or atheism. It may be so with some; must it, therefore, be so with all? The same, of course, might have been said, and probably was said, freely, and just as truly, by the Jews of St Paul and others, and, in later times, by members of the Romish Church of our own Reformers. Our duty, surely, is to follow the Truth, wherever it leads us, and to leave the consequences in the hands of God. Moreover, in the only instance, where the writer in the Quarterly does attempt to remove a difficulty, he explains away a miracle by a piece of thorough "neologianism," – I mean, where he accounts for the sun "standing still," at the word of Joshua, by referring to "one of the *thousand other modes*, by which God's mighty power could have accomplished that miracle, rather than by the actual suspension of the unbroken career of the motion of the heavenly bodies in their appointed courses," which last the Bible plainly speaks of to a common understanding, though the writer seems not to believe in it.[1]

[1] So, too, Archd. Pratt writes, *Scripture and Science not at variance*, p. 25, – 'The accomplishment of this [miracle] is *supposed by some* [N.B.] to have been *by the arresting of the earth in its rotation*. In what other words, then, could the miracle have been expressed? Should it have been said, "So the earth ceased to revolve, and made the sun appear to stand still in the midst of heaven?" This is not the language we should use, even in these days of scientific light. Were so great a wonder again to appear, would even an astronomer, as he looked into the heavens, exclaim, "The earth stands still!"? Would he not be laughed at as a pedant? Whereas, to use the language of appearances, and thus to imitate the style of the Holy Scriptures themselves, would be most natural and intelligible.'
It will be observed that Archd. Pratt does not commit *himself* to maintaining the above view: he says, 'it is supposed by some' to have been accomplished thus. But he argues as if this explanation were possible, and not improbable; that is to say, he lends the weight of his high position and mathematical celebrity to the support of a view, which every natural philosopher will know to be wholly untenable. For, – not to speak of the fact, that, if the earth's motion were suddenly stopped, a man's *feet* would be arrested, while his *body* was moving at the rate (on the equator) of 1,000 miles an hour, (or, rather, 1,000 miles a *minute*, since not only must the earth's diurnal rotation on its axis be stopped, but its annual motion also through space, so that every human being and animal would be dashed to pieces in a moment, and a mighty deluge overwhelm the earth, unless all this were prevented by a profusion of miraculous interferences, – one point is at once fatal to the above solution. Archd. Pratt quotes only the words, 'So the *sun* stood still in the midst of heaven, and hasted not to go down about a whole day;' and, although this is surely one of the most prominent questions, in respect of which it is asserted that 'Scripture and Science are at variance,' he dismisses the whole subject in a short note, and never even mentions the *moon*. But the Bible says, '*The sun stood still, and the moon stayed*,' Jo. x. 13; and the arresting of the earth's motion, while it might cause the appearance of the sun 'standing still,' would not account for the moon 'staying.'
It is impossible not to feel the force of Archd. Pratt's own observation, p. 30, 'The leasson we learn from this example is this: How possible it is that, even while we are contending for truth, our minds may be enslaved to error by long-cherished prepossessions!'

J. W. COLENSO

'After reading that article, I felt more hopelessly than ever how hollow is the ground, upon which we have so long been standing, with reference to the subject of the Inspiration of Scripture. I see that there is a very general demand made upon the clerical authors of "Essays and Reviews," that they should leave the Church of England, or, at least, resign their preferments. For my own part, however much I may dissent, as I do, from some of their views, I am very far indeed from judging them for remaining, as they still do, as ministers within her pale, – knowing too well, by my own feelings, how dreadful would be the wrench, to be torn from all one has loved and revered, by going out of the Church. Perhaps, they may feel it to be their duty to the Church itself, and to that which they hold to be the truth, to abide in their stations, unless they are formally and legally excluded from them, and to claim for *all* her members, clerical as well as lay, that freedom of thought and utterance, which is the very essence of our Protestant religion, and without which, indeed, in this age of advancing science, the Church of England would soon become a mere dark prison-house, in which the mind both of the teacher and the taught would be fettered still with the chains of past ignorance, instead of being, as we fondly believed, the very home of religious liberty, and the centre of life and light for all the world. But, whatever may be the fate of that book or its authors, it is surely impossible to put down, in these days, the spirit of honest, truth-seeking, investigation into such matters as these. To attempt to do this, would only be like the futile endeavour to sweep back the tide, which is rising at our very doors. This is assuredly no time for such trifling. Instead of trying to do this, or to throw up sand-banks, which may serve for the present moment to hide from our view the swelling waters, it is plainly our duty before God and Man to see that the foundations of our faith are sound, and deeply laid in the very Truth itself.

'For myself, if I cannot find the means of doing away with my present difficulties, I see not how I can retain my Episcopal Office, in the discharge of which I must require from others a solemn declaration, that they "unfeignedly believe all the Canonical Scriptures of the Old and New Testament," which, with the evidence now before me, it is impossible wholly to believe in.[1]

'I need not say to you that, whatever support and comfort I may feel in the consciousness of doing what appears to be right, it would be no

[1] This was written before the recent decision of the Court of Arches, by which, of course, the above conclusion is materially affected.

light thing for me, at my time of life, to be cast adrift upon the world, and have to begin life again under heavy pressure and amidst all unfavourable circumstances, – to be separated from many of my old friends, to have my name cast out as evil even by some of them, and to have it trodden under foot, as an unclean thing, by others, who do not know me, – not to speak of the pain it would cause me to leave a work like this, which has been committed to me in this land, to which my whole heart and soul have been devoted, and for which, as it seemed, God had fitted me in some measure more than for others, – a work in which I would joyfully still, if it please God, spend and be spent.

'But God's Will must be done. The Law of Truth must be obeyed. I shall await your reply, before I take any course, which may commit me in so serious a matter. And I feel that I shall do right to take time for careful deliberation. Should my difficulties not be removed, I shall, if God will, come to England, and there again consult some of my friends. But then, if the step must be taken, in God's name I must take it; and He Himself will provide for me future work on earth, of some kind or other, if He has work for me to do.'

The above letter I wrote, but did not forward, in the early part of 1861. I had not then gone so deeply into the question as I have done since. And, as I do not wish to be misunderstood by some, whom I truly esteem and love, – to whom I owe all duty and respect, but allegiance to the Truth above all, – I may here say that, at the time when I took counsel with my Episcopal Brethren at the Capetown Conference in January, 1861, I had not even begun to enter on these enquiries, though I fully intended to do so on my return to Natal. Then, however, I had not the most distant idea of the results at which I have now arrived. I am sensible, of course, that, in stating this, I lay myself open to the objection, that the views, which I now hold, are comparatively of recent date, and, having been adopted within less than two years, may be found after a while untenable, and be as quickly abandoned. I do not myself see any probability or possibility of this, so far as the *main* question is concerned, viz. the unhistorical character of the story of the Exodus, which is exhibited in the First Part of this work. But, however this may be, I have thought it right to state the simple truth. And, though these views are, comparatively speaking, new to me, – and will be new, as I believe, to most of my English readers, even to many of the Clergy, of whom, probably, few have examined the Pentateuch *closely* since they took Orders, while parts of it some of them may never really have *studied* at all, – yet I am by this time well aware that most of the points here considered have been already brought forward, though not exactly in the present form, by various continental writers, with whom the critical and scientific study of the Scriptures has made more progress than it has yet done in England.[1]

Some, indeed, may be ready to say of this book, as the Quarterly says of the Essayists, 'the whole apparatus is *drawn bodily* from the German Rationalists.' This, however, is not the case; and I will, at once, state plainly to what extent I have been indebted to German sources, in the original composition of this work. Having determined that it was my duty, without loss of time, to engage myself thoroughly in the task, of examining into the foundations of the current belief in the historical credibility of the Mosaic story, I wrote to a friend in England, and requested him to send me some of the best books for entering on such a course of study, begging him to forward to me books on both sides of the question, 'both the bane and the antidote.' He sent me two German works, Ewald (*Geschichte des Volkes Israel*, 7 vols.) and Kurtz (*History of the Old Covenant*, 3 vols.), the former in German, the latter in an English translation (*Clark's Theol. Libr.*), and a book, which maintains the ordinary view, of the Mosaic origin and historical accuracy of the Pentateuch, with great zeal and ability, as will be seen by the numerous extracts which I have made from it in the body of this work. On receiving these books, I laid, for the present, Ewald on the shelf, and devoted myself to the close study of Kurtz's work, – with what result the contents of this volume will show. I then grappled with Ewald's book, and studied it diligently, the parts of it, at least, which concern the O.T. history. It certainly displays an immense amount of erudition, such as may well entitle it to be called, as in the Ed. Review on 'Essays and Reviews,' a 'noble work.' But, with respect to the Pentateuch, anyone, who is well acquainted with it, will perceive that my conclusions, on many important points, differ materially from his. Besides these, I had, at first, two books of Hengstenberg, on the *Psalms* and on the *Christology of the O.T.* And these comprised the whole of my stock of German Theology, when the substance of this book was

[1] Hengstenberg is very fond of representing almost all his opponents as *followers* of De Wette: 'They supply themselves very freely from his stores, and have made scarcely the least addition to them.' *Pent.* ii. p. 3. This, if true, would tend to diminish the force of their multiplied testimony, and to reduce it to the single voice of De Wette. But the *same* difficulties, *if they really exist*, must, of course, occur to *all*, who bring a fair and searching criticism to bear upon the subject, however they may differ in their mode of stating them.

written. Since then, however, and while rewriting it with a view to publication, De Wette's *Einleitung*, and Bleek's excellent posthumous work, *Einleitung in das A.T.*, have come into my hands. I have also carefully studied the most able modern works, written in defence of the ordinary view, such as Hengstenberg's *Dissertations on the Genuineness of the Pentateuch*, Hävernick's *Introduction to the O.T.*, &c., with what effect the contents of the present work will show. At a still later period, I have been able to compare my results with those of Kuenen, in his *Historisch-Kritisch Onderzoek*, of which Part I, on the Historical Books of the O.T. has just been published at Leyden, (Sept. 1861,) – a work of rare merit, but occupied wholly with critical and historical questions, such as do not come into consideration at all in the First Part of the present work. And, since my return to England, I have had an opportunity of consulting Dr Davidson's *Introduction to the O.T.*, Vols. I and II, the most able work which has yet appeared in England on the subject of Biblical Criticism.

It will be observed that I have quoted repeatedly from Kurtz, Hengstenberg, &c., as well as from English works of eminence, written in support of the ordinary view. I have made these quotations on principle, in order that the reader may have before him all that, as far as I am aware, can be said by the best writers on that side of the question, and may perceive also that I have myself carefully considered the arguments of such writers, and have not hastily and lightly adopted my present views; and I have often availed myself of their language, in illustration of some point occurring in the course of the enquiry, as being not only valuable on account of the information given on good authority, but liable also to no suspicion of having been composed from my own point of view, for the purpose of maintaining my argument.

Being naturally unwilling in my present position, as a Bishop of the Church, to commit myself even to a friend on so grave a subject, if it could possibly be avoided, I determined to detain my letter when written, for a time, to see what effect further study and consideration would have upon my views. At the end of that time, – in a great measure, by my being made more fully aware of the utter helplessness of Kurtz and Hengstenberg, in their endeavours to meet the difficulties, which are raised by a closer study of the Pentateuch, – I became so convinced of the unhistorical[1] character of very considerable portions

---

[1] I use the expression 'unhistorical' or 'not historically true' throughout, rather than 'fictitious,' since the word 'fiction' is frequently understood to imply *a conscious dishonesty* on the part of the writer, an *intention* to deceive. Yet, in writing the

of the Mosaic narrative, that I decided not to forward my letter at all. I did not now need counsel or assistance to relieve my own personal doubts; in fact, I had no longer any doubts; my former misgivings had been changed to certainties. The matter was become much more serious. I saw that it concerned the whole Church, – not myself, and a few more only, whose minds might have been disturbed by making too much of minor difficulties and contradictions, the force of which might be less felt by others. It was clear to me that difficulties, such as those which are set forth in the First Part of this book, would be felt, and realised in their full force, by most intelligent Englishmen, whether of the Clergy or Laity, who should once have had them clearly brought before their eyes, and have allowed their minds to rest upon them.[1]

story of the Exodus, from the ancient legends of his people, the Scripture writer may have had no more consciousness of doing wrong or of practising historical deception, than Homer had, or any of the early Roman annalists. It is *we*, who do *him* wrong, and do wrong to the real excellence of the Scripture story, by maintaining that it must be historically true, and that the writer *meant* it to be received and believed as such, not only by his own countrymen, but by all mankind to the end of time. Besides which, it should be remembered always (as a friend has very justly observed) that, 'in forming an estimate of ancient documents, of the early Scriptures especially, we are doing that, which is like examining judicially the case of one who is absent, and unable to give his account of the matter. We should be very scrupulous about assuming that it is impossible to explain satisfactorily this or that apparent inconsistency, contradiction, or other anomaly, and charging him with dishonesty of purpose, considering that ours is an *ex parte* statement, and incapable of being submitted to the party against whom it is made.'

[1] The following passage is written with a just appreciation of that 'love of positive, objective, truth,' which marks at least, if it does not specially distinguish, the English character. I cannot, however, give my assent to the closing words, which I have italicised, with the examples of Lycurgus, Numa, Zoroaster, &c., before me.

'One great characteristic of Englishmen, – the characteristic, in fact, on which they may justly rest their claims to a foremost (indeed *the* foremost) position among the representative races of humanity, is the belief in, and the love of, positive, objective, truth. . . . The Englishman may be narrow-minded or prejudiced, unapt to deal with abstract speculations. But he has, at least, had this training, – he has been accustomed to weigh evidence, *to seek for matter-of-fact truth in the first place*, and to satisfy himself as to the good faith and correct information of those, from whom he expects to receive knowledge or instruction. One thing with him is fixed and certain; whatever else is doubtful, this at least is sure: a narrative purporting to be one of positive facts, which is wholly or in any essential or considerable portion untrue, *can have no connection with the Divine, and cannot have any beneficial influence on mankind.*' – Rev. Preb. Cook, *Aids to Faith*, p. 146.

To the same effect writes the Rev. H. J. Rose, *Replies to Essays and Reviews*, p. 65: 'We must never forget the difference between the German and the English mind. The paradise of the German appears to consist in unlimited license of speculation, while the *practical element* is the prevailing characteristic of the English.

I considered, therefore, that I had not a right to ask of my friend privately beforehand a reply to my objections, with respect to which, as a Divinity Professor, he might, perhaps, ere long be required to express his opinion in his public capacity.

This conviction, which I have arrived at, of the *certainty* of the ground on which the *main* argument of my book rests, (viz. the proof that the account of the Exodus, whatever value it may have, *is not historically true*,) must be my excuse to the reader for the manner in which I have conducted the enquiry. A friend, to whom I had submitted the work, before I had decided to publish it, was afraid that I might give offence by stating too plainly at the outset the end which I had in view. He thought then – though now approving fully of the course which I am taking – that such an open declaration of the sum and substance of my work 'might tend to prejudice the reader, and probably make him more inclined to become hardened against the force of the arguments.' And he suggested that I might do more wisely to conceal, as it were, my purpose for a time, and lead the reader gradually on, till he 'would arrive of himself, almost unawares,' at the same conclusions as my own. But, however judicious for a merely rhetorical purpose such a course might have been, I could not allow myself to adopt it here, in a matter where such very important consequences are involved. I *must* state the case plainly and fully from the first. I do not wish to take the reader by surprise or to entrap him by guile. I wish him to go forward with his eyes open, and to watch carefully every step of the argument, with a full consciousness of the momentous results to which it leads, and with a determination to test *severely*, with all the power and skill he can bring to the work, but yet to test *honestly* and *fairly*, the truth of every inference which I have drawn, and every conclusion at which I have arrived. As Dr Moberly has well said, (*Some Remarks on Essays and Reviews*) –

Those, who have the means of knowing, must not be content with a religion on sufferance. The difficulties must be solved, and the objections must be met, when they are produced in a serious and argumentative form. p. xxv.

A serious statement of difficulties is a thing to be highly respected and seriously replied to; and, as to discussion, it would show great want of con-

---

And thus it often happens that a German will not cast off a certain phase of faith, when he has demolished every ground, *which an Englishman would deem a rational and logical foundation for holding it.*'

To this strong, practical, love of truth in my fellow-countrymen, whether Clergy or Laity, I appeal in the present volume.

J. W. COLENSO

fidence in what we believe to be the truth of God, if we were afraid of allowing it, or of entering upon it, when gravely purposed and conducted. p. lxiii.

So, too, a plain and full statement of the case has been loudly called for by the most strenuous English defenders of the ordinary view of Scripture Inspiration. Thus the Rev. J. W. Burgon writes, *Inspiration and Interpretation*, p. xxxvi,

> We desiderate nothing so much as 'searching enquiry.' . . . If the writer would state a single case with its evidence, we should know how to deal with him. We should examine his arguments *seriatim*, and either refute them, or *admit their validity*. From such 'free handling' the cause of sacred Truth can never suffer.

And Prof. Mansel writes, *Aids to Faith*, p. 12:

> Let us, at the outset, be clearly convinced of the vital importance of the question, in order that we may enter on its examination, prepared, if necessary, to sacrifice our most valued convictions at the demand of Truth, but, at the same time, so convinced of their value, as to be jealous of sacrificing them to anything but Truth.

I have, therefore, decided that it was my duty to give no 'uncertain sound,' but to set down openly at the outset the nature of the issue involved; and I trust that any plainness of speech in this respect will not be misinterpreted by my readers, as implying any wish or readiness on my part to utter what it may be painful to them, in their present state of mind, to hear. If my conclusions, indeed, were only *speculations*, if they were only matters of higher or lower *probability*, I feel that I should have no right to express them at all in this way, and thus, it may be, disturb painfully the faith of many. But the main result of my examination of the Pentateuch, – viz. that the narrative, whatever may be its value and meaning, cannot be regarded as historically true, – is not – unless I greatly deceive myself – a doubtful matter of speculation at all; it is a simple question of *facts*.

That the phenomena in the Pentateuch, to which I have drawn attention in the first instance, and which show so decisively its unhistorical character, have not yet, as far as I am aware, been set forth, in this form, before the eyes of English readers, may, perhaps, be explained as follows:

(i) Some of these difficulties would only be likely to occur to one in the same position as myself, engaged as a Missionary in translating the Scriptures, and, therefore, compelled to discuss all the minutest details with intelligent natives, whose mode of life and habits, and even the nature of their country, so nearly correspond to those of the ancient

Israelites, that the very same scenes are brought continually, as it were, before our eyes, and *vividly realised in a practical point of view*, in a way in which an English student would scarcely think of looking at them.

(ii) Such studies as these have made very little progress as yet among the Clergy and Laity of *England*; and so the English mind, with its practical common-sense, has scarcely yet been brought to bear upon them. Add to which, that the study of the Hebrew language has, till of late years, been very much neglected in England in modern times.

(iii) The difficulties, which have been usually brought forward in England, as affecting the historical character of the Pentateuch, are those which concern the Creation, the Fall, and the Deluge; and many, who feel these difficulties very strongly, are able to get over them, by supposing the first two to embody some kind of allegorical teaching, and the last to be a report of some dread catastrophe, handed down in the form of a legend from hoar antiquity, without questioning at all the general historical truth of the story of the Exodus, upon which such important consequences depend. Hence such minds are little impressed by discussions mooted upon these points, and, indeed, are rather irritated by having these questions brought before them at all, when, as they think, they can be fairly disposed of.

(iv) Thus it is that English Books, upon the historical credibility of the Mosaic narrative, are at present very few, and still fewer those, which treat the subject with the reverence due to a question, which involves the dearest hopes, and fondest beliefs, of so many; while others again, as the essays in 'Aids to Faith' and 'Replies to Essays and Reviews,' which are written in defence of the ordinary view while, professing a desire for candid and free, though reverential, examination of the subject, yet pass by entirely the main points of difficulty, as if they were wholly unknown to the writers.

(v) It is not unlikely that the works of the (so-called) *orthodox* German writers, Hävernick, Kurtz, Hengstenberg, Keil, &c., which are now being translated, and published in *Clark's Theological Library*, might before long have effected indirectly a considerable change in the current theology of England, by its being seen how feebly they reply to some of the more striking objections, which occur on a close study of the Pentateuch, – and which many an English reader will often learn first from these very attempts to answer them, – and also how often they are obliged, by the force of the Truth itself, to abandon ground long held sacred in England, of which several instances will appear in the body of this book. But, even then, these portions of their works are often so overlaid with a mass of German erudition, in illustration of other questions of no consequence, about which there is no doubt or dispute, that the reader is carried on from one real difficulty to another, without being exactly satisfied on each point as he passes, but yet without feeling very forcibly the failure in each particular instance, his attention being distracted, and his patience and perseverance often rather painfully tasked, in the labour of going through the intermediate matter.

(vi) On the other hand, writers of the liberal school in Germany take so completely for granted, – either on mere *critical* grounds, or because they assume from the first the utter impossibility of miracles or supernatural revelations, – the unhistorical character and non-Mosaic origin of the greater portion, at least, if not the whole, of the Pentateuch, that they do not generally take the trouble to test the credibility of the story, by entering into such matter-of-fact enquiries, as are here made the basis of the whole argument.

There can be no doubt, however, that a very wide-spread distrust does exist among the intelligent Laity in England, as to the soundness of the ordinary view of Scripture Inspiration. But such distrust is generally grounded on one or two objections, felt strongly, perhaps, but yet imperfectly apprehended, not on a devout and careful study of the whole question, with deliberate consideration of all that can be said on both sides of it. Hence it is rather secretly felt, than openly expressed; though it is sufficiently exhibited to the eye of a reflecting man in many outward signs of the times, and in none more painfully than in the fact, which has been lamented by more than one of the English Bench of Bishops, and which every Colonial Bishop must still more sorrowfully confess, that the great body of the more intelligent students of our Universities no longer come forward to devote themselves to the service of the Church, but are drafted off into other professions. How can it be otherwise, when in an age like the present, – which has been well described as one 'remarkable for fearlessness, and it may be hoped, for sincerity, in the pursuit of truth,' (Rev. Preb. Cook, *Aids to Faith*, p. 133,) – the very condition of a young man's entering the Ministry of the Church of England is, that he surrender henceforth all freedom of thought, or, at least, of utterance, upon the great questions which the age is rife in, and solemnly bind himself for life to 'believe unfeignedly all the Canonical Scriptures;' while he probably knows enough already of geology, at all events, if not of the results of critical enquiry, to feel that he cannot honestly profess to believe in them implicitly?[1] The Church of England must fall to the ground by its own internal weakness, – by losing its hold upon the growing intelligence of all classes, – unless some remedy be very soon applied to this state of things. It is a miserable policy, which now prevails, unworthy of the Truth itself, and one which cannot long be maintained, to 'keep things quiet.'

Meanwhile, a restraint is put upon scientific enquiry of every kind, by the fear of transgressing in some way the bounds, which the Scripture statements are supposed to have set to such speculations, and by the necessity of propitiating to some extent the popular religious feeling on the subject.[2] Men of science, generally, have not the leisure to pursue very far for themselves such investigations as these. And, if men of devout minds, they will feel obliged to acquiesce, more or less, in the *dicta* of the Church and the Clergy, while conscious oftentimes that such *dicta* are painfully at variance with truths, which they have begun to glimpse at as the results of their own researches. They must proceed, and, probably, very many do proceed, far enough to see that there is something hollow in the popular belief, and that the modern view of Scripture Inspiration cannot possibly be true in all points. But the work of examining into its truth or falsehood is a work for theologians, not for natural philosophers, and, to be done thoroughly, it requires great labour and a special training. Hence they will probably drop the subject altogether, some sinking into practical, if even unavowed, unbelief of

1 This passage I have written, notwithstanding the relief given to the consciences of many of the clergy by Dr Lushington's recent judgment, because, if I mistake not, the answer in the Ordination Service is not the only part of our formularies, that will be generally understood, until explained by judicial authority, to involve implicit belief in the historical truth of the facts recorded in the Pentateuch.

2 A remarkable illustration of this may be seen in the fact that, even in such a work as the English translation of Humboldt's *Cosmos*, 'undertaken in compliance with the wish of Baron von Humboldt,' 'under the superintendence of Lieut. Col. Edward Sabine, R.A., For. Sec. R.S.,' an important passage is omitted altogether, in which the expression of the author's views, as to the origin of the human race from one pair, would have, perhaps, offended the religious prejudices of English readers. That the passage in question was not suppressed, by reason of any change of view in Humboldt himself, is shown by the fact that it is found in the French translation, and the translator, M. Faye, states as follows: 'Another part, relative to the great question of human races, has been translated by M. Guignaut. This question was foreign to my habitual studies. Moreover, it has been treated in the German work with such superiority of views and of style, that M. de Humboldt had to seek, among his friends, the man most capable of giving its equivalent to French readers. M. de Humboldt naturally addressed himself to M. Guignaut; and this *savant* has been pleased to undertake the translation of the last ten pages of the text, as well as of the corresponding note.' (See *Indigenous Races of the Earth*, Trübner and Co., London, pp. 402–409.)

the whole Mosaic story, as told in the Pentateuch, others smothering up their misgivings with a general assumption that the account must be substantially true; while there are very many, who appreciate to some extent the difficulties of the ordinary view, but yet are unable to satisfy themselves that it is wholly untenable, and live in a state of painful uncertainty, which they would gladly have terminated, though even by the sharp pang of one decisive stroke, which shall sever their connection with it once and for ever.

I believe that there are not a few among the more highly educated classes of society in England, and multitudes among the more intelligent operatives, who are in danger of drifting into irreligion and practical atheism, under this dim sense of the unsoundness of the popular view, combined with a feeling of distrust of their spiritual teachers, as if *these* must be either ignorant of facts, which to themselves are patent, or, at least, insensible to the difficulties which those facts involve, or else, being aware of their existence, and feeling their importance, are consciously ignoring them. It has been said by some, 'Why make this disturbance? Why publish to the world matters like these, about which theologians may have doubts?' I answer, that they are not theologians only, who are troubled with such doubts, and that we have a duty to discharge towards that large body of our brethren, – *how* large it is impossible to say, but, probably, much larger than is commonly imagined, – who not only doubt, but disbelieve, many important parts of the Mosaic narrative, as well as to those, whose faith may be more simple and unenquiring though not, therefore, necessarily, more deep and sincere, than theirs. We cannot expect such as these to look to us for comfort and help in their religious perplexities, if they cannot place entire confidence in our honesty of purpose and good faith, – if they have any reason to suppose that we are willing to keep back any part of the truth, and are afraid to state the plain facts of the case.

On this subject I commend to the reader's attention the following admirable remarks of Archbishop Whately, (*Bacon's Essays*, with Annotations, p. 11):

We are bound never to countenance any erroneous opinion, however seemingly beneficial in its results, – never to connive at any salutary delusion (as it may appear), but to open the eyes (when opportunity offers, and in proportion as it offers) of those we are instructing, to any mistake they may labour under, though it may be one which leads them ultimately to a true result, and to one of which they might otherwise fail. The temptation to depart from this principle is sometimes excessively strong, because it will often be the case that men will be in some danger, in parting with a long-admitted error, of abandoning, at the same time, some truth they have been accustomed to connect with it. Accordingly, censures have been passed on the endeavours to enlighten the adherents of some erroneous churches, on the ground that many of them thence become atheists, and many, the wildest of fanatics. That this should have been in some instances the case, is highly probable; it is a natural result of the pernicious effects on the mind of any system of blind unenquiring acquiescence. Such a system is an evil spirit, which, we must expect, will cruelly rend and mangle the patient as it comes out of him, and will leave him half dead at its departure. There will often be, and oftener appear to be, danger in removing a mistake, – the danger that those, who have been long used to act rightly on erroneous principles, may fail of the desired conclusions when undeceived. In such cases, it requires a thorough love of truth, and a firm reliance on Divine support, to adhere steadily to the straight course. If we give way to a dread of danger from the inculcation of any truth, physical, moral, or religious, we manifest a want of faith in God's power, or in the will to maintain His own cause. There may be danger attendant on every truth, since there is none that may not be perverted by some, or that may not give offence to others; but, in the case of anything which plainly appears to be truth, every danger must be braved. We must maintain the truth as we have received it, and trust to Him, who is 'the Truth,' to prosper and defend it.

That we shall indeed best further His cause by fearless perseverance in an open and straight course, I am firmly persuaded. But is is not only when we *perceive* the mischiefs of falsehood and disguise, and the beneficial tendancy of fairness and candour, that we are to be followers of truth. The trial of our faith is when we *cannot* perceive this; and the part of a lover of truth is, to follow her at all seeming hazards, after the example of Him, who 'came into the world, that He should bear witness to the Truth.'

For such persons especially, as I have indicated above, I have written this book, and for all, who would really see and know the actual Truth in this matter. I have desired to set before the reader at full length the arguments, by which I have been myself convinced upon the subject, and to take him with me, as it were, along the path, which I have followed in the search after the Truth. It is not sufficient merely to make general statements, or to refer to this or that writer, as having irrefragably proved the truth of certain results.[1] I have wished to enable the

[1] This is a great defect in more than one of the Essays contained in the 'Aids to Faith,' arising chiefly, no doubt, from the very wide extent of ground which the whole controversy covers, and the limited space that could be allotted for each individual reply. But it is very unsatisfactory to be told, p. 248, that 'it has been shown by Hävernick,' or, p. 240, that 'Hengstenberg has established beyond all possibility of refutation' some point under consideration, when (as will appear in numberless cases in the course of this work) an actual quotation and discussion of the arguments used in such cases would very probably show that they are anything but convincing or indisputable. So, too, the Essays, above referred to, deal for the most part with general questions, upon which it is easy to say much

reader to satisfy his own mind on each point as it arises, precisely as I have satisfied mine, by a thorough discussion of all that can be said on both sides of the question.

Much labour has thus been bestowed, in the course of this work, in exposing the fallacy of very many of the arguments, which have been adduced by Hengstenberg and others, in support of the ordinary view. With reference to this point I sympathise entirely with the sentiments expressed in the following extract, quoted in *Types of Mankind,* Trübner and Co., p. 655:

> We should feel a humiliation to contend with such sophistries seriously and in detail, were we not firmly convinced that to do so is not merely the *most legitimate,* but also the *only,* mode, by which truth can be rendered permanently triumphant. Wit and sarcasm may obtain a temporary success; they may awaken minds otherwise prepared for freedom; but they are often unjust, usually un-benevolent, and consequently, in the majority of cases, they merely awaken antagonism, and cause men to cling with increased fondness to their opinions. Nothing but minute, searching, inexorable, argument will ever obtain a speedy or a permanent triumph over deep-seated prejudice.

And, although by adopting this course, I have necessarily increased the size of my book, I could not do otherwise, if I would effectually compass the end which I have in view, and place the whole subject fairly and fully within the grasp of any earnest intelligent enquirer, whether Clerk or Layman.

I have here confined my enquiries chiefly to the Pentateuch and book of Joshua, though, in so doing, I have found myself compelled to take more or less into consideration the other books of the Old Testament also. Should God in His Providence call me to the work, I shall not shrink from the duty of examining on behalf of others into the question, in what way the interpretation of the New Testament is affected by the unhistorical character of the Pentateuch. Of course, for the satisfaction of my own mind, and in the discharge of my duties to those more immediately dependent on me, I cannot avoid doing so, if health and strength are granted me, as soon as I have completed the present work, and ascertained that the ground is sure, on which I here take my stand. For the present, I have desired to follow the leading of the Truth itself, and not to distract my attention, or incur the temptation of falsifying

---

that is very true, and would be readily admitted, at least by one arguing from my point of view; whereas the *details* of the Scripture narrative, in which the real difficulties lie, are left by these writers for the most part unnoticed.

the conclusions, to which the argument would honestly lead me, by taking account *à priori* of the consequences; and I would gladly leave to other hands the work of conducting the above enquiry at greater length for the general reader.

On one point, however, it may be well to make here a few observations. There may be some, who will say that such words as those in John vi. 46, 47, 'For had ye believed Moses, ye would have believed Me, for *he wrote* of Me. But, if ye believe not his writings, how shall ye believe my words?' – or in Luke xx. 37, 'Now, that the dead are raised, even *Moses shewed* at the bush, [i.e. in the passage about the 'bush,'] when he called the LORD, the God of Abraham, and the God of Isaac, and the God of Jacob,' – or in Luke xvi. 29, '*They have Moses and the Prophets*; let them hear them,' and v. 31, '*If they hear not Moses and the Prophets*, neither will they be persuaded, though one rose from the dead,' – are at once decisive upon the point of Moses' authorship of the Pentateuch, since they imply that our Lord Himself believed in it, and, consequently, to assert that Moses did *not* write these books, would be to contradict the words of Christ, and to impugn His veracity.

To make use of such an argument is, indeed, to bring the Sacred Ark itself into the battle-field, and to make belief in Christianity itself depend entirely upon the question whether Moses wrote the Pentateuch, or not. There is, however, no force in this particular objection, as will appear from the following considerations.

(i) First, such words as the above, if understood in their most literal sense, can only be supposed, at all events, to apply to *certain parts* of the Pentateuch; since most devout Christians will admit that the last chapter of Deuteronomy, which records the death of Moses, could not have been written by his hand, and the most orthodox commentators are obliged also to concede the probability of *some* other interpolations having been made in the original story. It would become, therefore, even thus, a question for a reverent criticism to determine what passages give signs of *not* having been written by Moses.

(ii) But, secondly, and more generally, it may be said that, in making use of such expressions, our Lord did but accommodate His words to the current popular language of the day, as when He speaks of God 'making His sun to rise,' Matt. v. 45, or of the 'stars falling from heaven,' Matt. xxiv. 29, or of Lazarus being 'carried by the angels into Abraham's bosom,' Luke xvi. 22, or of the woman 'with a spirit of infirmity,' whom 'Satan had bound eighteen years,' Luke xiii. 16, &c.,

without our being at all authorized in drawing from them scientific or psychological conclusions.

(iii) Lastly, it is perfectly consistent with the most entire and sincere belief in our Lord's Divinity, to hold, as many do, that, when He vouchsafed to become a 'Son of Man,' He took our nature fully, and voluntarily entered into all the conditions of humanity, and among others, into that which makes our growth in all ordinary knowledge *gradual* and *limited*. We are expressly told, in Luke ii. 52, that 'Jesus increased in *wisdom*,' as well as in 'stature.' It is not supposed that, in His human nature, He was acquainted, more than any educated Jew of the age, with the mysteries of all modern sciences; nor, with St Luke's expressions before us, can it be seriously maintained that, as an *infant* or *young child*, He possessed a knowledge, surpassing that of the most pious and learned adults of His nation, upon the subject of the authorship and age of the different portions of the Pentateuch. At what period, then, of His life upon earth, is it to be supposed that He had granted to Him, as the Son of Man, *supernaturally*, full and accurate information on these points, so that He should be expected to speak about the Pentateuch in other terms, than any other devout Jew of that day would have employed? Why should it be thought that He would speak with certain *Divine* knowledge on this matter, more than upon other matters of ordinary science or history?

While confining, however, as I have said, my present investigations to the Pentateuch and Book of Joshua, I have spared no pains to make them as complete as possible, with the means at my disposal, so far as these books are concerned. If it should be said that a work of this kind may well require years for its consideration, before it can be matured and fitted for publication, I answer that, situated as I am, I have had no alternative. Being invested with the episcopal office, I cannot, as an ordinary clergyman might, obtain leave of absence from my duties for a year or two, and have them carried on by a substitute. Nor can I, arriving in England as a Missionary Bishop, and receiving, therefore, calls from many quarters to plead the cause of Missions, decline acceding to such calls, without assigning, as I do by the publication of this book, the reason why, with my present work in hand, I cannot comply with them. The question, however, has been to me a matter of life and death, and I have laboured upon it incessantly, with all the powers which God has given me. Yet this toil has been mainly bestowed upon the critical and subsidiary portion of my book; and, by a careful comparison of my own conclusions with those of Bleek and Kuenen, which contain the latest results of continental criticism in Germany and Holland, I believe that I have made myself sufficiently master of the subject, to be able to place confidence in the general soundness of the views that will be here maintained, even though on some points, as will be seen, I feel obliged to differ with the above eminent critics. The essential portions, however, of this work, viz. the result arrived at in Part I, required comparatively very little labour. The facts have only to be stated, as I have endeavoured to state them, in a form intelligible to the most unlearned layman; and the truth of the conclusions drawn will, as it appears to me, be self-evident to most of my readers, who have courage to face the truth, and courage to confess it.

Finally, I am not aware of any breach of the Law of the Church of England, as declared by the recent judgment in the Court of Arches, which is involved in this publication. It is now ruled that the words in the Ordination Service for Deacons, 'I do unfeignedly believe all the Canonical Scriptures,' must be understood to mean simply the expression of a *bonâ fide* belief, that 'the Holy Scriptures contain everything necessary to salvation,' and 'to that extent they have the direct sanction of the Almighty.'

I am not conscious of having said anything here, which contravenes this decision. Should it be otherwise, and should the strange phenomenon be witnessed, of a Bishop of the Protestant Church of England, – more especially one, who has been expressly occupied in translating the Scriptures into a foreign tongue, – being precluded by the Law of that Church from entering upon a close, critical, examination of them, and from bringing before the great body of the Church, (not the Clergy only, but the Clergy and Laity,) the plain, honest, results of such criticism, I must, of course, bear the consequences of my act.

But, meanwhile, I cannot but believe that our Church, representing, as it is supposed to do, the religious feeling of a free, Protestant, nation, requires us now, as in the days of the Reformation, to protest against all perversion of the Truth, and all suppression of it, for the sake of Peace, or by mere Authority. As a Bishop of that Church, I dissent entirely from the principle laid down by some, that such a question, as that which is here discussed, is not even an open question, for an English clergyman, – that we are bound by solemn obligations to maintain certain views, on the points here involved, to our lives' end, or, at least, to *resign* our sacred office in the Church, as soon as ever we feel it impossible any longer to hold them.

On the contrary, I hold that the foundations of our National Church are laid upon the Truth itself, and not upon mere human prescriptions, and that the spirit of our Church, as declared in the days of the Reformation, fully recognises my right to use all the weight of that office, with which the Providence of God has invested me, in declaring the Truth, and recommending the subject of this work to the thoughtful consideration of English Churchmen. Nine years ago, I was deemed not unworthy to be called to this high office. I trust that the labours of those years may be accepted as an evidence that, to the best of my power, I have striven to discharge faithfully the duties entrusted to me, and may serve also as a guarantee, that, in putting forward this book, I am acting in no light spirit, but with the serious earnestness of one, who believes that he owes it as a duty to the Church itself, of which he is a minister, to do his part to secure for the Bible its due honour and authority, and save its devout readers from ascribing to it attributes of perfection and infallibility, which belong to God only, and which the Bible never claims for itself. More than all others, I believe, is a Bishop bound to do this, if his conscience impels him to it, – inasmuch as he, above others, is bound to be an example to the Flock of that walking in the Light, without which there cannot be true Life in a Church, any more than in an individual soul, – 'renouncing the hidden things of dishonesty, not walking in craftiness nor handling the word of God deceitfully, but, by manifestation of the Truth, commending himself to every man's conscience in the sight of God.'

If the arguments, on which the conclusions of these first chapters rest, shall be found, upon a thorough examination, to be substantially well-grounded and true, I trust that we shall not rest until the system of our Church be reformed, and her boundaries at the same time enlarged to make her what a National Church should be, the Mother of spiritual life to all within the realm, embracing, as far as possible, all the piety, and learning, and earnestness, and goodness, of the nation. Then, at last, would a stop be put to that internecine war between the servants of one God and the professed followers of the same religion, which now is a reproach to our Christian name, and seriously impedes the progress of truth and charity, both at home and abroad. Should the reception of this book, by the more thoughtful portion of the community, indicate that such a Reform is possible and probable, and will be but a question of time, so that, being able meanwhile to speak out plainly the truth, we shall have only to bear with the inconveniences and inconsistencies, which must attend a state of transition, it would not be necessary for me, or for those who think with me, to leave the Church of England voluntarily, and abandon the work to which we have devoted ourselves for life.

In conclusion, I commend this subject more especially to the attention of the Laity. *They* are happy enough to be able to lay aside such questions as these, if they will, while still continuing members of the National Church. I implore them to consider the position, in which the *Clergy* will be placed, if the facts, brought forward in this book, are found to be substantially true. Let them examine their own hearts solemnly, in the sight of God, on these points. Would they have the Clergy bound, under pains and penalties, to profess belief in that, which they do not themselves believe in, to which they would not on any account commit themselves? Are they willing that their own sons, who may feel the Divine call to devote themselves to the ministry of souls, should be entangled in these trammels, so galling to the conscience, so injurious to their sense of truth and honesty, so impeding to the freedom and heartiness of their ministrations? *We*, indeed, who are already under the yoke, may have for a time to bear it, however painful it may be, while we struggle and hope on for deliverance. But what youth of noble mind, with a deep yearning for truth, and an ardent desire to tell out the love of God to man, will consent to put himself voluntarily into such fetters? It may be possible to represent some of the arguments in this book as invalid, others as unimportant. But, if the main results of it be true, as I believe it will be found to be, it seems to me impossible that, five years hence, unless liberty of speech on these matters be frankly acknowledged to belong to the Clergy as well as the Laity, any of the more hopeful and intelligent of our young men will be able, with clear consciences, to enter the ministry of the Church of England.

I now commit this First Part of my work into the Hands of Almighty God, beseeching Him mercifully to accept and bless it, as a feeble effort to advance the knowledge of His Truth in the world.

J. W. NATAL

LONDON: *Oct.* 4, 1862

I I

A. P. STANLEY: *'Sermons on Special Occasions':*
The Religious Aspects of Geology (Funeral Sermon
on Sir Charles Lyell)

Lyell's *Principles of Geology* (1830) was influential in spreading the idea
that the age of the earth was far greater than the conventional 6,000
years. Much later, his *Antiquity of Man* (1863) came to anticipate, in
part, the argument of Darwin's more famous *Descent of Man* (1871).
Stanley is here speaking as Dean of Westminster at the solemn interment
of a famous man in Westminster Abbey, as he did for so many other
famous men, including Palmerston, Dickens and Carlyle. The year is
1875, and the fiercest conflicts and intensest agonies excited by Darwin's
Origin of Species sixteen years before were moderating. Stanley's great
aim, as always, is to see things in perspective; and because he is so determined to do this, he is very often the most detached and reliable
commentator on the religious controversies of his age. His point about
Scripture and science is really this: two completely different modes of
thought and description can be in harmony, but they can never, in any
obvious sense, be reconciled. The experience of looking at an architect's
plan, and at a building can never be at all alike. Yet the plan may be a
truthful account of the building in some of its aspects. On this analogy,
the misguided attempt to deal with the tricky case of the hare by alter-
ing the text, would be comparable to a pretence that a pencil line on the
architect's plan was really just like the line of stone or brick.

Stanley takes occasion to point out also, as against the *idée reçue* of an
unending conflict between religion and science, that Lyell himself had
been a believer, and that two noted early geologists, Sedgwick and
Buckland, had been Anglican clerics.

In general, one can see in Stanley's measured words the results of a
time of calmer reflection on the searing controversies of the 60's. No
one did more than Stanley to help bring that cold war to an end.

February 28, 1875, after the funeral of Sir Charles Lyell

The earth was without form and void; and darkness was upon the face of the deep. And the Spirit of God moved upon the face of the waters. – Genesis i. 2.

THESE words, from the Book of Genesis, of which the lessons are now in our church services drawing to a close, convey a sense wider than their mere literal transcript. They express the transition from that gulf which by the ancient Greeks was called 'Chaos,' to that grace and order which, under the name of 'Kosmos,' has been adopted by a famous modern philosopher to describe the system of the universe. The words which portray the formless void of the earth, convey in the original, in the most forcible manner, the image of the old discordant elements of conflict, whilst the word used for the moving of the Divine Spirit on the face of the waters expresses the gentle brooding and yearning as of a parent-bird over the troubled deep.[1] The language, however poetic, childlike, parabolical, and unscientific, yet impresses upon us the principle in the moral and the material world, that the law of the Divine operation is the gradual, peaceful, progressive redaction and development of discord into harmony, of confusion into order, of darkness into light.

To unfold and to exemplify that law is in various degrees one of the chief missions of the nobler souls in whom the Divine Spirit, according to the diversity of its gifts, leads on the human race towards perfection. It has so chanced that within this short month of February, by a most unusual coincidence of mortality, twice have the gates of this Abbey been opened to pay the last honours to two men, widely apart in all else, but alike in the fulfilment of this Divine Law – the one the acknowledged chief[2] of the English musicians of our time; the other, who was yesterday laid in his grave, the acknowledged chief of those who have devoted themselves to the study of our mother-earth.

I. Suffer me before passing to this, the main subject of our thoughts, to say a few words of the first of these two gifted persons; the more so, that his special work was no unapt commentary on the sacred text, no unsuitable prelude to that which shall follow.

Of all the branches of art and letters, none more reveals the hidden capacities of the human soul, or of 'the fearful and wonderful' structure of the human frame, than the slow and yet certain process through

1 'Dove-like sat brooding o'er the vast abyss.' – Milton's *Paradise Lost*, Book I.
2 Sir William Sterndale Bennett, who was buried in the Abbey on Feb. 6, 1875.

which from the simplest and the most barbarous sounds that Art, which
both heathens and Christians have not scrupled to call Divine, has called
into being worlds of melody and harmony, which have entranced the
ear, and calmed the heart, and elevated the mind of succeeding generations of mankind, gaining in volume and complexity and force, as time
has rolled on. The spirit which brooded over the rude lyre of Orpheus
or the rough harp of David, is the same spirit which breathes through
the anthems of our great cathedrals or the choral strains of our oratorios;
but what a pathos, what a majesty, what a glory, of which David[1] never
dreamed, has been inspired into these sounds, by the genius of a Purcell
or a Beethoven, a Handel or a Mendelssohn! Some of us may recall the
well-known words in which the contrast of this development has been
drawn out by one whose insight into the secrets of musical art, and
whose complete mastery over the musical cadences of our English
tongue are unquestioned, however much we may lament the uncertain
tone of his theological trumpet, or wonder at the oblique march of his
wayward genius.

There are seven notes in the scale; make them fourteen; yet what a slender
outfit for so vast an enterprise! What science brings so much out of so little?
Out of what poor elements does some great master in it create his new world!
. . . Is it possible that that inexhaustible evolution and disposition of notes, so
rich yet so simple, so intricate yet so regulated, so various yet so majestic,
should be a mere sound, which is gone and perishes? Can it be that those mysterious stirrings of heart, and keen emotions, and strange yearnings after we
know not what, and awful impressions from we know not whence, should be
wrought in us by what is unsubstantial, and comes and goes, and begins and
ends in itself? No, they have escaped from some higher sphere; they are the
outpourings of eternal harmony in the medium of created sound; they are
echoes from our Home; they are the voice of Angels; or the Magnificat of
Saints; or the living laws of Divine Governance; or the Divine Attributes;
something are they besides themselves which we cannot compass, which we
cannot utter – though mortal man, and he, perhaps not otherwise distinguished
above his fellows, has the gift of eliciting them.[2]

To elicit these marvels, to elevate that glorious art, was the mission
of the gentle musician who, three weeks ago, was laid beside those who,
in earlier days in the church or nation, in the words of the sacred[3]
writers, have 'handled the harp and organ,' and 'found out musical

[1] 'I think,' said Luther, in the sixteenth century, 'that if David rose from the
dead, he would wonder much to find how far we have advanced in music.'
[2] Dr Newman's *University Sermons*, pp. 348, 349.
[3] Gen. iv. 21; Ecclus. xliv. 5.

tunes;' by such heavenly strains he soothed his own soul and the souls of others, when they have sat down 'wearied with the journey'[1] of life; and again and again will his memory be recalled to us, as we hear the sacred melody on which he has written, as on waves of light, those Divine words which describe, as it were, the second creation of the world, which ought to stand as the principle of all Christian worship – 'God is a spirit, and they that worship Him must worship Him in spirit and in truth.'

II. I have said that this passing allusion to the departed musician, this indication of the latent capacities for spiritual emotion wrapped up even in abstract and inanimate things, in elements seemingly without form and void, is no unfitting prelude to the consideration of that study of nature, of which he who has just followed to the same long home was so bright an example. A celebrated teacher of our age, to whom music was a sealed book, but to whom objects of natural beauty were full of enjoyment, used to say 'Wild flowers are my music;'[2] and so, in like manner, to all students of nature, earth and sea, with their hidden harmonies, have indeed a music of their own, which, like the secrets of the vocal art, have to be drawn out by the fire of genius, by the preserving vigilance, by the active search, of scientific study. In this spirit I propose to call your attention for a brief space to the religious aspect of 'that noble science of Geology,' which a great historian has called 'the boast of our age,'[3] and of which the words of the text might well, especially in regard to the work of him whom we now commemorate, be called the first germ and the abiding motto.

It is well known that when the science of Geology first arose, it was involved in endless schemes of attempted reconciliation with the letter of Scripture. There were, there are perhaps still, two modes of reconciliation of Scripture and science, which have been each in their day attempted, and have each totally and deservedly failed. One is the endeavour to wrest the words of the Bible from their natural meaning, and force them to speak the language of science. Of this, the earliest, and perhaps the most memorable, example was set by the Greek translators in the time of the Ptolemies – the Seventy, as they were called. They came, in the course of their[4] translation, to that verse of Leviticus[5] containing the well-known stumbling-block which they

---

1 *The Woman of Samaria*, by Sir W. Sterndale Bennett.
2 Arnold's *Life*, p. 185.
3 Hallam's *Hist. of Literature*, vol. iii. pt. iv. ch. 8.
4 The *Septuagint* version.   5 Lev. xi. 6

probably were the first to discern, which speaks of the hare as one of the animals that chew the cud. In the old world, before the birth of accurate observation, that which had the appearance of rumination was mistaken for the reality, and was so described. But, by the time that the Greek translation of the Bible was undertaken, the greatest naturalist of antiquity, the world-famous Aristotle, had already devoted his sagacious mind to the study of the habits of animals, and through his writings the true state of the case had become known in Alexandria. The venerable scholars who were at work on the translation were too conscientious to reject the clear evidence of science; but they were too timid to allow the contradiction to appear, and therefore, with the usual rashness of fear, they boldly interpolated the word 'NOT' into the sacred text, and thus, as they thought, reconciled it to science by making the whole passage mean exactly the reverse of that which was intended. This is the earliest instance of the falsification of Scripture to meet the demands of science; and it has been followed in later times by the various efforts which have been made to twist the earlier chapters of the Book of Genesis into apparent agreement with the last results of geology – representing days not to be days, morning and evening not to be morning and evening, the deluge not to be the deluge, and the ark not to be the ark. On the other hand, there has sprung up in later times the equal error of falsifying science to meet the supposed requirements of the Bible. Of this, the most signal example was when the discoveries of Galileo were condemned by the Supreme Judge of faith and morals in the Roman Church, and when the Jesuits in their edition of Newton's 'Principia' announced in the preface that they were constrained to treat the theory of gravitation as a fictitious hypothesis, because else it would conflict with the 'decrees of the Popes against the motion of the earth.' This mode of reconciliation has also been tried in our times, at each successive advance of science. Every generation of the ecclesiastical or religious world has been tempted to the hazardous enterprise of denying the voice of God as He speaks to us in His words, and in His laws, and often the plain conclusions of careful observation have been set aside as impious and dangerous.

But there is another reconciliation of a higher kind which, we humbly trust, will never fail – or rather not a reconciliation at all, but an acknowledgment of the affinity, the identity which exists between the *spirit* of Science and the *spirit* of the Bible. And this is of two kinds – first, there is the likeness of the general spirit of the truths of science to the general spirit of the truths of the Bible; and, secondly, there is the likeness of the general spirit of the method of science to the general spirit of the method of the Bible.

1. Let me exemplify both of these in the instance of Geology, and of the illustrious student of geology who has just passed away from us. First, let us see what is the geological truth which he was the chief instrument in clearly setting forth and establishing on a new foundation. It was the doctrine, wrought out by careful, cautious inquiry in all parts of the world, that the frame of this earth was gradually brought into its present condition, not by violent or sudden convulsions, but by slow and silent action, the same causes operating, as we see operate now, through a long succession of ages, stretching back beyond the memory or imagination of man. We have already indicated that there need be no question raised whether or not this doctrine agrees with the letter of the Bible. We do not expect that it should; for if there were no such scientific researches and conclusions, we now know perfectly well, from our increased insight into the earlier Biblical records, that they were not, and could not be, literal and prosaic matter-of-fact descriptions of the beginning of the world, of which, as of its end, 'no man knoweth,' or can conceive except by figure and parable. It is now clear to diligent students of the Bible, that the first and second chapters of Genesis contain two narratives of the Creation, side by side, differing from each other in almost every particular of time and place and order. It is now certain that the vast epochs demanded by scientific observation are incompatible both with the six thousand years of the Mosaic chronology, and the six days of the Mosaic Creation. No one now infers from the Psalms that 'the earth is set so fast that it cannot be moved,' or that 'the sun' actually 'comes forth as a bridegroom from his chamber' – or that 'the morning stars sang' with an audible voice at the dawn of the creation. To insist on these details as historical or scientific, is as contrary to the style and character of the sacred books themselves as it is to the undoubted facts of science. But when from these we rise to the spirit, the ideal, the general drift and purpose of the Biblical accounts, we feel ourselves in an atmosphere of moral elevation which meets the highest requirements that philosophy can make; we find exactly that affinity which we should expect to find between the most sacred, the most majestic of ancient records (even if we say no more), and the most certain and sublime of modern discoveries.

I have often spoken before of this inner harmony between the highest flights of Scripture and the highest flights of science or genius. Look at the discoveries of Geology in this light, and they will appear to us not only not irreligious, but as filling the old religious truths with a new life of their own, and receiving from those truths a hallowing glory in return. When the historian of our planet points out to us that the successive layers of the earth's surface were formed not by strange and sudden shocks, but by the same constant action of wind and wave, of falling leaves, and silent stream, and floating ice, and rolling stones, that we see in operation daily before our eyes; that there were not separate centres of creation, but one primal law, which formed and governs all created beings; what is this but the echo of those voices which of old declared that 'in the beginning the heavens and the earth were created,'[1] not by conflicting deities, but by One supreme and indivisible; which told us that 'God's word endureth for ever in heaven;' that 'His faithfulness continues throughout all generations;' that 'as He established the earth, so it abideth;' that 'all things continue according to His ordinance;'[2] that 'He who laid out the foundation of the world above the waters, for His mercy endureth for ever,' is the same as He who 'daily giveth food to all flesh,' for it 'is the same mercy that endureth for ever;'[3] that 'He has given a law which shall not be broken.' And are we not reminded that long ago there was one who stood in the cave of the cliffs of Horeb, and waited for the sign of the Divine operations,[4] and that it was then borne in upon his soul that the Lord was not in the earthquake, the hurricane, or the fire, but in the still small whispering murmur of the gentle air, and the silence of the desert? Do we not in those deep descents into the ocean gulfs, those subtle transformations of land and sea and all that in them is, discern a reflex of that Presence which has 'searched us out and known us;' which 'did see our substance yet being imperfect, and in whose book were written all the members' of the human race, and its habitation, 'which day by day were fashioned while as yet there was none of them?'[5] And when, further, we contemplate the vast infinitudes of time and space, that long ascending order, that gradual, insensible progress, which Geology demands, do we not feel that much as the Bible may contain of detail and expression and imagery running in another direction, yet its general, though not its uniform teaching, its highest, though not its constant utterances, would encourage us to believe that the world is something deeper and wider than we in our narrow view should imagine it to be; that creation is something which reaches further back and deeper down than our childish and limited notions would suggest to us; that the distance of its

[1] Gen. i. 1. [2] Ps. cxix. 89–91. [3] Ps. cxxxvi. 6, 25.
[4] 1 Kings xix. 9–12. [5] Ps. cxxxix. 1–16.

first beginning, however remote, melts into a distance remoter still? It is only the doubly doubtful Second Book of the Maccabees[1] which contains the text that the world was made 'of things that were not.' The earlier loftier teaching of the Bible enters into no such metaphysical labyrinth. There 'deep still calls to deep.' There it is still the 'earth without form and void, and darkness gathering over the face of the deep.' In the Prophets of the Bible, as in the prophets of Science, there is a sense, dim and vague, yet strong and earnest, of the infinite variety of the treasure-house of creation, the infinite patience and perseverance of the Creator, 'A thousand years in Thy sight are but as yesterday, and one day as a thousand years.'[2] 'My Father worketh hitherto and I work.'[3] 'O the depth of the riches both of the wisdom and knowledge of God! How unsearchable are His judgments, and His ways past finding out!'[4] 'Where wast thou when I laid the foundations of the earth? whereupon are the foundations thereof fastened, or who laid the corner-stone thereof? . . . Hast thou entered into the springs of the sea, or walked in the search of the depth?'[5] 'There is one glory of the sun, and another glory of the moon, and another glory of the stars. The first is that which is natural, and afterward that which is spiritual.'[6]

Surely to expressions such as these, however little they can be pressed into scientific exactness, the correlative theory of science is not that which limits the duration of earth to the space of a few brief centuries, but that which expands it to illimitable ages. Surely the view which shows the long preparation of the earth for man gives a grander prelude to his appearance on this globe, than that which makes him coeval with the beasts that perish. Surely the intimations of future progress which are suggested by observing the latent faculties wherewith he is endowed, are more consonant to the hope of a glorious and fruitful immortality than the view which regards him as a stationary being, knowing at once all that he can ever know, and contented with the narrow horizon that is alone open to him. All honour to the peaceful conqueror who, by years of unhasting, unresting research, annexed these new provinces of thought to the knowledge of man, and therefore to the glory of God! All honour to the herald and archæologist of our race, who has un-rolled in all its length and breadth the genealogy of the antiquity of man, and the antiquity of his habitation! All honour to the bold yet reverent touch which, in the Temple of the Most High, not made with hands, rent assunder from the top to the bottom the veil that con-

---

[1] 2 Macc. vii. 28.   [2] Ps. xc. 2; 2 Pet. iii. 8.   [3] John v. 17.
[4] Rom. xi. 33.   [5] Job xxxviii. 4–16.   [6] 1 Cor. xv. 41–46.

cealed its full proportions, and revealed its ever-widening, ever-lengthening vistas backward into the furthest past of memory, and forward to the endless future of hope. Not the limitation, but the amplification of the idea of God, is the result of the labours of such a student. Not the descent, but the ascent of man is the final result of his speculations. If, as he used to say, 'we have in our bones the chill' of that contracted view in which we had been brought up, yet the enlargement which he effected for the view of the past ought to give a warmth, a fire to our heart of hearts, to our soul of souls, in proportion as we feel that we are not the creatures of yesterday, but 'the heirs of all the ages' – even the ages that cannot be numbered, and of worlds that have perished in the making of us; the ancestors, let us trust, of those who, compared with us, shall seem to have attained to 'a new heaven and a new earth,' wherein 'old things shall have passed away, and all things shall have become new,'[1] under the breath of that Spirit which is for ever brooding over the face of the troubled universe.

2. This leads me to the likeness of the general spirit of the method of the philosophic geologist, and the general spirit of the method of the Bible. If there be any one point in which the whole structure of the Bible and the whole plan of its teaching is a model to the student, whether of nature, of man, or of God, it is the slow 'increasing purpose' of Revelation, through 'sundry times and divers manners,' working as if with the persistence of unconscious instinct and the patience of deliberate will towards the fulness of time, with the constant warning to each succeeding age to have the eyes and ears of its mind open to the reception of Light and Truth. Thus, as in art, so in science, the whole race of mankind, and each individual member of it, must aim to deserve that proud yet lowly title by which the Founder of Christianity called His followers – Disciples, that is, 'scholars,' learners even to the very end; scholars bent on the attainment of the Truth in all its parts, 'to bear witness to which He was born, and for which cause He came into the world.'[2] To invest the pursuit of Truth with the sanctity of a religious duty, to make Truth and Goodness meet together in one holy fellowship, is the high reconciliation of Religion and Science for which all scientific and all religious men should alike labour and pray. 'Sacred, no doubt,' said one of the greatest of astronomers, 'sacred is the authority of the Fathers; sacred was Lactantius, who denied the earth's rotundity; sacred was Augustine, who admitted the earth to be round, but denied the antipodes; sacred is the authority of the moderns, who admit the

---

[1] 2 Pet. iii. 13; 2 Cor. v. 17.   [2] John xviii. 37.

smallness of the earth, yet deny its motion; yet, more sacred to me than all these is – TRUTH.' So spoke Kepler. Yes, more sacred than all things is Truth, next after or along with Goodness, and therefore to be sought calmly, temperately, deliberately, as in the Holy of Holies and in the presence of the Most High.

Such a union of patient research and reverential piety has been the special glory of the great school of English Geology. Amidst all the alarms of the religious world, and all the embitterments of the scientific world, it has been our just pride in England that the two pioneers of this newborn science, at a time when it had to fight its way against prejudice, and ignorance, and apathy, towards its present hard-won place, were honoured dignitaries of the National Church. One was the illustrious Professor of Cambridge, whose generous heart, and brilliant fancy, and heavenward hope enlightened and warmed his whole being, and continued to irradiate a life prolonged beyond the allotted term of man's existence. The other was the eager, indefatigable student, who left his chair at Oxford only to preside over this ancient Church, whose very stones and dust were dear to him, but by him examined and sifted as never before by hand or eye of English layman or ecclesiastic. And now within these walls, beneath the monument of Woodward, the earliest of English geologists, lies the latest of that distinguished group, the friend of Sedgwick and the pupil of Buckland. The tranquil triumph of Geology, once thought so dangerous, now so quietly accepted by the Church, no less than by the world, is one more proof of the groundlessness of theological panics in the face of the advances of scientific discovery.

Of him, who is thus laid to rest, if of any one of our time, it may be said that he followed Truth with a zeal as sanctified as ever fired the soul of a missionary, and with a humility as child-like as ever subdued the mind of a simple scholar. For discovering facts, confirming or rectifying conclusions, there was no journey too distant to undertake. Never did he think of his own fame or name in comparison with the scientific results which he sought to establish. From early youth to ex-treme old age it was to him a solemn religious duty to be incessantly learning, constantly growing, fearlessly correcting his own mistakes, always ready to receive and reproduce from others that which he had not in himself. Science and Religion for him not only were not divorced, but were one and indivisible. He felt with another eminent votary of science in our time, that this divorce, unhappily so welcome to some on either side, is 'a mere pretence,' neither true in fact, neither Christian

nor philosophic in idea.[1] 'The spiritual world and the intellectual world
are no more to be separated in this fashion,' than are the secular and the
religious, the Church and the Commonwealth. The instinct which
impels us to seek for harmony between the highest truths of science and
the highest truths of the Bible is an instinct far nobler and truer than
that which would seek to part them asunder. In this higher instinct, he
who has departed fully shared. The great religious problems of our
time were never absent from his mind. The infinite possibilities of
nature gave him fresh ground for his unshaken hope in the unknown,
immortal future. His conviction of the peaceful, progressive combination of natural causes towards the formation of our globe filled him
with a profound and ever profounder sense of 'the wonder and the
glory of this marvellous universe.' The generous freedom allowed to
religious inquiry in the National Church, the cause of humanity in the
world at large, were to him as dear as though they were his own personal
and peculiar concern. With that one faithful, beloved, and beautiful
soul, who, till within the last two years of his life, shared all his joys and
all his sorrows, all his labours and all his fame, he walked the lofty path,
'which the vulture's eye hath not seen, nor the lion's whelp trodden'[2]
– the pathway of the just, 'that shineth more and more unto the perfect
day,' in which we humbly trust that they are now at last reunited in the
presence of that light which they both so sincerely sought.

There is an unusual solemnity in the last thought of one who passes
into that Eternal World, on which, as in a shadow or mirror, he had so
long and anxiously meditated, in the unknown ages of which he was,
as it were, the first discoverer. That 'lofty and melancholy Psalm,' as
a famous historian has called it, which ancient tradition has ascribed to
Moses, the man of God, well represents the feeling of one grown gray
with vast experience, who here takes his stand at the close of his earthly
journeyings, and contrasts the fleeting generations of men with the
huge forms of the granite mountains at whose feet they have so long
wandered, and contrasts yet more mountains and men alike with the
eternity of Him who existed and exists before, above, and beyond them
all. 'Lord, Thou hast been our refuge, our dwelling-place from generation to generation. Before the mountains were brought forth, or ever
the earth and the world were made, from everlasting to everlasting
Thou art God.'[3] Whether or not it was the funeral hymn of the Lawgiver of Israel, it has become the funeral hymn of the world. And it

1 The Duke of Argyll in *The Reign of Law*, pp. 57, 58.
2 Job xxviii. 7.   3 Psalm xc. 1, 2. (See Ewald.)

seems to sum up with peculiar force the inner life of the Christian philosopher, who concluded his chief work with the contrast of 'the relations which subsist between the finite powers of man and the attributes of an Infinite and Eternal Being,'[1] who felt persuaded that after all the magnificent discoveries and speculations on mountain and valley, on earth and sea and sky, the religious sentiment still remained the grandest and most indestructible instinct of the human race; strongest, most sublime in those individuals of our race that are most fully and perfectly developed. At such a solemn farewell to the benefactors of mankind, we feel that the True, the Just, the Good is the Eternal Principle and Cause which outlasts and outweighs all outward and visible things. 'Before the mountains were brought forth, or ever the earth and the world were made, from everlasting to everlasting Thou art God.'

[1] *Principles of Geology*, ii. 621.

12

FREDERICK TEMPLE: *The Relations between Religion and Science*

Bampton Lectures 1884, Lecture VI

Temple, born in 1821, had been one of the less controversial contributors to *Essays and Reviews* in 1860. In 1884 when he delivered the
Bampton Lectures from which this piece is taken, he had been, despite
protests, bishop of Exeter for some fifteen years, and he ended his life
as Archbishop of Canterbury, appointed with remarkable disregard of
their theological differences by the High Church Prime Minister, Lord
Salisbury, in 1896. Salisbury was, however, like Temple in taking a
keen interest in science.

Headmaster of Rugby, like the more famous Thomas Arnold,
Temple possessed a clear and efficient rather than a profound or original
mind. His succession to the primacy in his old age shows the traditional
Anglican respect for administrative ability and sound scholarship, and
is also perhaps a reminder that a little, but not too much, rebellion
against authority is often the road to success in the Church of England. But he found his road to success by accident not design, for it
is clear that his regard for truth was a much stronger motive than
ambition.

His method of reconciling Darwin with Christianity is balanced and
sensible. It is perfectly true, and Darwin freely admitted it, that his
doctrine cannot explain the origin of life itself, or of some of the specifically human qualities. It is worth noticing, though, that Temple is a
true Victorian in his stress on the moral sense as the essential point of
religious consciousness. This is perhaps a weakness, for it ignores Kier-
kegaard's famous 'teleological suspension of the ethical', as in the story
of Abraham and Isaac, and, indeed, in the orthodox doctrine of Redemption by the Blood of Christ. It also ignores, though Temple himself certainly would not have wished to deny, the evident fact that it is

possible to have a strongly developed moral sense without having any overtly religious sense at all.

There appears to be one definite error in Temple's reasoning .When he says, 'But there is no evidence whatever to show that what we have observed is not a fair sample of the whole,' it is difficult to see how there ever could, in principle, be any such evidence.

Apparent Collision between Religion and the Doctrine of Evolution

Know ye that the Lord He is God: it is He that hath made us, and not we ourselves. Psalm c. 3.

RELIGION is rooted in our spiritual nature and its fundamental truths are as independent of experience for their hold on our consciences as the truths of mathematics for their hold on our reason.

But as a matter of fact Religion has taken the form of a revelation. And this introduces a new contact between Religion and Science, and of necessity a new possibility of collision. There is not only possible opposition or apparent opposition of Science in what is revealed, in what we may call the actual substance of the revelation; but also in the accessories and evidences of the revelation, which may be no actual part of the revelation itself, but nevertheless are, to all appearance, inseparably bound up with it. It is therefore no more than might have been expected that the general postulate of the uniformity of nature should appear to be contravened by the claim to supernatural power made on behalf of revelation, and that the special, but just at present leading scientific doctrine, the doctrine of Evolution, should be found inconsistent with parts, or what appear to be parts, of the revelation itself. And we have to consider the two questions, What has Revelation to say concerning Evolution? and what has Science to say concerning Miracles?

Concerning Evolution, we have first to consider how much in this direction has been made fairly probable, and what still remains to be determined.

It cannot then be well denied that the astronomers and geologists have made it exceedingly probable that this earth on which we live has been brought to its present condition by passing through a succession of changes from an original state of great heat and fluidity, perhaps even from a mixture mainly consisting of gases; that such a body as the planet Jupiter represents one of the stages through which it has passed, that such a body as the moon represents a stage toward which it is tend-

ing; that it has shrunk as it cooled, and as it shrank has formed the eleva-
tions which we call mountains, and the depressions which contain the
seas and oceans; that it has been worn by the action of heat from within
and water from without, and in consequence of this action presents the
appearance when examined below the surface of successive strata or
layers; that different kinds of animal and vegetable life have followed
one another on the surface, and that some of their remains are found
in these strata now; and that all this has taken enormous periods of
time. All this is exceedingly probable, because it is the way in which,
as Laplace first pointed out, under well-established scientific laws of
matter, particularly the law of gravitation and the law of the radiation
of heat, a great fluid mass would necessarily change. And the whole
solar system may and probably did come into its present condition in
this way. It certainly could have been so formed, and there is no reason
for supposing that it was formed in any other way.

Once more, if we begin, as it were, at the other end, and trace things
backwards from the present, instead of forwards from the remote past,
it cannot be denied that Darwin's investigations have made it exceedingly probable that the vast variety of plants and animals have sprung
from a much smaller number of original forms.

In the first place, the unity of plan which can be found pervading any
great class of animals or plants seems to point to unity of ancestry. Why,
for instance, should the vertebrate animals be formed on a common
plan, the parts of the framework being varied from species to species,
but the framework as a whole always exhibiting the same fundamental
type? If they all descended from a common ancestor, and the variations
were introduced in the course of that descent, this remarkable fact is at
once accounted for. But, in the second place, observation shows that
slight variations ARE perpetually being introduced with every successive generation, and many of these variations are transmitted to the
generations that follow. In the course of time, therefore, from any one
parent stock would descend a very large variety of kinds. But if, in the
third place, it be asked why this variety does not range by imperceptible
degrees from extreme forms in one direction to extreme forms in the
other, the answer is to be found in the enormous prodigality and the
equally enormous waste of life and living creatures. Plants and animals
produce far more descendants than ever come even to such maturity
as to reproduce their kind. And this is particularly the case with the
lower forms of life. Eggs and seeds and germs are destroyed by millions,
and so in a less but still enormous proportion are the young that come

from those that have not been destroyed. There is no waste like the waste of life that is to be seen in nature. Living creatures are destroyed by lack of fit nourishment, by lack of means of reproduction, by accidents, by enemies. The inevitable operation of this waste, as Darwin's investigation showed, has been to destroy all those varieties which were not well fitted to their surroundings, and to keep those that were. One species of animal has been preserved by length of neck, which enabled it to reach high-growing fruits and leaves; another by a thicker skin, which made it difficult for enemies to devour; another by a colour which made it easier to hide. One plant has been preserved by a bright flower which attracted insects to carry its pollen to other flowers of its kind; another by a sweet fruit which attracted birds to scatter its seed. Meanwhile other animals and plants that had not these advantages perished for the lack of them. The result would be to maintain, and perpetually, though with exceeding slowness, more and more to adapt to the conditions of their life, those species whose peculiarities gave them some advantage in the great struggle for existence.

Here again we have the working of known laws of life, capable of accounting for what we see. And the high probability cannot be denied that by evolution of this kind the present races of living creatures have been formed. And to these arguments the strongest corroboration is given by the frequent occurrence, both in plants and animals, of useless parts which still remain as indications of organs that once were useful and have long become useless. Animals that now live permanently in the dark have abortive eyes which cannot see, but indicate an ancestor with eyes that could see. Animals that never walk have abortive legs hidden under their skin, useless now but indicating what was useful once. Our knowledge no doubt in this as in any other province of nature is but the merest fraction of what may be known therein. But there is no evidence whatever to show that what we have observed is not a fair sample of the whole. And so taking it, we find that the mass of evidence in favour of the evolution of plants and animals is enormously great and increasing daily.

Granting then the high probability of the two theories of Evolution, that which begins with Laplace and explains the way in which the earth was fitted to be the habitation of living creatures, and that which owes its name to Darwin and gives an account of the formation of the living creatures now existing, we have to see what limitations and modifications are necessarily attached to our complete acceptance of both.

First, then, at the very meeting point of these two evolutions we have the important fact that all the evidence that we possess up to the present day negatives the opinion that life is a mere evolution from inorganic matter. We know perfectly well the constituents of all living substances. We know that the fundamental material of all plants and all animals is a compound called protoplasm, or that, in other words, organic matter in all its immense variety of forms is nothing but protoplasm variously modified. And we know the constituent elements of this protoplasm, and their proportions, and the temperatures within which protoplasm as such can exist. But we are quite powerless to make it, or to show how it is made, or to detect nature in the act of making it. All the evidence we have points to one conclusion only, that life is the result of antecedent life, and is producible on no other conditions. Repeatedly have scientific observers believed that they have come on instances of spontaneous generation, but further examination has invariably shown that they have been mistaken. We can put the necessary elements together, but we cannot supply the necessary bond by which they are to be made to live. Nay, we cannot even recall that bond when it has once been dissolved. We can take living protoplasm and we can kill it. It will be protoplasm still, so far as our best chemistry can discover, but it will be dead protoplasm, and we cannot make it live again; and as far as we know nature can no more make it live than we can. It can be used as food for living creatures, animals or plants, and so its substance can be taken up by living protoplasm and made to share in the life which thus consumes it; but life of its own it cannot obtain. Now here, as it seems, the acceptance of the two evolutions lands us in acceptance of a miracle. The creation of life is unaccounted for. And it much more exactly answers to what we mean by a miracle than it did under the old theory of creation before Evolution was made a scientific doctrine. For under that old theory the creation of living creatures stood on the same footing as the creation of metals or other inorganic substances. It was part of that beginning which had to be taken for granted, and which for that reason lay outside of the domain of Science altogether. But if we accept the two evolutions, the creation of life, if unaccounted for, presents itself as a direct interference in the actual history of the world. There could have been no life when the earth was nothing but a mass of intensely heated fluid. There came a time when the earth became ready for life to exist upon it. And the life came, and no laws of inorganic matter can account for its coming. As it stands this is a great miracle. And from this conclusion the only escape that has been suggested is to suppose that life came in on a meteoric stone from some already formed habitable world; a supposition which transfers the miracle to another scene, but leaves it as great a miracle as before.

Nor, if it was a miracle, can we deny that there was a purpose in it worthy of miraculous interference. For what purpose can rank side by side with the existence and development of life, the primary condition of all moral and spiritual existence and action in this world? In the introduction of life was wrapped up all that we value and all that we venerate in the whole creation. The infinite superiority, not in degree only, but in kind, of the living to the lifeless, of a man to a stone, justifies us in believing that the main purpose of the creation that we see was to supply a dwelling-place and a scene of action for living beings. We cannot say that the dignity of the Moral Law requires that creatures to be made partakers in the knowledge of it, and even creatures of a lower nature but akin to them, must have been the results of a separate and miraculous act of creation. But we can say that there is a congruity in such a miracle, with the moral purpose of all the world, of which we are a part, that removes all difficulty in believing it. Science, as such, cannot admit a miracle, and can only say, 'Here is a puzzle yet unsolved.' Nor can the most religious scientific man be blamed as undutiful to religion if he persists in endeavouring to solve the puzzle. But he has no right to insist beforehand that the puzzle is certainly soluble; for that he cannot know, and the evidence is against him.

Secondly, if we look at the Darwinian theory by itself, we see at once that it is incomplete, and the consideration of this incompleteness gravely modifies the conclusion which would otherwise be rightly drawn from it, and which, indeed, Darwin himself seems disposed to draw. For the theory rests on two main pillars, the transmission of characteristics from progenitor to progeny, and the introduction of minute variations in the progeny with each successive generation. Now, the former of these may be said to be well established, and we recognise it as a law of life that all plants and animals propagate their own kind. But the latter has, as yet, been hardly examined at all. Each new generation shows special slight variations. But what causes these variations? and what determines what they shall be? In Darwin's investigations these questions are not touched. The variations are treated as if they were quite indefinite in number and in nature. He concerns himself only with the effect of these variations after they have appeared. Some have the effect of giving the plant or animal an advantage in the struggle of life; some give no such advantage; some are hurtful. And hence follows the permanent preservation or speedy destruction of the plants and animals themselves. But we are bound to look not only to their effects but to their causes, if the theory is to be completed. And then we cannot fail to see that these variations in the progeny cannot be due to something in the progenitors, or otherwise the variations would be all alike, which they certainly are not. They must, therefore, be due to external circumstances. These slight variations are produced by the action of the surroundings, by the food, by the temperature, by the various accidents of life in the progenitors. Now, when we see this, we see also how gravely it modifies the conclusions which we have to draw concerning the ancestry of any species now existing. Let us take, for instance, the great order of vertebrate animals. At first sight the Darwinian theory seems to indicate that all these animals are descended from one pair or one individual, and that their unity of construction is due to that fact; but if we go back in thought to the time at which the special peculiarities were introduced which really constituted the order and separated it from other animals, we see that it is by no means clear that it originated with one pair or with one individual, and that, on the contrary, the probabilities are the other way. Although the separation of this order from the rest must have taken place very early, it cannot well have taken place until millions of animals had already come into existence. The prodigality of nature in multiplying animal life is fully acknowledged by Darwin, and that prodigality is apparently greatest in the lowest and most formless type of animal. There being, then, these many millions of living creatures in existence, the external surroundings introduce into them many variations, and among these the special variations to which the vertebrate type is due. It is quite clear that wherever the external surroundings were the same or nearly the same, the variations introduced would be the same or nearly the same. Now, it is far more probable that external surroundings should be the same or nearly the same in many places than that each spot should be absolutely unlike every other spot in these particulars. The beginnings of the vertebrate order would show themselves simultaneously, or at any rate independently, in many places wherever external conditions were sufficiently similar. And the unity of the plan in the vertebrata would be due, not to absolute unity of ancestry, but to unity of external conditions at a particular epoch in the descent of life. Hence it follows that the separation of animals into orders and genera and even into species took place, if not for the most part yet very largely, at a very early period in the history of organic evolution. Of course the descendants of any one of the original vertebrata might, and probably in not a few cases did, branch off into new subdivisions and yet again into further subdivisions, and we are always justified in looking for unity of ancestry among all the species. But it is also quite possible that any species may be regularly descended, without branching off at all, from one of the originals, and that other species that resemble it may owe the resemblance simply to very great similarity of external conditions. To find, for instance, the unity of ancestry between man and the other animals, it will certainly be necessary to go back to a point in the history of life when living creatures were as yet formless, undeveloped – the materials, as we may call them, of the animal creation as we now see it, and not in any but a strictly scientific sense, what we mean when we ordinarily speak of animals. The true settlement of such questions as these can only be obtained when long and patient study shall have completed Darwin's investigations by determining under what laws and within what limits the slight variations which characterise each individual animal or plant are congenitally introduced into its structure. As things stand the probabilities certainly are that a creature with such especial characteristics as man has had a history altogether of his own, if not from the beginning of all life upon the globe, yet from a very early period in the development of that life. He resembles certain other animals very closely in the structure of his body; but the part which external conditions had to play in the earliest stages of evolution of life must have been so exceedingly large that identity or close similarity in these external conditions may well account for these resemblances. And the enormous gap which separates his nature from that of all other creatures known, indicates an exceedingly early difference of origin.

Lastly, it is quite impossible to evolve the Moral Law out of anything but itself. Attempts have been made, and many more will no doubt be made, to trace the origin of the spiritual faculty to a development of the other faculties. And it is to be expected that great success will ultimately attend the endeavours to show the growth of all the subordinate powers of the soul. That our emotions, that our impulses, that our affections should have had a history, and that their present working should be the result of that history, has nothing in it improbable. There can be no question that we inherit these things very largely, and that they are also very largely due to special peculiarities of constitution in each individual. That large part of us which is rightly assigned to our nature as distinct from our own will and our own free action, it is perfectly reasonable to find subject to laws of Evolution. Much of this nature, indeed, we share with the lower animals. They, too, can love; can be angry or pleased; can put affection above appetite; can show generosity and nobility of spirit; can be patient, persevering, tender, self-sacrificing; can take delight in society: and some can even organise it, and thus enter on a kind of civilisation. The dog and the horse, man's faithful servants and companions, show emotions and affections rising as far as mere emotions and affections can rise to the human level. Ants show an advance in the arts of life well comparable to our own. If the bare animal nature is thus capable of such high attainments by the mere working of natural forces, it is to be expected that similar forces in mankind should be found to work under similar laws. We are not spiritual beings only, we are animals, and whatever nature has done for other animals we may expect it to have done and to be doing for us. And if their nature is capable of evolution, so too should ours be. And the study of such evolution of our own nature is likely to be of the greatest value. This nature is the main instrument, put into the grasp as it were of that spiritual faculty which is our inmost essence, to be used in making our whole life an offering to God. It is good to know what can be done with this instrument and what cannot; how it has been formed in the past, and may be still further formed for the future. It is good to study the evolution of humanity. But all this does not touch the spiritual faculty itself, nor the Moral Law which that faculty proclaims to us. The essence of that law is its universality; and out of all this development, when carried to its very perfection, the conception of such universality cannot be obtained. Nothing in this evolution ever rises to the height of a law which shall bind even God Himself, and enable Abraham to say, 'Shall not the Judge of all the earth do right?' The very word right in this, its fulness of meaning, cannot be used.

Evolution may lead the creature to say what is hateful and what is lovable, what is painful and what is delightful, what is to be feared and what is to be sought; it may develop the sentiment which comes nearest of all to the sentiment of reverence, namely, the sentiment of shame; but it cannot reveal the eternal character of the distinction between right and wrong. Nay, there may be, as was pointed out in the last Lecture, an evolution in our knowledge even of the Moral Law, just as there is an evolution in our knowledge of mathematics. The fulness of its meaning can become clearer and ever clearer as generation learns from generation. But the principle of the Moral Law, its universality, its supremacy, cannot come out of any development of human nature any more than the necessity of mathematical truth can so come. It stands not on experience, and is its own evidence. Nor indeed have any of the attempts to show that everything in man (religion included) is the product of Evolution ever touched the question how this conception of universal supremacy comes in. It is treated as if it were an unauthorised extension from our own experience to what lies beyond all experience. This, however, is to deny the essence of the Moral Law altogether: that Law is universal or it is nothing.

Now, when we compare the account of the creation and of man given by the doctrine of Evolution with that given in the Bible, we see at once that the two are in different regions. The purpose of giving the accounts is different; the spirit and character of the accounts is different; the details are altogether different. The comparison must take note of the difference of spirit and aim before it can proceed at all.

It is then quite certain, and even those who contend for the literal interpretation of this part of the Bible will generally admit, that the purpose of the revelation is not to teach Science at all. It is to teach great spiritual and moral lessons, and it takes the facts of nature as they appear to ordinary people. When the creation of man is mentioned there is clearly no intention to say by what processes this creation was effected, or how much time it took to work out those processes. The narrative is not touched by the question, Was this a single act done in a moment, or a process lasting through millions of years? The writer of the Book of Genesis sees the earth peopled, as we may say, by many varieties of plants and animals. He asserts that God made them all, and made them resemble each other and differ from each other. He knows nothing and says nothing of the means used to produce their resemblances or their differences. He takes them as he sees them, and speaks of their creation as God's work. Had he been commissioned to teach his people the science of the matter, he would have had to put a most serious obstacle in the way of their faith. They would have found it almost impossible to believe in a process of creation so utterly unlike all their own experience. And it would have been quite useless to them besides, since their science was not in such a condition as to enable them to coordinate this doctrine with any other. As science it would have been dead; and as spiritual truth it would have been a hindrance.

But he had, nevertheless, great ideas to communicate, and we can read them still.

He had to teach that the world as we see it, and all therein contained, was created out of nothing; and that the spiritual, and not the material, was the source of all existence. He had to teach that the creation was not merely orderly, but progressive; going from the formless to the formed; from the orderless to the ordered; from the inanimate to the animate; from the plant to the animal; from the lower animal to the higher; from the beast to the man; ending with the rest of the Sabbath, the type of the highest, the spiritual, life. Nothing, certainly, could more exactly match the doctrine of Evolution than this. It is, in fact, the same thing said from a different point of view. All this is done by casting the account into the form of a week of work with the Sabbath at the end. In so constructing his account, the writer made use of a mode of teaching used commonly enough in the Bible. The symbolical use of the number seven is common in other inspired writers. The symbolical use of periods of time is not without example. That the purpose of the account was not to teach great truths, but to give men information upon scientific questions, is incredible. And, in fact, if we look in this account for literal history, it becomes very difficult to give any meaning to what is said of the seventh day, or to reconcile the interpretation of it with our Lord's words concerning the Sabbath, 'My Father worketh hitherto, and I work.' There is no more reason for setting aside Geology, because it does not agree in detail with Genesis, than there is for setting aside Astronomy because all through the Old Testament the sun is spoken of as going round the earth.

And when the writer of Genesis passes from creation in general to man in particular, it is still clear that he has no mission to tell those for whom he was writing by what processes man was formed, or how long those processes lasted. This was as alien from his purpose as it would have been to tell what every physiologist now knows of the processes by which every individual man is developed from a small germ to a breathing and living infant. He takes men – and he could not but take men as he sees them – with their sinful nature, with their moral and spiritual capacity, with their relations of sex, with their relations of family. He has to teach the essential supremacy of man among creatures, the subordination in position but equality in nature of woman to man, the original declension of man's will from the divine path, the dim and distant but sure hope of man's restoration. These are not, and cannot be, lessons of science. They are worked out into the allegory of the Garden of Eden. But in this allegory there is nothing whatever that crosses the path of science, nor is it for reasons of science that so many great Christian thinkers from the earliest age of the Church downwards have pronounced it an allegory. The spiritual truth contained in it is certainly the purpose for which it is told; and evolution such as science has rendered probable had done its work in forming man such as he is before the narrative begins.

It may be said that it seems inconsistent with the dignity of man's nature as described in the Bible to believe that his formation was effected by any process of evolution, still more by any such process of evolution as would represent him to have been an animal before he became a man.

But, in the first place, it is to be observed that Science does not yet assert, and there is no reason to believe that it ever will assert, that man became a fully developed animal, with the brute instincts and inclinations, appetites and passions, fully formed, an animal such as we see other animals now, before he passed on into a man such as man is now. His body may have been developed according to the theory of Evolution, yet along a parallel but independent line of its own; but at any rate it branched off from other animals at a very early point in the descent of animal life. And, further, as Science cannot yet assert that life was not introduced into the world when made habitable by a direct creative act, so too Science cannot yet assert, and it is tolerably certain will never assert, that the higher and added life, the spiritual faculty, which is man's characteristic prerogative, was not given to man by a direct creative act as soon as the body which was to be the seat and the instrument of that spiritual faculty had been sufficiently developed to receive it. That the body should have been first prepared, and that when it was prepared the soul should either have been then given, or then first made to live in the image of God, – this is a supposition which is inconsistent neither with what the Bible tells nor with what Science has up to this time proved.

And to this must be added that it is out of place for us to define what is consistent or inconsistent with the dignity of man in the process or method by which he was created to be what he is. His dignity consists in his possession of the spiritual faculty, and not in the method by which he became possessed of it. We cannot tell, we never can tell, and the Bible never professes to tell, what powers or gifts are wrapped up in matter itself, or in that living matter of which we are made. How absolutely nothing we know of the mode by which any single soul is created! The germ which is to become man can be traced by the physiologist through all the changes that it has to undergo before it comes to life. Is the future soul wrapped up in it from the first, and dormant till the hour of awakening comes? or is it given at some moment in the development? We see in the infant how its powers expand, and we know that the spiritual faculty, the very essence of its being, has a development like the other faculties. It has in it the gift of speech, and yet it cannot speak. Judgment, and taste, and power of thought; self-sacrifice and unswerving truth; science and art, and spiritual understanding, all may be there in abundant measure and yet may show no sign. All this we know; and because it is common and well known we see nothing inconsistent with the dignity of our nature in this concealment of all that dignity, helpless and powerless, within the form of an infant in arms. With this before us it is impossible to say that anything which Science has yet proved, or ever has any chance of proving, is inconsistent with the place given to man in Creation by the teaching of the Bible.

In conclusion, we cannot find that Science, in teaching Evolution, has yet asserted anything that is inconsistent with Revelation, unless we assume that Revelation was intended not to teach spiritual truth only, but physical truth also. Here, as in all similar cases, we find that the writer of the Book of Genesis, like all the other writers in the Bible, took nature as he saw it, and expressed his teaching in language corresponding to what he saw. And the doctrine of Evolution, in so far as it has been shown to be true, does but fill out in detail the declaration that we are 'fearfully and wonderfully made; marvellous are Thy works; and that my soul knoweth right well.' There is nothing in all that Science has yet taught, or is on the way to teach, which conflicts with the doctrine that we are made in the Divine Image, rulers of the creation around us by a Divine superiority, the recipients of a Revelation from a Father in Heaven, and responsible to judgment by His Law. We know not how the first human soul was made, just as we know not how any human soul has been made since; but we know that we are, in a sense in which no other creatures living with us are, the children of His special care.